THE MANY FACES OF SOCIAL WORKERS

THE MANY FACES OF SOCIAL WORKERS

Armando T. Morales

University of California at Los Angeles

Bradford W. Sheafor

Colorado State University

Allyn and Bacon

Boston   London   Toronto   Sydney   Tokyo   Singapore

To my wife, Cynthia,
and my children: Christina Mia, Roland, Gary, and Soo
—ATM

To my wife, Nadine,
and my children: Christopher, Perry, Brandon, and Laura
—BWS

Series Editor, Social Work and Family Therapy: Patricia Quinlin
Editor in Chief, Social Sciences: Karen Hanson
Editorial Assistant: Annemarie Kennedy
Marketing Manager: Jackie Aaron
Editorial Production Service: Omegatype Typography, Inc.
Composition and Prepress Buyer: Linda Cox
Manufacturing Manager: Suzanne Lareau
Cover Administrator: Kristina Mose-Libon
Electronic Composition: Omegatype Typography, Inc.

Copyright © 2002 by Allyn & Bacon
A Pearson Education Company
75 Arlington Street
Boston, MA 02116

Internet: www.ablongman.com

Portions of this material appeared in *Social Work: A Profession of Many Faces,* 9th Edition, by Armando T.
Morales and Bradford W. Sheafor, copyright © 2001 by Allyn & Bacon.

Between the time web site information is gathered and published, some sites may have closed. Also, the
transcription of URLs can result in typographical errors. The publisher would appreciate notification
where these errors occur so that they may be corrected in subsquent editions. Thank you.

Library of Congress Cataloging in Publication Data

Morales, Armando.
    The many faces of social workers / Armando T. Morales, Bradford W. Sheafor.
      p.   cm.
    Includes bibliographical references and index.
    ISBN 0-205-34434-8
    1. Social service—United States.   2. Social workers—United States.   3. Social
    service—Vocational guidance—United States.   I. Sheafor, Bradford W. II. Title.

HV91 .M653 2002
361.3'2'02373—dc21

                                       2001034328

Printed in the United States of America

10 9 8 7 6 5 4 3 2 1   06 05 04 03 02 01

Photo Credits:
Frontispiece: Robert Harbison; Chapter 1: Robert Harbison; Chapter 2: Robert Harbison; Chapter 3: AP/Wide World
Photos; Chapter 4: Bryce Flynn/Stock Boston; Chapter 5: Spencer Grant/Stock Boston; Chapter 6: Robert Harbison;
Chapter 7: Robert Harbison; Chapter 8: Robert Harbison; Chapter 9: Jeffry D. Scott; Chapter 10: Robert Harbison.

CONTENTS

PREFACE

During the three decades since we began preparing the parent text of this book, called *Social Work: A Profession of Many Faces,* the social work profession has changed significantly. Through nine editions of that textbook we have recorded many changes in the profession, as well as in U.S. society, that have affected social work practice.

Throughout this period we have portrayed social work as the helping profession that focuses on helping people interact more effectively with their environments. Simultaneously, we have maintained that social work's mission is also to help change those environments to make them more supportive of people's needs; that is, to prevent problems from occurring in the first place. This, we believe, is social work's niche among the helping professions. We recognize that some social workers are more focused on changing people, while others emphasize changing social structures. Yet we conclude that social workers must do both if they are to be true to the mission of this profession. In fact, we are convinced that clients are shortchanged if social workers perform only one of these two basic functions. Social workers cannot be exclusively clinical or exclusively policy oriented if they are to be of maximum effectiveness.

We have also recognized that social work's historical roots were in giving priority to the members of the society who are the most vulnerable to social issues. People who experience poverty, oppression, disabling conditions, chronic physical or mental illness, abuse, or some combination of these factors deserve first call on the efforts of social workers. Drawing on our own knowledge or the expertise of valued colleagues in social work, we have provided a set of chapters that help to understand why these special population groups are vulnerable to social issues and how social workers might intervene at both the micro and macro levels to prevent, treat, or care for people experiencing these conditions. Periodically, we have added new chapters and updated the older ones to present the most current information available to our readers.

Finally, because social work is an action-oriented profession, we have provided case material to help our readers understand how this profession uses its understanding of the human condition and its intervention competencies to facilitate change that will improve people's lives. This case material has been in the form of short cases related to the content of individual chapters.

Throughout the years, the structure of that book has stayed essentially the same. However, we have learned that some instructors and the nature of some curricula in social work education programs suggest an uncoupling of the two content sections of the book. In some courses, a smaller and less expensive book that describes social work, social workers, and what they do meets the course objectives. In these courses, instructors typically assign supplemental reading materials to more briefly address the populations that social workers serve—reserving the more in-depth material for courses that focus on ethnic and cultural sensitivity in social work practice. Similarly, instructors in the ethnic and cultural sensitivity courses often favor a more general text on the fundamentals of culture and ethnicity, supplemented by the content we provide relative to the several vulnerable population groups served by social workers.

In response to these two needs, the ninth edition of *Social Work: A Profession of Many Faces* is available in three forms. For the past eight editions it was released as a single text. Now it is being split into two books—one focused on social work and social workers (Chapters 1 through 10 of the ninth edition) and the other focused on the populations with whom social workers work (Chapters 11 through 23). The substantial case that makes up Chapter 23 is included with the other text, but might also be used to examine the work of a social worker by applying the content describing social work.

This book, *The Many Faces of Social Workers,* is divided into three parts. It begins with a wide view of the profession of social work as it has evolved in U.S. society. To understand social work, you must appreciate the context in which it functions. Thus, you must understand the extent of the commitment society is willing to make to ensure that its members have the opportunity to function at their maximum capacity. For example, do our social systems lead to a distribution of income that provides basic food, clothing, and shelter for all children and adults? If we were to accomplish this, no one would be living in poverty. Yet, the U.S. government reports that, according to the prevailing definition of the poverty line, in 1998 11.2 percent of the families and 12.7 percent of the individuals in the United States were considered to be living in poverty. And, for a child under age 18 or a person of African American or Hispanic origin, the rates are doubled.[1] Is a society that is organized so that the highest 20 percent of the households hold 49.2 percent of the income and the lowest 20 percent hold only 3.6 percent likely to have all its citizens leading full and satisfying lives? Given the strong economy in the 1990s and early years of the twenty-first century, one would expect the society to move in the direction of improving this unequal distribution of income. Not true! Since 1990, the mean income of the lowest 20 percent increased (in constant 1998 dollars) by 2.8 percent, while the mean income of the highest 20 percent increased by 17.4 percent.[2]

Similar measures related to people experiencing physically and mentally disabling conditions or discrimination based on gender, age, ethnicity, sexual orientation, or family dysfunction yield a similar result. Clearly, many people in today's complex society require assistance in dealing with various social issues, and the society needs the assistance of social workers if they are to understand and change the conditions that create these issues. The demand is such that the U.S. Bureau of Labor Statistics projects social work as one of the fastest growing occupations in the United States, with an estimated need of 36.1 percent more social workers from 1998 to 2008[3]—more than twice the growth rate for all jobs in the United States.

When social work emerged as a recognized profession in the United States during the 1900s, it included a number of different service functions such as caring for the poor and infirm, assisting new immigrants adapt to U.S. society, and helping families improve the lives of their children. Although a common approach to service provision is expected of all social workers, what they do and how they do it continues to vary somewhat when working in different settings, with different client

[1]http://www.census.gov/hhes/poverty/poverty98/pv98est1.html.
[2]http://www.census.gov/hhes/income/income98/in98dis.html.
[3]http://stats.bls.gov/emphome.htm.

populations, and when addressing different social problems. Thus, a career ladder for social workers has evolved, reflecting the educational and skill levels required for performing different job functions. The middle section of *The Many Faces of Social Workers* is intended to help readers understand the reasons for the different expressions of social work and the varied requirements for social workers as background for making career decisions.

In the final section of this book, we address some of the central factors that underpin social work practice. Because it is a text intended to provide an overview of social work, we do not attempt to describe how to practice social work. Instead we describe the fundamental values and ethics that guide social workers and identify the tasks that they typically perform. We then detail the knowledge and competencies needed to carry out those tasks. This analysis indicates that one task social workers are expected to perform, preventing social problems, is typically not central to the work of social workers. Therefore, we provide a chapter (Chapter 9) that identifies some primary prevention approaches as a means of helping new social workers appreciate how this aspect of social work might be incorporated in their future practice.

Finally, we have prepared a chapter that extends beyond social work in the United States. The changing times since this book was first launched in the 1970s clearly have led to a shrinking of the perceived distance and differences among the countries of the world. As many countries have undergone rapid change and various forms of industrial and technical advancement, the need for social work has also expanded. Chapter 10, "Social Work Throughout the World," provides a global view of this profession.

A special note to our readers. It is our perception that mastery of the content in these ten chapters will provide a solid background for understanding social work as one of the central professions in today's society. We believe, too, that this is just a start to becoming a social worker. The curriculum of a social work education program will, no doubt, revisit many of the themes we present and address them in greater depth. We particularly want to emphasize that early in your social work education, you should examine the factors that make various population groups more vulnerable than others to social problems, and should consider how social workers might adapt their practice when serving those groups.

In our closely related book, *The Many Faces of Social Work Clients,* we offer a series of chapters that provide an overview of this material. This might be the text for a separate course on ethnic and cultural sensitivity in social work practice, or simply be obtained by the student as a useful reference for subsequent practice activities. Specifically, we draw on an ecosystems perspective to organize different approaches of looking at each population group. The following chapter titles identify the groups we address in that book.

- Social Work Practice with Women
- Social Work Practice with Lesbian, Gay, and Bisexual People
- Social Work Practice with Children and Youth
- Social Work Practice with the Elderly
- Social Work Practice with People with Disabilities
- Social Work Practice in Rural Areas: Appalachia as a Case Example

- Urban and Suburban Gangs: The Psychosocial Crisis Spreads
- Social Work Practice with Asian Americans
- Social Work Practice with American Indians and Alaskan Natives
- Social Work Practice with Mexican Americans
- Social Work Practice with African Americans
- Social Work Practice with Puerto Ricans
- The Social Worker in Action: A High School Homicide Case

A note to our instructors. To support your instruction based on *The Many Faces of Social Workers,* we have developed an accompanying *Instructor's Manual/Test Bank.* The *Manual* contains a synopsis of the most important content in each chapter, suggested teaching activities to help engage students in the material, and sample discussion, essay, and multiple-choice questions. This *Manual* contains all of the material for the combined version of *Social Work: A Profession of Many Faces* and you only need to use the items related to the first ten chapters when teaching from this book. Also, a computerized version of the test bank is available from Allyn and Bacon that is formatted for both Macintosh and IBM personal computers. Other useful information can be found at our web site (http://www.ablongman.com/morales).

The popular Baez Family Fire case continues to be available for teaching purposes in the *Instructor's Manual* as well as on our web site. We have organized that case material so that the story unfolds a few pages at a time, allowing an instructor to process the content with students before continuing to the next events in the case. We believe this format provides the necessary flexibility for using this case material in discussion groups, assigning term papers, and even providing the context for exam questions. Instructors may use this case material without seeking permission from Allyn and Bacon. Also, Allyn and Bacon sends copies of this book to Recording for the Blind (20 Rosel Road, Princeton, New Jersey 08540) when the first copies are printed in anticipation that an audio version will be available for people who are visually impaired as soon as it is needed for the classroom. Once again, requesting the version for *Social Work: A Profession of Many Faces,* 9th edition, and assigning only the first ten chapters will be the most efficient way to obtain this recorded version of the material.

We thank our students and colleagues at the University of California at Los Angeles and Colorado State University; our families and loved ones—especially our wives Cynthia and Nadine—for supporting us in the preparation of this material on top of already crowded schedules; and the staff at Allyn and Bacon, who have been gracious and creative in helping make our material more readable and available to faculty members and students. Also, thanks to the reviewers who provided helpful feedback and comments on this edition: Carmen A. Aponte, SUNY College at Brockport; Carol J. Bridges, East Central University; and Leon F. Burrell, University of Vermont.

THE MANY FACES OF
SOCIAL WORKERS

Social Work in U.S. Society

If the world were a perfect place, it would provide for everyone warm and safe housing, an adequate supply of nutritious food, challenging jobs, good health care, and love and caring from friends and family. It would be a world with minimal stress, crime, and suffering. All people would find their lives satisfying and fulfilling. Social work exists because the world is less than perfect. Social workers serve people and the institutions of society as they confront this imperfection.

The social worker is not satisfied with this imperfect world that sends too many children to bed hungry at night, has effectively declared too many older people useless, restricts too many physically disabled people from productive living, allows too many women and children to be physically and sexually abused, deprives too many members of minority groups of the full opportunity to share in the benefits of this affluent society, has too many single parents trying to raise children in substandard housing without enough money for proper nutrition and food, and deprives too many emotionally and intellectually impaired people of satisfying lives because they behave or learn differently from the majority in the society. In fact, when even one person suffers from loneliness, hunger, discrimination, poor housing, domestic violence, or emotional upset, there is a need for social work.

Social work emerged during the twentieth century as an important profession in U.S. society. Its development has paralleled a seeming roller coaster of public interest in human welfare and social services. At times, when the national political climate placed a high priority on human welfare, social work jobs became plentiful and the number of bright and socially concerned people entering social work increased dramatically. However, the tides of the political climate periodically yield a conservative orientation more concerned with economic prosperity than human welfare, with big business than human rights, and with reducing taxes for the wealthy than maintaining or improving social programs. In such times, the appeal of social work to many young people tends to decline, and the supply of competent social workers is reduced. Clearly, social work is closely tied to the political and social philosophy that dominates at any period of time.

Although the supply of social workers may increase or decline from time to time, it is likely that there will always be a strong demand for this profession. The places of employment or the type of services needed from social workers may change, but the need for social work services will undoubtedly continue. It has become a central part of the fabric of U.S. society.

Why is social work important to U.S. society? Social workers provide important services to help people solve problems that limit their social functioning and services to enhance the quality of their lives. Social workers provide these services in a variety of ways.

Sometimes social workers offer a *direct service* or help individuals, families, or other groups on a face-to-face basis. In some situations they help people solve specific problems, while at other times they counsel people to solve problems or engage in activities that will enhance the quality of their lives—whether or not they experience an identifiable problem.

Services might also be provided indirectly on behalf of individuals or groups of people. These *indirect services* help to make social institutions such as organizations, neighborhoods, communities, or even the policies of a government or laws of a country more responsive to the needs of people.

Providing needed human services and contributing to improvement of the quality of life for all people are personally rewarding experiences. Each social worker can enjoy the satisfaction of knowing that he or she makes a small but important contribution to the well-being of society.

This book presents an overview of social work for the person considering this profession as a possible career choice. It does not attempt to "sell" social work but to portray it honestly, with its strengths and limitations in clear view. Because we are interested in recruiting qualified people to our profession—a profession in which we take great pride—we hope this book will enable people to discover whether social work is for them. Social work is not easy work. It can be as emotionally draining as it is rewarding. It can be as frustrating as it is satisfying. The prerequisite to developing the knowledge, values, and skills necessary for competent social work practice must be a basic commitment to social betterment and a willingness to invest oneself in facilitating the process of change.

To understand the current status of social work in the United States, one must first understand the historical context in which it developed. Chapter 1 begins with a quotation from the Preamble to the U.S. Constitution that commits this nation to "promoting the general welfare" of its people. Although there has been considerable fluctuation in the degree to which members of the society choose to share their resources to fulfill that commitment and continuing disagreement about how meeting social needs

should be accomplished, a fundamental strength of this nation has been its basic assurance that at least the minimum needs of all people would be met. In Chapter 1 we examine the efforts of U.S. society to respond to the needs of its members. A summary of some of the important events and philosophies that have shaped society's social programs and its methods of delivering human services is presented. In addition, some of the continuing issues regarding the provision of human services are highlighted because, as it will later become evident, they affect the tools that social workers have available to serve their clients.

Within the framework of an evolving social welfare institution that today combines public, voluntary, and for-profit forms of service delivery, a profession concerned with helping people interact more effectively with the world around them, and simultaneously change that world to make it more supportive of human welfare, has emerged. An overview of that profession, social work, is the substance of Chapter 2. Social work is presented as a profession characterized by breadth and versatility. While the central focus of social work is seemingly obscured when one looks at the many different expressions of social work in the wide range of human service organizations and the varied practice activities in which social workers engage, its central feature—attending to the quality of people's social functioning—makes it an important profession in fulfilling society's commitment to the welfare of its people.

Building on the concept of social work as a comprehensive helping profession concerned with enhancing social functioning, Chapter 3 charts its evolution as a profession from well-meaning volunteers to a recognized and respected helping profession. Of particular note is Table 3-1; it presents major events in the history of the United States and displays parallel events in the evolution of the social welfare institution and the social work profession in an effort to integrate the historical information found throughout the book.

Part One, then, establishes the position of social work in U.S. society. Like all professions, social work exists because it fulfills important social needs and because this society sanctions its role in meeting those needs. That is not true everywhere. In certain parts of the world societies do not take on that responsibility. Those societies leave such efforts entirely to friends, family, and neighbors, and these informal efforts may or may not prove helpful.

CHAPTER 1

Social Welfare: A Response to Human Need

Prefatory Comment

To understand social work and the activities of social workers, we must begin with an examination of U.S. society's commitment to the well-being of its members. How a society responds to the Biblical question, "Am I my brother's (and sister's) keeper?" is perhaps the acid test of that society's real interest in its people. Individuals and political parties regularly disagree about when our society should accept responsibility for assisting our brothers and sisters, as well as who should pay for it and how much money or other resources should be invested in meeting their needs. Nevertheless, it is evident that in a complex industrialized society such as the United States, a formalized battery of social programs and human services is required if minimum standards of living are to be achieved by most (if not all) citizens. Those programs and services make up an essential element of U.S. society—its social welfare institution.

What social workers do and the resources they have available to help people meet their social needs are highly dependent on the degree to which the society supports its human service programs. Therefore, we have initiated this book's exploration of social work with a chapter that examines the evolution of U.S. society's social welfare institution.

From its very beginning the United States has been committed to "promoting the general welfare" of its people:

> We, the people of the United States, in order to form a more perfect Union, establish justice, insure domestic tranquility, provide for the common defense, promote the general welfare, and secure the blessings of liberty to ourselves and our posterity, do ordain and establish this Constitution for the United States of America.
>
> —Preamble to the Constitution

During the ensuing years since the Constitution was adopted, there have been continuing debate and changing public policy about how to fulfill this promise.

How is a nation to promote the welfare of its citizens? Clearly, a first step is to meet their basic needs. To achieve that objective, programs must be provided that ensure at least minimum levels of safety, health, and personal well-being. The design of such programs, however, requires sufficient flexibility to respond to changing needs. For example, moving from an agriculture-based economy to one based on machines and then to one based on electronic technology radically altered the structure of the workforce and the opportunity for many to hold meaningful jobs. Similarly, the movement from an agricultural to an industrial society influenced the ability of the primary social institution, the family, to perform many of its traditional functions in meeting the needs of its members. Extended family members are often scattered geographically where jobs are located, and many cannot readily interact with other family members when they need help. Also, the effect of such factors as racism, sexism, and ageism has created large groups of citizens who do not have equal access to many of the established ways of having needs met (e.g., rewarding jobs, police protection, quality housing), making them especially vulnerable. These and other trends have moved social welfare programs from a relatively minor role in U.S. society to an increasingly central place.

To reach people in need, social programs must be designed to serve the people for whom they are intended and delivered in such a manner that those people can benefit from them. In most cases, these programs require skilled professionals to serve the people needing assistance. Depending on the need being addressed, the helpers must have various kinds of knowledge and unique competencies to effectively serve their clients. As the knowledge and skill requirements have become more than any one person can master, a division of labor has occurred and several helping professions have evolved to provide these programs. One of these professions is social work. Social work's unique contribution among the helping professions is to assist individuals to interact more effectively with the people and social institutions (e.g., family members, neighbors, schools, hospitals, courts, nursing homes, and even whole communities) that are important parts of their lives.

Some Social Workers in Action

Examining the day-to-day work of several social workers helps one to appreciate how social workers serve their clients and the kind of human needs they address. Consider the following case examples of social workers as they go about their tasks:

In twenty minutes, Nadine Harrison, a social worker with the local public social services department, has an appointment with Ms. Kim Lee. Ms. Lee is terribly worried about her future and that of her two small children. Her husband was killed two months ago in a robbery at the neighborhood market where he worked. In addition to her grief and loneliness, Ms. Lee found that, after paying funeral expenses, little money was left for raising the children. She asks Ms. Harrison for help.

Laura Jackson is executive director of the Council on Aging in her community. This council identifies and seeks solutions to problems experienced by older people in that community. As executive director, Ms. Jackson provides leadership to the citizen board as it considers new programs. Tonight the board will consider initiating a new program for older people: a telephone hook-up between shut-ins.

Brandon Ford is a social worker employed in a psychiatric hospital. Although he works with some patients individually, this afternoon he will meet with a group of adolescent boys who expect to be released from the hospital in a few weeks. Mr. Ford will help the boys explore their feelings about leaving the hospital and their friends, and will discuss the problems they may face when they return to their homes. He will also help to connect them and their parents with a local mental health clinic where they can receive support after their hospitalization is ended.

Perry Garcia is a social worker at a storefront neighborhood center in a large city. His job is to help residents rectify substandard housing conditions in the area. Tonight Mr. Garcia is helping a group from the neighborhood plan a strategy for pressuring some of the landlords to improve the quality of housing.

This afternoon Christopher Warren will testify before a committee of the state legislature that is considering the need for new laws and programs related to the state parole system. After seven years as a probation officer, Mr. Warren is well prepared to provide the Senate committee with expert testimony about problems with the existing approach to parole and probation.

Each of these social workers is either carrying out a social program intended to meet some human need or, in the case of Christopher Warren, is attempting to improve a program. All are employed by human service agencies—some are *public* or tax-supported organizations created by government, while others are *private* agencies supported through donations and governed by a volunteer board. Some of these social workers serve an area as small as a neighborhood, while others have a whole state as their service area. Most work directly with individuals and families, although some work primarily through committees or other groups in an effort to achieve a high quality of life for all.

In short, the many faces of social work reveal a profession serving a wide range of people by assisting them to improve their general well-being. Social workers play a central role in helping the society realize its commitment to promoting the general welfare of its citizens.

Identifying Human Needs

Each individual has his or her own special needs. The configuration of these needs, the intensity with which they are felt, and the ability to discover ways to meet them are part of what makes humans unique. Individuals vary, for example, in the degree of need for expressions of affection, for approval from friends and family, and for intellectual stimulation. Some people can manage pain and illness or limited financial resources quite satisfactorily, while others suffer greatly. Some can ignore the many injustices that prevail, while others are motivated to action when they observe injustices.

It is not necessary for a society to develop programs that respond to each and every human need. People are expected to develop their own means of satisfying most of their needs without help from others. If that fails, they typically look to family and friends and natural helpers in the community. If they still are unable to find help, only then will they turn to the various human services to meet these needs. Social programs, then, are often a "resource of last resort."

There are fundamental differences of opinion about the appropriate role of human services in U.S. society. A *conservative* philosophy argues for placing primary responsibility on the individual and family; a *liberal* position favors a more substantial role for social programs in meeting those needs. The society must ultimately determine the degree to which its function is to provide for people's needs and/or wants. At any time, that decision is determined by the society's prevailing philosophy regarding social responsibility. As the political climate moves between conservative and liberal philosophies, the human services are impacted—sometimes dramatically.

Although each of us has his or her own unique constellation of needs, there are some common needs that affect all people. Romanyshyn described these as needs of the flesh (survival and creature comforts), needs of the heart (love, intimacy, and exchange of tenderness), needs of the ego (sense of adequacy and self-assertiveness), and needs of the soul (transcending self to define the meaning of life beyond one's own biological existence).[1] Which of these needs should the society attempt to serve? Logically an effort should be made first to address the most basic needs and then, if there is sufficient interest, to deal with those of lesser priority. Maslow suggests the following priorities, or *hierarchy of human needs,* beginning with the most basic:[2]

- *Physiological survival needs:* nourishment, rest, and warmth

- *Safety needs:* preservation of life and sense of security

- *Belongingness needs:* to be a part of a group and to love and be loved

- *Esteem needs:* approval, respect, acceptance, and appreciation

- *Self-actualization needs:* opportunity to fulfill one's potential

The more basic the need, the more likely it is that society will make some provision for assisting people to meet that need. Thus, human service programs that respond to the hungry child or homeless family (i.e., physiological survival need) are more likely to be supported than marital counseling (i.e., belongingness need) or programs that offer growth-enhancing experiences for the "normal" or "healthy" person (i.e., self-actualization need).

Social Welfare Programs

Some of society's efforts to meet human needs are labeled "social welfare programs." The term *social,* when applied to humans, addresses the interactions of individuals or groups with other people, groups, organizations, or communities. The term *welfare* implies concern for the "well-being" of people. Social welfare programs, then, are developed to help people function more satisfactorily in their interactions with others and thus lead more fulfilling lives.

Social welfare programs take many forms. Some, for example, are income-transfer programs intended to achieve greater economic equity in the society by taxing the more wealthy and providing financial assistance to the poor. Other social programs are intended as society's efforts to prevent physical, psychological, or sexual abuse, for example, those programs that protect children from harmful parental behavior. Still other social welfare programs might be found in hospitals where patients are helped to adjust to changed capacities or to obtain needed resources to deal with a medical problem. These programs are not intended to replace individual caring, but rather to express formal (or institutionalized) social concern.

How individual and institutionalized caring should interact has been an issue in U.S. society from its founding. In the early years of this "land of opportunity" with its abundant resources and vast, unsettled lands, the "rugged individualist mentality" prevailed. It was thought that individuals and families should take care of themselves and, if that failed, neighbors or churches and synagogues should take care of their members. Only when those sources failed to meet the need would the community and more formal social programs be used to serve those in need.

While the spirit of caring about those in need is inherent in the U.S. historical commitment to the ethics embodied in Judaism and Christianity, it has not played out as unrestrained willingness to provide services. In practice, most human service programs have been limited to problem solving. The emphasis has been on "fixing" problems or "curing" harmful conditions. Thus, programs aimed at enhancing social functioning or preventing emerging problems generally have been neglected.

It is evident that society holds different views about the people who are the recipients of various social programs. For example, in relation to financial aid programs it is considered quite acceptable to assist the farmer facing fluctuations in the price of crops by providing price supports. It is similarly acceptable for small business owners or college students to receive government-subsidized grants or loans. However, it is much less acceptable, even for single mothers and their children, to receive food stamps or direct cash assistance as indicated by the passage of the Personal Responsibilities and Work Opportunity Reconciliation Act in 1996, popularly known as the "welfare reform law." Financial aid is even more unacceptable when it is provided to the alcoholic or substance abuser who cannot hold a job, though the person's need may be just as great as in many other situations. These examples demonstrate an important point: The conditions that create the need for human services affect the willingness of society to provide social programs to address those needs.

The Evolution of Social Programs

An index of the nation's continued commitment to its people is its investment in social programs. These programs are the mechanisms by which public concerns are translated into methods of serving individual people. They are expressed in laws and other policies that represent the society's plans to provide for selected needs. Social programs not only include giving tangible resources (i.e., food, housing, and clothing), but also incorporate a variety of activities like counseling or group facilitation provided by skilled professionals. To make these services available to clients, programs must be delivered by an organization where clients and service providers can come together to address the need.

In the United States, social welfare programs have been subject to ever-changing philosophies and, therefore, support for these programs has increased and decreased at various periods. A brief review of the emergence of social welfare in the United States provides an important context for understanding the social programs offered today and the place of social work among the helping professions.

COLONIAL TIMES TO THE GREAT DEPRESSION

Picture life in the rural United States in the 1700s when land was plowed and families worked to tame the wilderness. Although there were many trials and tribulations in an agricultural society, the person with average intelligence and a willingness to work hard could usually succeed. Given an open frontier and liberal government policies for staking a claim to fertile land, an individual could readily acquire property and produce at least the necessities of life. Because the family was strong and each member had sharply defined roles that contributed to the family's welfare, people survived and, in time, usually prospered. The "American Dream" could become a reality for most (unless one was of African, Asian, Mexican, or Native American background) in this simple agrarian society.

The family was not usually alone or completely self-supporting. All members of the family (i.e., grandparents, children, and other relatives) were supportive and, perhaps as important, were needed. Even the mentally or physically disabled person could find meaningful ways to contribute. For mutual protection, social interaction, and opportunity to trade the goods they produced, families would band together into loosely knit communities. Trade centers eventually emerged as small towns; a market economy evolved; and merchants opened stores, bought and sold products, and extended credit to people until their products were ready for market.

Efforts to meet human needs in this environment can best be characterized as *mutual aid*. When special problems arose, neighbors and the community responded. The barn that burned was quickly rebuilt, widows and orphans were cared for, and the sick were tended to. People shared what they had with needy friends and neighbors, knowing that the favor would be returned some day. In this preindustrial society, the quality of life depended on the "grace of God" and hard work. Society rarely needed to respond to unmet human needs; but when it did, churches and synagogues usually provided that service.

Conditions began to change in the 1800s and early 1900s when industrialization and urbanization created rapid and dramatic changes in both the family and the market system. People congregated in cities where there were jobs, the individual breadwinner rather than the family unit became the key to survival, and interactions with others were increasingly characterized by impersonality. Those from the vulnerable population groups (e.g., immigrants, the aged, minorities, women, persons with disabilities) in particular experienced reduced opportunity for employment or, if employed, access to meaningful and personally rewarding jobs. Not only were social problems increased, but with the changed roles of the family and market system, society had to create new means of responding to human needs.

Early social welfare programs were heavily influenced by the *Puritan ethic* that argued that only those people with a moral defect failed. According to Puritan reasoning, those who failed must suffer from a moral weakness and were viewed as sinful and ethically weak. It is not uncommon even today for clients to feel that their troubles represent God's means of punishing them for some sin or act of immoral behavior. Following the same philosophy, grudging taxpayers often resent contributing to human services when they believe the client is at fault for needing assistance. This view, however, does not take into consideration the structural factors in the society that contribute to or even may cause an individual's problems.

The United States was not settled by wealthy people—the wealthy had no reason to leave Europe. When social needs were addressed by this developing society, small voluntary organizations were formed to provide services. Puritan judgmentalism was evident in the names of organizations such as the "Home for Intemperate Women" or the "Penitent Females Refuge." If voluntary organizations did not meet needs, town meetings were held and actions taken to provide assistance, thus creating the first public social services. Any assistance was considered charity, not a right. Requests for help were either supported or rejected, depending on the judgments made by the townsfolk.

The philosophy derived from the *French Enlightenment* of the eighteenth century contradicted the Puritan view. It argued that people are inherently good and that need for assistance is not necessarily tied to morality. People needing help were considered worthy of that assistance depending on the causes of their problems. Persons with limited income, for example, were classified as worthy poor and unworthy poor. The *worthy poor* were viewed as good people who required help because they were afflicted with an ailment or were women and children left destitute by the death or desertion of the breadwinning husband and father. The *unworthy poor* were thought to have flaws of character. In one attempt to better understand the factors that contributed to the presence of the unworthy poor, a report of the Society for the Prevention of Pauperism in the City of New York in 1818 identified the following causes of poverty: ignorance, idleness, intemperance in drinking, want of economy, imprudent and hasty marriages, lotteries, pawnbrokers, and houses of ill fame.[3] That one's plight may have been caused by others, by chance, or even by structural conditions in the society was only beginning to be recognized.

There were, of course, those who held a more sympathetic view of persons in need and attempted to reform the punitive and uncaring approaches to providing services. For example, as early as 1776, in Philadelphia, the Society for Alleviating the Miseries of Public Prisons was formed. Later, one of the first great social reformers, Dorothea Dix, chronicled the deplorable conditions in prisons and almshouses (also referred to as "poor farms") and sought to establish government responsibility for meeting human needs. Her effective lobbying contributed to the passage of a bill in the U.S. Congress to grant federal land to states to help them finance care for the mentally ill. The veto of that bill in 1854 by President Franklin Pierce established a precedent that was to dominate thinking about society's responsibility for social welfare for the next three-quarters of a century—that the federal government should play no part in providing human services. As late as 1930, President Herbert Hoover relied on the precedent established by the Pierce veto when he approved an appropriation of $45 million to feed livestock in Arkansas during a drought while opposing an additional $25 million to feed the farmers who raised that livestock.[4]

Other social reformers, too, began to advocate for programs to meet needs—mostly through voluntary associations such as the Charity Organization Societies,

Settlement Houses, the Mental Hygiene Movement, and programs to assist former slaves to integrate into the dominant society. When the federal government refused to engage in providing human services, the states sporadically offered services, with several states creating state charity boards or public welfare departments. However, not until the Great Depression of the 1930s led to severe economic crisis and the ensuing New Deal programs of President Franklin D. Roosevelt was it recognized that private philanthropy, even in combination with limited state and local government support, could not adequately address the major human needs.

The human services would never again be the same. New partnerships and a division of responsibility among local, state, and federal governments had to be forged, and it was necessary for the ensuing social programs to be articulated with programs offered by the private sector.

THE GREAT DEPRESSION TO THE PRESENT

The Great Depression was also the great equalizer. People who had previously been successful suddenly required help. These were moral, able-bodied people who needed assistance. Could they be blamed for their condition or did other factors contribute to their troubles? Did they have a right to some form of assistance when they were in trouble? In this case it was the deterioration of the worldwide economy that forced many people into poverty. U.S. society began to recognize that indeed there were structural factors in modern society responsible for many social problems. Thus began an unprecedented period of expansion in social welfare in the United States.

World War II rallied the United States to a common cause and helped people recognize their interdependence. Each person was counted on to contribute to the common good during wartime conditions, and the nation could ill afford to create "throwaway" people by failing to provide for their basic needs. By the 1960s economic recovery was complete, and a brief period of prosperity and responsiveness to human needs followed. The Kennedy and Johnson administrations fostered the War on Poverty and Great Society programs, and the Human Rights Revolution was in its heyday. These activities focused public concern on the poor, minorities, women, the aged, the mentally and physically disabled, and other population groups that had previously been largely ignored. Legislation protecting civil rights and creating massive social programs was passed; court decisions validated the new legislation, and a vast array of new social programs emerged. For example, poverty rates, the prime indicator of social well-being, dropped by half, from 22.4 percent in 1959 to a low of 11.1 percent in 1973. [5]

With the exception of the cost of the Vietnam War and the military buildup during the Reagan and Bush administrations, examination of federal expenditures reveals a continuous decline in expenditures on national defense. At the same time, only the conservative Reagan era has countered the trend for the United States to increasingly invest in its human resources. Even the George H. Bush presidency saw a rather dramatic increase in human resource spending. At the beginning of the Kennedy Administration in 1962, almost twice as much was spent on defense as on human resources. By the end of the Clinton Administration, the amount of money invested in national defense was only slightly more than one-fourth of that spent on human resources. Figure 1-1 reflects the annual expenditures in billions of dollars from the federal budget on human resources and national defense with the value of the dollar held constant (i.e., all years translated to the value of the dollar in 1992).

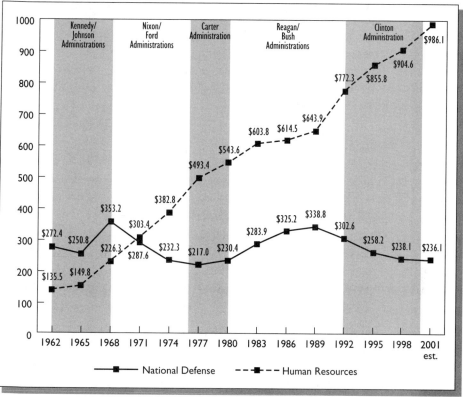

FIGURE 1-1   **U.S Expenditures on National Defense and Human Resources (in billions of constant FY 1992 dollars): 1962–2001 (est.)**

Source: U.S. Office of Management of the Budget, "The Budget for Fiscal Year 2000," Historical Tables, Table 3.1. http://www.access.gpo.gov/usbudget/fy2000/buddocs/html budget

The bloom on social programs began to fade in the middle of the 1970s, and public apathy replaced public concern. A deteriorating economy was accompanied by a growing political conservatism, and the continued commitment to human services was placed in direct competition with military buildup and the maintenance of U.S. superpower status. By the 1980s, the time was ripe for conservatives to attempt to dismantle the social programs that had developed over the last two decades. Echoing the political rhetoric based on the distrust of government that had characterized the philosophies of Presidents Franklin Pierce and Herbert Hoover, and mixed with punitive, moralistic views regarding the recipients of human services that revealed vestiges of the Puritan philosophy, President Ronald Reagan set out to limit the federal government's social programs. As reflected in Figure 1-2, the Reagan administration had only moderate influence over expenditures for mandated social programs such as Social Security, but was able to decrease by almost 15 percent the expenditures on discretionary social programs.

The Reagan administration set out not only to cut federal expenditures, but also to shift responsibility to state and local governments or, where possible, to the private sector of the human services. However, the combination of a more liberal Congress

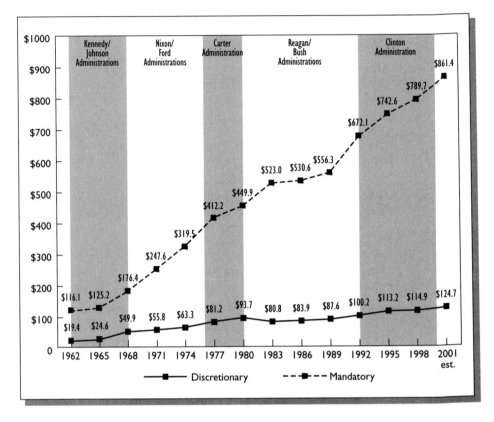

FIGURE 1-2 **Mandatory and Discretionary U.S. Government Expenditures on Human Resource* (in billions of constant FY 1992 dollars): 1962–2001 (est.)**

*U.S. Budget areas included in these data are mandatory and discretionary outlays for (1) education, training, employment, and social services; (2) health; (3) Medicare; income security and housing; and (5) veteran's benefits.

Source: U.S. Office of Management of the Budget, "The Budget for Fiscal Year 2000," Historical Tables, Table 3.1. http://www.access.gpo.gov/usbudget/fy2000/buddocs/html budget

and a series of Supreme Court decisions that protected the gains made in human services and civil rights during the prior two decades partially blunted the radical changes that President Reagan had promised. With per capita expenditures remaining somewhat constant during this period at about $2,500 per person, the 1983 poverty rate* reached the highest point (15.2 percent of the population) in twenty years, began to

---

*The poverty level is adjusted annually to reflect the amount of money required by families of different sizes to be able to provide a minimum level of nutritious food, obtain adequate housing, sufficiently clothe family members for work and school, and provide needed health care. The poverty threshold in 1998 was approximately $8,200 for a single-person household; $11,200 for two persons; $13,000 for a family of three including one child; $16,600 for a family of four with two children; and so on. As a reference point, median income for all families in the United States in 1997 was $45,347. Poverty thresholds for households of varying sizes can be found at http://www.census.gov/hhes/poverty/threshold/threshold98.html.

decline in the late 1980s, and then bounced back to another high point (14.8 percent) at the end of the George H. Bush era (see Figure 1-3). Implementation of President Clinton's moderate social agenda, although blunted somewhat by a very conservative Congress, resulted in a small increase in per capita human resource expenditures and a slight decrease in the poverty rate to 13.3 percent.

A major piece of the Clinton social agenda was to strengthen the health care system and make some form of health care available to all citizens. Meaningful health care reform was not accomplished during the Clinton era, but a second central agenda item, welfare reform, was passed and signed by the president in 1996 in the form of the Personal Responsibilities and Work Opportunity Reconciliation Act. The upbeat title of the act belied its more mean-spirited intent, which was to roll back key provisions of the Social Security Act and drive people off welfare—even if their condition might worsen. Under this act the unconditional guarantee of cash aid

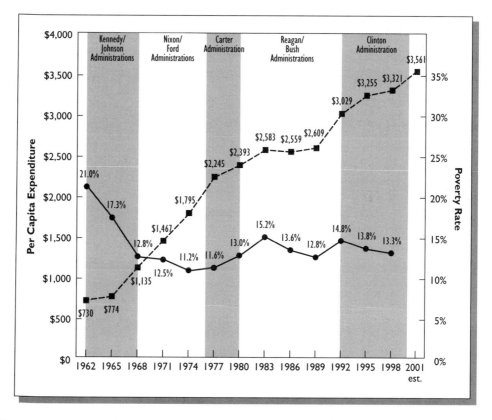

FIGURE 1-3 **Per Capital U.S. Government Expenditures on Human Resources* (in constant FY 1992 dollars) and Poverty Rate: 1962–2001 (est.)**

*U.S. Budget areas included in these data are mandatory and discretionary outlays for (1) education, training, employment, and social services; (2) health; (3) Medicare; (4) income security and housing; and (5) veteran's benefits.

Sources: Joseph Dalaker and Mary Naifeh. *Poverty in the United States: 1997.*
Current Population Reports, Consumer Income, p. 60–201. Washington, D.C.: U.S. Department of Commerce, September 1998: 55–58. http://www.census.gov/hhes/www/poverty97.html

for persons in need (i.e., an entitlement) was eliminated. Aid to Families with Dependent Children (AFDC) was replaced by Temporary Assistance to Needy Families (TANF), reflecting the expectation that the help was only temporary (i.e., a maximum of five years in a family's life). In addition, many legal immigrants became ineligible for services; the definition of disabilities was narrowed, making many previously eligible people ineligible for continuing aid; and there was a work requirement that limited families to two consecutive years of assistance if job training has not been secured and employment not obtained. The states and various American Indian tribes were given the authority and funds ($16.5B) per year in the form of block grants to design and implement the TANF program within their jurisdictions.[6] The result has been little consistency in these programs across the United States.

For clients, it is fortunate that TANF was implemented at the time of a booming economy and the labor market was able to absorb the large number of persons seeking employment, usually with limited job skills. In fact, before the implementation of TANF, the economy had improved and the number of people receiving public assistance had begun to decline. With government funds used to reward businesses that hired welfare recipients and the provision of assistance to clients with child-care costs, by 1998 the number of people receiving financial aid had declined substantially, from 12.3 million in 1996 to 8 million.[7] It is thought that the first two years of TANF creamed off the recipients who had the potential to enter and remain in the employment market. Finding a way to support the remaining less employable recipients who will have used up their lifetime benefits by the year 2001 will be a major challenge for the next administration. It is evident that removing people from the welfare rolls does not necessarily mean that they are no longer living in poverty. The 3 percent decline in the poverty rate from 13.7 percent in 1996 to 13.3 percent in 1998 does not match the 35 percent decline in the number of persons receiving financial aid.

The emphasis on federal government expenditures should not detract from the recognition that considerable financial investment is made to support the general welfare of the people of the United States. Local and state governments, as well as the private/nonprofit sector of the economy, contribute a considerable amount of money to the health, education, and welfare of the people. Table 1-1 provides an indication of the amounts expended by these three sources of funds.

The dollars reported in the column for the federal government in Table 1-1 omit the $329.5B Social Security expenditures that are derived from employee/employer social insurance taxes and are administered by the government. Shoring up Social Security is another serious challenge facing the United States. High on the political agenda for the next few years must be the development of a plan to assure the survival of Social Security, because at the current rate by the year 2014 the revenues generated by the Social Security Trust Fund will not equal the expenditures required by the retired population.[8] Nevertheless, it is important to note that people in the United States contribute almost $1,392 billion each year to improve the general well-being of the people. For those of us more accustomed to dealing in $100 increments, the billions of dollars invested in these services is sometimes difficult to comprehend. In 1997, for example, an average of approximately $5,179 from tax-generated and voluntary funds was spent to support each of the 269 million people in the United States.

TABLE 1-1	Government and Private Sector Allocations to Health, Education, and Social Welfare (in billions of dollars)			
	Federal Govt. (1998)	State/Local Govt. (1995)	Private/Nonprofit (1997)	Total
Health, hospitals, Medicare	$342.2B	$108.8B	$14.0B	$465.0B
Elementary, secondary, higher education and training programs	37.5	358.8	21.5	417.8
Human services (social services, recreation, housing, community planning)	55.8	41.8	21.7	110.3
Income security (cash assistance and other public welfare)	204.5	195.5	0	400.0
TOTAL	$640.0B	$704.9B	$48.2B	$1,393.1B

Note: The dates in Table 1-1 are derived from the latest reports for each source. It takes considerable time for the federal government to secure and summarize data from each of the state and local governments. Also, categories for reporting (e.g., health, education, human services) are not identical for each source and the above data should be viewed as approximate.

Sources:
(Federal Government) U.S. Office of Management and Budget, "The Budget for Fiscal Year 2000," Historical Tables, Table 3.1. http://www.access.gpo.gov/usbudget/fy2000/buddocshtml#budget
(State and Local Governments) U.S. Bureau of the Census [http://www.census.gov/govs/estimate/96stlus.txt].
(Private/Nonprofit) Ann E. Kaplan, ed., *Giving USA: The Annual Report on Philanthropy for the Year 1997.* New York: American Association of Fund-Raising Counsel Trust for Philanthropy, 1998, p. 23.

Further examination of Table 1-1 reveals that the major financial responsibility for health care rests with the federal government and that state and local governments are the primary contributors to education and training programs. These two sources almost equally fund the income security programs. It is also noteworthy that human services receive only limited funding from any source. Had the philosophy of the Pierce Doctrine that government should not be involved in human services prevailed, it is clear that, generous as it is, the private sector voluntarily contributes only 3 percent of the funds to support health, education, and social welfare would not meet the need. Without a substantial tax base, the United States could not begin to adequately assist in carrying out the mandate of the Constitution to promote the general welfare of the people.

Continuing Issues in Social Welfare

It is within the context of changing philosophies of social welfare that the social work profession emerged and established its role among the helping professions. The manner in which the following issues are resolved when establishing the various social programs affects the type of work performed by social workers and their ability to respond to client needs.

PURPOSES AND GOALS FOR SOCIAL PROGRAMS

Social programs are created to accomplish three general purposes. First, most are designed for the *remediation* of a social problem. When a sufficient number of people experience difficulty in a particular aspect of social functioning, social programs are created to provide services intended to correct that problem—or at least to help the clients deal with it more effectively. Remediation programs include services such as income support for the poor, counseling for the mentally ill, and job training for the displaced worker. Remediation has historically been the central form of human service.

A second general purpose of human services has evolved more recently—the *enhancement* of social functioning. In this form of social program the emphasis is on the growth and development of clients in a particular area of functioning without a "problem" having necessarily been identified. Well-baby clinics, parent-effectiveness training, and various youth recreation programs are all examples of social programs designed for personal enhancement.

Finally, the purpose of some social programs is the *prevention* of social problems. As opposed to treating symptoms, prevention programs attempt to identify the basic causes of difficulties in social functioning and seek to stimulate changes that will keep problems from ever developing. Prevention programs, for example, might include helping parents learn appropriate ways to discipline children or conducting community education to make the public aware of the negative impact racism or sexism has on the growth and development of children.

Social programs have been created to serve at least four specific goals: socialization, social integration, social control, and social change. Each goal responds to different human needs—some programs are focused on the needs of individuals or families and others address the needs of the society.

One goal of social programs is to facilitate the *socialization* of people to the accepted norms and behaviors of society. Such programs are designed to help people develop the knowledge and skills to become full participating and contributing members of society and include, for example, such programs as scouting, Boys Clubs and Girls Clubs, and YMCA or YWCA activities. A goal of other social programs is to assist in *social integration* where people are helped to become more successful in interacting with the world around them. Counseling, therapy, and rehabilitation programs, for example, attempt to achieve this goal. A third goal of social programs is, at times, to provide *social control* by removing people from situations when they might place themselves or others at risk or when they require some period of isolation from their usual surroundings in order to address problems. Examples of these programs are found in mental hospitals and correctional facilities. Finally, some programs are intended to achieve *social change*, that is, to express the conscience of society by stimulating changes that will enhance the overall quality of life. For example, public education to encourage the practice of safe sex to reduce the risk of AIDS and the solicitation of employers to hire the developmentally disabled are activities that help to bring about social changes that benefit the society.

RESPONSIBILITY FOR MEETING HUMAN NEEDS

A somewhat controversial issue affecting human services is the assignment of responsibility for meeting basic needs. Our historical review of social programs indicated that the expectation in the most simple form of U.S. society was that the individual would take care of himself or herself or, if not, that families would see that their members' needs were met. Laws in the United States have placed primary responsibility on the family unit for caring for its members and, to a larger extent than in many societies, have protected the sanctity of the family's decisions about how to achieve this goal. It is only in cases where family members are being damaged (e.g., child abuse or neglect, domestic violence, elder maltreatment) that society reluctantly intervenes.

Although some important human services are provided under the auspices of religious organizations, a second level of responsibility for addressing unmet needs increasingly has been assigned to secular nonprofit human service organizations. U.S. society first looked to these voluntary organizations, such as those associated with a local United Way, to meet needs that the family could not provide. Today the most conservative viewpoint would argue that even this auspice for service provision inappropriately relieves families of their responsibility to care for their members. Most people, however, recognize that private human services are an important means of promoting the general welfare in today's mobile and complex society.

As massive social problems persisted, such as the continuing high poverty rate, it became evident that voluntary donations would not be sufficient to achieve even minimal levels of well-being for a large number of people. Therefore, it became necessary for government to enter the business of providing social programs where taxes could be levied to ensure the availability of sufficient funds to meet the most basic needs. One perspective about government-sponsored programs is that they should be developed locally where they can respond to the uniqueness of the region—whether that be a city, county, state, or some other governmental unit. Those supporting the other side of this issue seek a strong federal role in social programs and argue that the causes of many human problems are such factors as chronic unemployment, institutionalized discrimination, inflation, an international trade deficit, and even the volatile price of goods and services on the worldwide market. They argue that individuals and local areas have little, if any, influence over these factors and that it is necessary to create national programs to equalize the burden of responding to the victims of these largely uncontrollable events.

Finally, what had been a sharply increasing role of government in human services was blunted during the 1980s and early 1990s when government agencies initiated a pattern of contracting with private for-profit sources to provide services. The conservative viewpoint contends that it is inefficient for government agencies to commit to employment of staff and construction of facilities where social programs are offered. Instead, they argue it is better to allow the competition of private enterprise to shape service provision by allowing government-funded programs to contract with private practitioners and for-profit corporations. Opponents of this argument for privatization, in contrast, contend that this activity has allowed private enterprise to "cream off" the clients most amenable to help, leaving the more hard-core problems for public and voluntary (nonprofit) human service agencies.

The presence of diverse and sometimes contradictory social programs has resulted in a complex and confusing patchwork of programs and services. For most people seeking help, finding one's way through the network of services with differing sponsorship and differing eligibility requirements is virtually impossible. Professional assistance is often required to negotiate the human services system.

HUMAN SERVICE AS A RIGHT

Regardless of the auspices (i.e., sponsorship) of a social program, the problem of whether clients have a right to receive or refuse the services must be addressed. Historically, social services were viewed as charity—that is, benevolent gifts that a righteous public bestowed on the worthy poor and begrudgingly provided for the not-so-worthy. When human services are based on charity, the recipient is expected to be grateful for any help given, and the donors expect to be appreciated for their contributions to these good works.

A contrasting view is that any member of the society may someday be a victim of factors beyond his or her control and, therefore, has a right to receive services. Given this perspective, some clients have taken the position that they are entitled to services and increasingly have organized or sought legal remedy to ensure that help is provided when needed. Groups advocating for the rights of the poor, the aged, the developmentally disabled, and the physically disabled are found throughout the United States. Once the view is adopted that one has a right to service, the matter of one's having the right to refuse service also arises. For example, should the homeless be required to accept shelter? Or, is it the right of a mental patient to refuse medication? The answers to these questions affect the manner in which professions provide human services.

SOCIAL PROGRAM CONCEPTIONS

The design of social programs also reflects differing philosophical views about who should be served and when services should be given. Programs based on the *safety net approach* are planned as a way for the society to assist people when other social institutions have failed to resolve specific problems. An alternative conception of social programs, the *social utilities approach,* views human services as society's frontline manner of addressing common human needs.

THE SAFETY NET APPROACH.   One conception views human services as a safety net that saves people who have not had their needs met by their primary resources such as the family or employment/economic systems. This approach begins with the presumption that a predefined problem exists—for example, that a family's income is too low, that a person's behavior is deviant, that a child is at risk. Services are then provided to address the problems, and, when a satisfactory level of problem reduction is achieved, the services are terminated. One negative aspect of such programs is that to be eligible for a safety net program, a client must also take on the stigma of having failed in some aspect of social functioning. Further, at times clients must be terminated from service because they have reached a predefined level of functioning, even though the service providers recognize that the clients would benefit from additional assistance.

Safety net programs are thought of as *residual* because they are designed to deal with the residue of human problems—that is, those problems that are left after all other processes of helping are exhausted. Programs based on this approach are also *selective* in the sense that they are designed to serve a specific population experiencing a specific need. Finally, safety net programs are *time-limited* in the sense that services are terminated when a problem is solved (or at least reduced) or a predetermined level of functioning is achieved.

THE SOCIAL UTILITIES APPROACH. The social utilities conception of human services views social programs as one of society's first-line social institutions for meeting needs. Like public utilities for water and electricity, these social utilities are available to all people who wish to make use of them. They do not assume that the person who receives services is at fault or has necessarily failed if he or she requires services. Rather, this concept recognizes that society creates conditions where all people can benefit from social programs, whether the program is designed to help people solve problems or enhance already adequate functioning.

Social utility programs are *universal* in the sense that they do not have strict eligibility requirements. Such programs are also based on an *institutional* conception of human services that considers social programs a regular or institutionalized way of meeting human needs. They do not assume that the individual, family, or any other social institution has failed if, for example, parents place a child in day care, if a young person joins a scouting program, or if a senior citizen takes advantage of a senior center's lunch program.

Different social programs in the United States reflect the safety net and social utilities philosophies. Some human service agencies provide programs representing both philosophies. For example, a public human services department might administer safety net programs such as financial assistance and child protection services and, at the same time, carry responsibility for Medicare and adoption services that are based on the social utilities concept.

HUMAN SERVICE PROGRAM CATEGORIES

Finally, it is useful to recognize that social programs can be divided into three distinct categories: social provisions, personal services, and social action. Each category serves an important function in promoting the general welfare of persons in U.S. society.

SOCIAL PROVISIONS. This category of social programs is designed to meet the most fundamental needs of the population, and such programs are typically viewed as part of the safety net. *Social provisions* are the tangible resources given to persons in need, either as cash or as direct benefits, such as food, clothing, or housing.

Social provisions are the most costly programs in outlay of actual dollars. As social programs have evolved, governmental agencies have assumed the primary responsibility for providing these services, and the private sector has taken the role of providing backup for those people who slip through the mesh of the public safety net. Such major social provision programs as Temporary Assistance to Needy Families (TANF), Supplemental Security Income (SSI), Food Stamps, Low-rent Public Housing, and many others are provided under governmental auspices. Meals and lodging for transients and the homeless, emergency food programs, financial aid in response to crisis situations, shelters for battered wives, and many other social provision programs, however, are offered by voluntary social agencies.

PERSONAL SERVICES. The personal services category of programs includes both problem-solving and enhancement programs. Unlike social provisions, *personal services* are intangible services that help people resolve issues in their social functioning. Examples of personal service programs are marriage and family counseling, child protection services, client advocacy, family therapy, care for the disabled, job training, family planning and abortion counseling, foster care programs, human service brokering and referral activities, and many other programs aimed at helping clients strengthen their social functioning.

SOCIAL ACTION. When one works with people, it quickly becomes evident that it is often inadequate just to help a person or group cope with an unjust world. Efforts must be made to create a more just and supportive environment. For example, it is not enough to help a woman understand and cope with discrimination in the workplace. Although these activities may be important for her ability to keep her job, they do not resolve the basic problem, and they place the burden of change and adjustment on the victim. *Social action* programs help change conditions that create difficulties in social functioning. They require specialized knowledge and skill to effect change in organizations and communities. These efforts involve fact finding, analysis of community needs, research and interpretation of data, and other efforts to inform and mobilize the public to action in order to achieve change.

Concluding Comment

Nearly two hundred and twenty-five years ago the United States of America was formed with a goal of joining people to promote, among other things, the general welfare of all. To achieve that purpose, a variety of programs have been created to meet basic human needs. As the society has changed, so have the programs.

Programs that address needs related to people's social functioning have increasingly been created. Beginning with the expectation that families would take care of their members and, if not, then voluntary associations or local government would make needed provisions, the period since the Great Depression has seen the evolution of a welfare state where public programs primarily support the basic social provisions of food, clothing, and housing. Yet, private philanthropy remains an important resource for personal services and social action programs. Although a considerable share of the nation's resources has been applied to the human services, the principal indicator of its social health, poverty, remains at a high level—particularly for households headed by single mothers and members of minority groups. The passage of the Personal Responsibilities and Work Opportunity Reconciliation Act in 1996 by the U.S. Congress—and the action by President Clinton to sign it into law—represents a major step backward in the society's taking responsibility for its poorest and most vulnerable members.

More effective provision of social programs will require skilled professionals to help clients achieve more desirable levels of social functioning. A group of professional helpers who are central to the efforts to improve the general well-being of people are social workers. Chapter 2 examines that profession and its evolution from a group of concerned volunteers to its role today as a critical part of U.S. society.

KEY WORDS AND CONCEPTS

Hierarchy of needs

Social welfare programs

Human services

Mutual aid philosophy

Puritan philosophy

French Enlightenment philosophy

Conservative/liberal philosophies

Social problem

Social program purposes (i.e., remediation, enhancement, prevention)

Social program goals (i.e., socialization, social integration, social control, social action)

Social program conceptions (i.e., safety net, social utilities)

Human service program categories (i.e., social provisions, personal services, social action)

SUGGESTED READINGS

Axinn, June, and Leven, Herman. *Social Welfare: A History of the American Response to Need*, 4th Edition. New York: Longman, 1997.

Chelf, Carl P. *Controversial Issues in Social Welfare Policy: Government and the Pursuit of Happiness*. Newbury Park, CA: Sage, 1992.

Day, Phyllis J. *A New History of Social Welfare*. Englewood Cliffs, NJ: Prentice Hall, 1989.

Miringoff, Marc, and Miringoff, Marque-Luisa. *The Social Health of the Nation: How America Is Really Doing*. New York: Oxford University Press, 1999.

O'Looney, John. *Redesigning the Work of Human Services*. Westport, CT: Quorum, 1996.

Trattner, Walter I. *From Poor Law to Welfare State*, 6th Edition. New York: Free Press, 1999.

ENDNOTES

1. John Romanyshyn, Victor Baez, and Bradford W. Sheafor, "Social Welfare, Organizational Structure, and Professionals" (Fort Collins: Colorado State University, 1976), videotape.

2. Abraham H. Maslow, *Motivation and Personality* (New York: Harper & Row, 1970), pp. 25–58.

3. Ralph E. Pumphrey and Muriel W. Pumphrey, eds., *The Heritage of American Social Work* (New York: Columbia University Press, 1961), p. 60.

4. Harold L. Wilensky and Charles N. Lebeaux, *Industrial Society and Social Welfare* (New York: Free Press, 1965), p. 42.

5. U.S. Census Bureau, "Poverty 1997" (Washington, D.C.: The Bureau, 1999). http://www.census.gov/hhes/poverty/poverty997/pv97/est1.html

6. U.S. Department of Health and Human Services, The Administration for Children and Families, June 30, 1999. http://www.acf.dhhs.gov/programs/opa/facts/majorpr.htm.

7. Ibid.

8. George W. Church, "How We Can Fix Social Security," *Time* 123 (18, May 10, 1999), unnumbered special insert.

CHAPTER 2

Social Work: A Comprehensive Helping Profession

Prefatory Comment

The human services have become a central part of the fabric of U.S. society. Founded on the goal of promoting the general welfare of its members, society has gradually assumed considerable responsibility for ensuring that its people have access to assistance in meeting their basic needs. One way society provides such assistance is through social programs that make available both tangible resources and various social services to aid people in solving problems or enhancing their social functioning.

The provision of social programs requires people who possess a variety of helping skills. Such helping is often rewarding to both the recipient and the provider of the services. From ancient times to the present all civilized societies have placed great value on helping others. Even in the most simple societies, family, friends, members of the clan or tribe, and other personal acquaintances were expected to care for people in need. As societies became more complex and social programs were created to respond to the more severe needs of people, volunteers associated with churches and community service agencies began to play an active role in providing assistance. In today's industrial and technological society the resolution of many social problems is quite complicated, requiring that human services be provided by highly trained professionals. It is within this context that social work was born.

Social work is one of several professions that has evolved to offer these human services. This chapter provides a general description, an overview, of social work with many of its elements to be revisited and examined in greater depth in subsequent chapters.

What is perhaps the most basic form of helping has been termed *natural helping*. Before reaching a social worker or other professional helpers, clients often have been counseled or assisted in some way by family, friends, neighbors, or volunteers. Natural helping is based on a mutual relationship among equals, and the helper draws heavily on intuition and life experience to guide the helping process. The complexity of social issues and the extensive knowledge and skill required to effectively provide some human services exceed what natural helpers can typically accomplish. This has resulted in the emergence of several occupations that deliver more complicated services to people in need.

Professional helping is different from natural helping in that it is a disciplined approach focused on the needs of the client and it requires specific knowledge, values, and skills to guide the helping activity. Both natural and professional helping are valid means of assisting people in resolving issues related to their social functioning. In fact, many helping professionals first became interested in these careers because they were successful natural helpers and found the experience rewarding. Social workers often work closely with natural helping networks both during the change process and as a source of support after professional service is terminated. However, natural helpers are not a substitute for competent professional help in addressing serious problems or gaining access to needed services.

Social work is the most comprehensive of human service occupations and, through time, has become recognized as the profession that centers its attention on helping people improve their social functioning. In simplest terms, social workers help people strengthen their interaction with various aspects of their world—their children, parents, spouse or other loved one, family, friends, coworkers, or even organizations and whole communities. Social work is also committed to changing factors in the society that diminish the quality of life for all people, but especially for those persons who are most vulnerable to social problems.

Social work's mission of serving both people and the social environment is ambitious. To fulfill that mission, social workers must possess a broad range of knowledge about the functioning of people and social institutions, as well as have a variety of skills for facilitating change in how individuals, organizations, and other social structures operate. This comprehensive mission has made social work an often misunderstood profession. Like the fable of the blind men examining the elephant with each believing that the whole elephant is like the leg, trunk, ear, and so on that he examined, too often people observe one example of social work and conclude that it represents the whole of professional activity. To appreciate the full scope of this profession, it is useful to examine its most fundamental characteristics—the themes that characterize social work.

The Central Themes Underpinning Social Work

Five themes can be identified that reflect the character of social work. No one theme is unique to this profession, but in combination they provide a foundation on which to build one's understanding of social workers and their practice.

A COMMITMENT TO SOCIAL BETTERMENT

Belief in the fundamental importance of improving the quality of social interaction for all people, that is, *social betterment,* is a central value of the social worker.

The social work profession has taken the position that all people should have the opportunity for assistance in meeting their social needs. The source of that assistance might be family, friends, or more formal social programs.

Social work has maintained an idealism about the ability and responsibility of this society to provide opportunities and resources that allow each person to lead a full and rewarding life. It has been particularly concerned with the underdog—the most vulnerable people in the society. This idealism must not be confused with naivete. Social workers are often the most knowledgeable people in the community about the plight of the poor, the abused, the lonely, and others who for a variety of reasons are out of the mainstream of society or experiencing social problems. When social workers express their desire for changes that contribute to the social betterment of people, it is often viewed as a threat by those who want to protect the status quo.

A GOAL TO ENHANCE SOCIAL FUNCTIONING

The commitment to social betterment precludes a narrow focus on specific social problems. In fact, social work takes the position that social betterment involves more than addressing problems—it also involves assisting those who want to improve some aspect of their lives, even though it may not be considered as problematic. Social work, then, is concerned with helping people enhance their *social functioning,* that is, the manner in which they interact with people and social institutions.

Social workers help people and social institutions change in relation to a rapidly changing world. The technology explosion, information explosion, population explosion, and even the threat of nuclear explosion dramatically impact people's lives. Those who can readily adapt to these changes—and are not limited by discrimination due to race, cultural background, gender, age, or physical, emotional, or intellectual abilities—seldom use the services of social workers. Others who have become victims of this too rapidly changing world and its unstable social institutions, however, are likely to require professional help in dealing with this change.

AN ACTION ORIENTATION

Social work is a profession of doers. Social workers are not satisfied just to examine social issues. Rather, they take action to prevent problems from developing, attack problematic situations that can be changed, and help people deal with troublesome situations that cannot be changed. To do this, social workers provide services that include such activities as individual counseling, family and group therapy, linking people to the network of services in a community, fund raising, and even social action. Indeed, social work is an applied science.

AN APPRECIATION FOR HUMAN DIVERSITY

To deal effectively with the wide range of individual and institutional change to which social work is committed, it has become a profession characterized by *diversity*—diversity of clientele, diversity of knowledge and skills, and diversity of services provided. In addition, social workers themselves come in all shapes, colors, ages, and descriptions.

Social workers view diversity as positive. They consider human difference desirable and appreciate the richness that can be offered a society through the culture, language, and traditions of various ethnic, racial, and cultural groups. They value the unique perspectives of persons of different gender, sexual orientation, or age groups, and they recognize and develop the strengths of persons who have been disadvantaged. What's more, social workers view their own diversity as an enriching quality that has created a dynamic profession that can respond to human needs in an ever-changing world.

A VERSATILE PRACTICE PERSPECTIVE

The wide range of human problems with which social workers deal, the variety of settings in which they are employed, the extensive scope of services they provide, and the diverse populations they serve make it unrealistic to expect that a single practice approach could adequately support social work practice. Rather, the social worker must have a comprehensive repertoire of knowledge and techniques that can be used to meet the unique needs of individual clients and client groups.

The versatile social worker, then, must have a solid foundation of knowledge about the behavior of people and social institutions in order to understand the situations their clients bring to them. He or she also needs to understand that differing beliefs may affect the way people will interpret and react to those situations. And, finally, the social worker must have mastered a number of helping techniques from which he or she can imaginatively select and skillfully use to help individuals, families, groups, organizations, and communities improve their social functioning.

How do these themes affect social work practice? The following case example* is just one of many situations where a social worker might help a client:

> Karoline Truesdale, a school social worker, interviewed Kathy and Jim Swan in anticipation of the Swans' oldest son, Danny, beginning school in the fall. The Swans responded to Ms. Truesdale's invitation to the parents of all prospective kindergartners to talk over any concerns they might have about their children's schooling. When making the appointment, Kathy Swan indicated that her son, Danny, was near the cut-off age for entering school and may not be ready yet for kindergarten. When questioned further, Kathy expressed considerable ambivalence indicating that having him in school would help to relieve other burdens at home, but may be too much for Danny.

> Karoline's notes from the interview contained the following information:

> *Kathy Swan is 20 years old and about to deliver her third child. She indicates that they certainly did not need another mouth to feed at this time, but "accidents happen" and she will attempt to cope with this additional child when it is born (although she already*

*Sonia Nornes and Bradford W. Sheafor originally developed this case material for the Fort Collins (Colorado) Family Support Alliance.

appears physically and emotionally depleted). Jim is 21 years old and holds a temporary job earning minimum wage. He moved the family to the city because "money in agriculture has gone to hell" and a maintenance job was available at a manufacturing plant here. However, he was laid off after three months when the plant's workforce was reduced. Jim is angry that he moved the family for this job, yet the company felt no obligation to keep him on. He stated that "people in the country don't treat others like that." He is also worried that his temporary job will last only a few more weeks and commented that Kathy "spends money on those kids like it was going out of style." Jim said in no uncertain terms that he did not want and they could not afford another baby, but Kathy had refused to even consider an abortion.

The children are quite active and Danny pays little attention to Kathy's constant requests that he calm down. When Jim attempts to control Danny, Kathy accuses him of being too physical in his discipline. When questioned about this, Jim reported that his Dad "beat me plenty and that sure got results." Kathy complains that Jim does not appreciate the difficulty of being home with the children all of the time, and she objects to the increasing amount of time he is away in the evenings. Jim replied rather pointedly that "it is not much fun being at home anymore." Tension between Kathy and Jim was evident.

When questioned about their social contacts since moving to the city, both Kathy and Jim reported that it had been hard to make friends. They knew "everyone in town" before they moved, but it is different now. With his changing employment, Jim has not made any real friends at work, and Kathy feels isolated at home since Jim takes the car to work each day and the bus is her only means of transportation. She did indicate that one neighbor has been friendly, and they have met two couples they liked at church.

When asked specifically about Danny, Kathy reported that he has been ill frequently with colds and chronic ear infections. She hesitantly described his behavior as troublesome and hoped the school's structure would help him. Kathy described a Sunday school teacher who called him hyperactive and suggested that she not take him to Sunday school anymore. Kathy wondered if there was some kind of treatment that would help Danny and allowed that she was "about at the end of her rope with that child."

It was clear to Karoline that both Kathy and Jim wanted Danny to begin school. But was Danny ready for school—and would the school be ready for Danny? Would Danny's entering school be best for him? Would it resolve the family's problems? Are there other things that could be done to help this family and, perhaps, prevent other problems from emerging?

Within the strict definition of her job, Ms. Truesdale could assist the Swans in reaching a decision about school attendance and complete her service to this family. With her "social betterment" concern, however, resolution of only the question about Danny's entering school would not be sufficient. As a social worker, Karoline would hope to help the Swan family address some of the more basic issues they face in order to improve the overall quality of their lives.

Social workers are not experts on all problems clients may experience. Ms. Truesdale's experience, for example, would not prepare her to make judgments about Danny's health and the possible relationship between his chronic colds and ear infections and his behavior problems. She might refer the Swans to a low-cost medical clinic where a diagnosis of Danny's health problems can be made. She is, however, an expert in "social functioning" and can help Jim and Kathy Swan work on their parenting skills, strengthen the quality of their communication, assist them in developing social relationships in the community, and, perhaps, help Jim obtain job training and stable employment. Karoline's "action orientation" would not allow her to procrastinate. She would be anxious to engage this family in assessing the issues it faces and would support Kathy and Jim as they take action to resolve them.

The Swan family represents at least one form of "human diversity." They are a rural family attempting to adapt to an urban environment. Ms. Truesdale knows that it will take time and probably some help to make this adjustment. She will explore strengths that may have been derived from their rural background. Perhaps Jim's skills in gardening and machinery repair would prove to be an asset in some lines of employment. Also, their rural friendliness may prove beneficial in establishing new social relationships, and they might be helped to build friendships through their church or neighborhood, or to use other resources where they can find informal sources of support (i.e., natural helping).

Service to the Swan family will require considerable practice "versatility." Ms. Truesdale will need to assist the family in problem solving around whether or not to send Danny to school. She will hopefully engage them in more in-depth family counseling. She might invite them to join a parents' group she leads to discuss child-rearing practices, link them with medical and psychological testing services for Danny, and help Mr. Swan obtain job training. If Danny does attend school next year, Karoline might work closely with his teacher and Mrs. Swan to monitor Danny's progress and address any problems in his social functioning that may arise. If he does not attend school, an alternative program might be found where he can develop the socialization skills required in the classroom. Clearly, a wide range of practice activities would be needed and Karoline must be versatile in her practice to apply them.

The Mission of Social Work

While social work practice requires considerable variation in activity, at a more abstract level the profession has consistently maintained that its fundamental *mission* is directly serving people in need and, at the same time, making social institutions more responsive to people. Although this unique mission has been steadfastly held for more than a century, it has been difficult to develop public understanding of its uniqueness among the helping professions. Carol Meyer accurately sums up the situation:

> All enduring professions adapt to social change and pursue their interests, but they maintain the same purposes at the core. Architects design buildings, doctors deal with sickness and health, lawyers practice law, and educators teach. Social workers are concerned with _____ ? With what? Fill in the blank. With people? Psychological functioning? Delivery of social services? Management of human service agencies? Policy analysis? Social change? . . . All of these or some of these?[1]

One way to identify the boundaries of social work is to examine its three primary purposes: caring, curing, and changing.

CARING

Throughout their history social workers have sought to improve the quality of life for the most vulnerable groups in the population. At times the best knowledge we can muster is inadequate to prevent or cure the many problems encountered by the disabled, elderly, terminally ill, and other persons with limited capacity for social functioning. From Dorothea Dix's concerns about the plight of people in mental hospitals in the mid-1800s to today's concerns about the negative experiences of people in some nursing homes, social workers have recognized that certain conditions in life cannot be corrected. Yet, the victims of these conditions deserve not only humane but high-quality care.

Caring that makes people comfortable and helps them cope with their limitations is frequently the most valuable service a social worker can provide. Sometimes caring takes the form of making social provisions available to people such as arranging for meals to be delivered or for income to be supplemented, and ensuring that adequate housing is provided. At other times, the person and/or family may require caring in the form of personal services such as counseling to better adjust to an unchangeable situation like a disability or terminal illness. There is an important leadership role for social work in helping communities create the necessary services to provide such care. The fundamental intention of caring for those in need continues to be a central purpose of social work practice.

CURING

Another thrust of social work practice has been to provide treatment for individuals and families experiencing problems in social functioning. Depending on client needs, direct service practices ranging from psychosocial therapy to behavioral modification, reality therapy, crisis intervention, and various group and family therapy approaches are used by social workers.[2] These approaches do not automatically cure social problems in the same way a physician might prescribe a medication to cure an infection. In fact, most social workers would argue that at best they can only help clients cure themselves. The contribution the social worker makes is the ability to engage the client in actively working toward change, to accurately assess the individual and societal factors that have created the need for change, to select appropriate techniques for a given client and situation, and to use these techniques effectively in conjunction with the clients to accomplish the desired results.

CHANGING THE SOCIETY

Social change is the third primary purpose of social work. Social workers are committed to reforming existing laws, procedures, and attitudes until they are more responsive to human needs. Many pioneer social workers were active reformers who worked to improve conditions in slums, hospitals, and poorhouses. Today, they actively influence social legislation in an effort to create new social programs or to change factors that contribute to damaging social conditions such as racism, sexism, and poverty.

Social workers also seek to change negative public attitudes about the more vulnerable members of society by providing public education and facilitating the empowerment of the affected members of the population to advocate for their own interests. Social workers, then, bring about change in the society by representing the interests of their clientele and/or helping clients convince decision makers at the local, state, or national levels to respond to human needs.

Defining Social Work

Three concerted efforts have been made to arrive at a clear definition of social work. The first occurred in the 1920s when the American Association of Social Workers convened a series of meetings of key agency executives in Milford, Pennsylvania. These representatives from a range of practice settings identified several factors that appeared to be common to all social work practice, but they could not agree on a concise definition of social work. However, the Milford Conference encouraged further efforts at articulating a definition of social work when it concluded that social work's common features were more substantial than the differences related to practice in different settings.[3]

The 1950s brought a second surge of interest in developing a clear conception of social work. The merger of several specialized social work practice organizations (e.g., American Association of Hospital Social Workers, National Association of Visiting Teachers, American Association of Psychiatric Social Workers, and the more generic American Association of Social Workers) into the National Association of Social Workers (NASW) was completed in 1955. For a time, a spirit of unity dominated the social work profession, and the effort to find a definition of social work that would reflect the commonality in diverse practice activities began in earnest. A critical step was the publication of the "Working Definition of Social Work Practice" in 1958. Although not yet providing a comprehensive definition of social work, the document established an important basis for subsequent definitions by identifying three common goals of social work practice:[4]

1. To assist individuals and groups to identify and resolve or minimize problems arising out of disequilibrium between themselves and their environment.
2. To identify potential areas of disequilibrium between individuals or groups and the environment in order to prevent the occurrence of disequilibrium.
3. To seek out, identify, and strengthen the maximum potential of individuals, groups, and communities.

Thus, the "Working Definition" established that social workers are concerned with curative or treatment goals, as well as emphasizing the importance of social change or prevention. In addition, the definition recognized the focus of social work on the interactions between people and their environments and the responsibility of social workers to provide services to people as individuals, as parts of various groups, and as members of communities.

Third, in the 1970s and 1980s, NASW published three special issues of its major journal, *Social Work*, that generated substantial debate and discussion, although not conclusions, about the nature of social work.[5] This activity enhanced understanding of the central features that characterize social work but did not lead to a definitive description of this profession.

Although NASW has never adopted a definition of social work, a one-sentence definition developed by one of its committees has gained widespread acceptance.

> Social work is the professional activity of helping individuals, groups, or communities enhance or restore their capacity for social functioning and creating societal conditions favorable to that goal.[6]

This statement provides a concise one-sentence "dictionary definition" of the profession. It draws important boundaries around social work. First, social work is considered professional activity. Professional activity requires a particular body of knowledge, values, and skills, as well as a discrete purpose that guides one's practice activities. When practice is judged professional, community sanction to perform these tasks is assumed to be present, and the profession, in turn, is expected to be accountable to the public for the quality of services provided.

Second, this definition captures a uniqueness of social work. It makes clear that social workers serve a range of client systems that include individuals, families or other household units, groups, organizations, neighborhoods, communities, and even larger units of society. For social work, the identification of one's client is tricky because a client or target of practice activity may range from an individual to a state or nation. The unique activities of the social worker are directed toward helping all of those systems interact more effectively and require professional education as preparation.

Finally, the last part of the definition concerns social work's dual focus on person and environment. Social workers help people enhance or restore their capacity for social functioning. At the same time, they work to change societal conditions that may help or hinder people from improving their social functioning. Herein lies another uniqueness of social work. Whereas some professions focus on change in the person and others on changing the environment, social work's attention is directed to the connections between person and environment.

When working with clients, social workers must take into consideration both the characteristics of the person and the impinging forces from the environment. In contrast, the physician is primarily prepared to treat physical aspects of the individual, and the attorney is largely concerned with the operation of the legal system in the larger environment (although both the physician and attorney should give secondary attention to other, related systems). Social work recognizes that each person brings to the helping situation a set of behaviors, needs, and beliefs that are the result of his or her unique experiences from birth. Yet it also recognizes that whatever is brought to the situation must be related to the world as that person confronts it. By focusing on transactions between the person and his or her environment, social interaction can be improved.

Figure 2-1 depicts this unique focus of social work. Social workers operate at the boundary between people and their environment. They are not prepared to deal with all boundary matters. Rather, they address those matters that are judged problematic

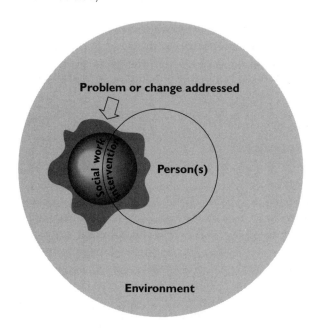

FIGURE 2-1 Focal Point of Social Work Intervention

or have been selected as a way to contribute to the enhancement of social functioning. In sum, social workers temporarily enter the lives of their clients to help them improve their transactions with important elements of their environment.

Social Work Practice Approaches

Arriving at a practice approach that is sufficiently flexible and encompassing to relate to this complex profession has proven difficult. In fact, social work might be characterized during much of its history as a profession in search of a practice approach. That search included the development of several distinct practice methods.

TRADITIONAL PRACTICE METHODS

As part of the drive to become a unique profession, social work sought to identify a distinctive method of practice that would distinguish it from other helping professions such as law, medicine, and psychology. The first practice method to develop, *social casework,* was first described in the 1917 classic social work book, *Social Diagnosis.*[7] In this book, Mary Richmond focused on the requirements for effective practice with individuals and families, regardless of the type of problem presented. The book filled an important void in social work by introducing a practice literature. The principles of social casework identified by Richmond were enthusiastically adopted by social workers, and the profession moved its primary focus to work with individuals and families. The popularity of Freudian psychology in the 1920s and 1930s also directed social work toward individual practice, rather than to the more controversial activities associated with changing social institutions that had previously characterized much of social work practice. Edith Abbott noted that Richmond later expressed concern over this trend to emphasize the person side of the person-environment mission of social work:

> The good social worker, says Miss Richmond, doesn't go on helping people out of a ditch. Pretty soon she begins to find out what ought to be done to get rid of the ditch.[8]

Social workers concerned with providing services to groups took longer to develop a set of guiding principles, partially because those social workers disagreed as to whether they should identify professionally with the emerging field of social work or with recreation or continuing education. This disagreement among *social group workers* was resolved in the 1930s in favor of identifying with social work, and thus a second distinct method evolved.

The third practice method to develop was *community organization*. With many social agencies and social programs evolving in each community, their coordination and the evaluation of their effectiveness became important and, to meet that need, another distinct practice area emerged. Community organization became the practice method primarily concerned with the distribution of financial resources and building linkages among existing services.

In addition to using one of these three primary practice methods in their work, many social workers found themselves responsible for administering social agencies and conducting research on the effectiveness of social programs. Their experience and education usually left them with little preparation for these indirect service activities. By the late 1940s *administration* and *research* had evolved as practice methods in social work. Viewed as secondary methods, they were seen as a supplement to a person's ability as a caseworker, group worker, or community organizer.

MULTIMETHOD PRACTICE APPROACH

Concurrent with the development of these five distinct practice approaches was the growing commitment to the evolution of social work as a single profession with a unifying practice method. A major study of social work and social work education, the Hollis–Taylor Report, was concluded in 1951. It recommended that, because the breadth of social work practice required social workers to intervene at more than one level of client system, social work education should prepare students with a beginning level of competence in each of the five practice methods.[9]

The multimethod practice approach proved a good fit with the varied demands for social work practice, but failed to yield the unifying practice theme the profession needed. Practitioners typically identified with a dominant method and used the others sparingly. Elitism based on practice method and setting persisted (e.g., it was preferable to be a psychiatric caseworker rather than "just" a social worker), creating an attitude that interfered with the search for commonality and unity within social work.

GENERALIST PRACTICE APPROACH

Supported by concepts drawn from social systems theory, the generalist approach to practice began to emerge in the late 1960s. As Balinsky stated, "The complexity of human problems necessitates a broadly oriented practitioner with a versatile repertoire of methods and skills capable of interacting in any one of a number of systems."[10] The generalist model provided that versatility and met the requirement for a flexible approach to social work practice demanded by the increasing complexity and interrelatedness of human problems.

Generalist practice contains two fundamental components. First, it provides a perspective from which the social worker views the practice situation. Social systems theory helps the social worker to maintain a focus on the interaction between systems—that is, the person–environment transactions—and to continually look for ways to intervene in more than one relevant system. Second, rather than attempting to make the client's situation fit the methodological orientation of the social worker, the situation is viewed as determining the practice approach to be used. Thus, the social worker is required to have a broad knowledge and skill base from which to serve clients or client systems and to have the ability to appropriately select from that base to meet the needs of the clients.

Although many social workers contend that the generalist approach has been part of social work practice since its inception, only recently have there been analysis and explication of this practice approach. With the accreditation requirement that both baccalaureate- and master's-level social workers be prepared as generalist practitioners, there has been a resurgence of activity aimed at clarifying the nature of generalist practice in recent years. In their article entitled "Milford Redefined: A Model of Initial and Advanced Generalist Social Work," Schatz, Jenkins, and Sheafor delineate the key elements of generalist social work at both the initial and advanced generalist levels.[11] Their model is based on research that documented areas of agreement among experts who have written about generalist social work practice or administered educational programs that prepared students as generalists.

This model recognizes that there is a *generic foundation* for all social work, whether generalist or specialist, that includes such factors as knowledge about the social work profession, social work values, the purpose of social work, ethnic/diversity sensitivity, basic communication skills, understanding of human relationships, and others.

The *generalist perspective,* according to the Schatz–Jenkins–Sheafor model: (1) is informed by sociobehavioral and ecosystems knowledge; (2) incorporates ideologies that include democracy, humanism, and empowerment; (3) requires a worker to be theoretically and methodologically open when approaching a practice situation; (4) is client-centered and problem-focused; (5) involves both direct and indirect intervention awareness; and (6) is research-based.

At the *initial generalist* level of practice, the social worker builds on the generic foundation and, using the generalist perspective, must at least be capable of: (1) engaging effectively in interpersonal helping; (2) managing change processes; (3) appropriately selecting and utilizing multilevel intervention modes; (4) intervening in multiple-sized systems as determined by the practice situation; (5) performing varied practice roles; (6) assessing and examining one's own practice; and (7) functioning successfully within an agency.

The *advanced generalist* social worker engages in more difficult practice tasks and, therefore, operates from an expanded knowledge base about individuals, groups, organizations, and communities. The advanced generalist must also develop increased skills to intervene in direct service provision with individuals, families, and groups at one end of the multiple-level practice spectrum, and, at the other end, address more complex indirect practice situations such as supervision, administration, and policy or program evaluation. Finally, the advanced generalist is expected to approach social work practice from an eclectic, but disciplined and systematic, stance and to simultaneously engage in both theoretical research and practice evaluation.

SPECIALIST PRACTICE APPROACH

In contrast to the generalist, a number of specialized practice approaches have emerged. *Specialist* social work practice is characterized by the application of selected knowledge and skills to a narrowed area of practice based on practice setting, population served, social problems addressed, and/or practice intervention mode used. In other words, this practice approach begins with a preference about the knowledge and skills required for practice in that specialized area and fits the client into those more narrow, but in-depth, worker competencies.

While education for generalist practice usually is offered in baccalaureate programs or the early part of master's-level programs, specialist education has increasingly been designated as the prerogative of the latter part of a master's degree. The Curriculum Policy Statement of the Council on Social Work Education that guides the accreditation of these programs identifies the following categories of specializations that schools might offer:

Fields of Practice: for example, services to families, children, and youth; services to the elderly; health; mental health; developmental disabilities; education; business and industry; neighborhood and community development; income maintenance; employment.

Problem Areas: for example, crime and delinquency; substance abuse; developmental disabilities; family violence; mental illness; neighborhood deterioration; poverty; racism; sexism.

Populations-at-Risk: for example, children and youth; the aged; women; single parents; ethnic populations; persons in poverty; migrants; gay and lesbian persons; the chronically mentally ill.

Intervention Methods or Roles: for example, specific practice approaches with individuals, families, and groups; consultation; community organization; social planning; administration; case management; social policy formulation; research.

Practice Contexts and Perspectives: for example, industry; hospitals; rural or urban areas.[12]

Today, like many disciplines, social work embraces both generalist and specialist approaches to practice. The generalist viewpoint supports the commonality that unites social work into one profession; the specialist approach helps to delineate unique areas for in-depth social work practice.

Social Workers: Their Many Faces

Three factors help to explain what it is like to be a social worker: career patterns at different educational levels; knowledge, values, and skills used in practice; and personal characteristics of social workers. For each factor there is considerable diversity expressed in the practice activities of social workers.

CAREER PATTERNS OF SOCIAL WORKERS

Varying career patterns have evolved as the practice of social work has changed over time. The early social workers were volunteers or paid staff who required no specific training or educational program to qualify for the work. When formal education programs were instituted at the turn of the century, they were training programs located in the larger social agencies. In fact, it was not until 1939 that accreditation standards required that all recognized social work education must be offered in institutions of higher education. There was also controversy over whether appropriate social work education could be offered at the baccalaureate level as well as at the more professionally respectable master's level. The reorganization of social work into one professional association (the National Association of Social Workers, NASW) and one professional education association (the Council on Social Work Education, CSWE) in the 1950s yielded a single-level profession. At that time, only the master's degree from an accredited school of social work was considered "legitimate" social work preparation. Today, the MSW degree still is considered the "terminal practice degree" in social work, but other professional practice levels are now recognized. In 1998, 13,660 persons received the MSW degree from one of the 126 accredited programs, making it the dominant qualification for social work practice.[13]

Another level of professional recognition was established in 1961 by the NASW—the Academy of Certified Social Workers (ACSW). The ACSW was the first step in creating a multilevel career pattern and represented the profession's method of identifying its more experienced practitioners. To be recognized as a member of the Academy, one must have completed an MSW, have at least two years of supervised practice experience, have favorable references, and pass a test on practice knowledge.

Increasingly, social workers are also completing doctoral degrees in social work, either the Doctor of Social Work (DSW) or the Doctor of Philosophy (Ph.D.). In 1998, for example, about 266 persons completed a doctorate in social work from sixty-two schools in the United States.[14] In addition, a number of other social workers also completed doctorates in related disciplines. Most doctoral-level social work-

ers are employed in teaching or research positions, but an increasing number of doctoral programs aimed at preparing people for direct social work are emerging. Doctoral programs, however, are not subject to accreditation by CSWE and are not
recognized as professional preparation for social work practice. Thus, the MSW
continues to be viewed as the terminal practice degree.

It was not until 1970 that the NASW recognized baccalaureate-level (BSW)
social workers as members of the Association. The Council on Social Work Education subsequently created accreditation standards, and, by 1998, 410 schools
throughout the United States graduated 11,435 persons with the BSW (at times this
may be a BA or a BS degree) from an accredited social work education program.[15]
Another career level had been recognized.

By 1981, NASW found it necessary to develop a classification system that would
help to clarify the various entry points to social work and define the educational and
practice requirements at each level. This system sorts out the somewhat mixed career
levels in social work:[16]

Basic Professional	Requires a baccalaureate degree from a program accredited by CSWE.
Specialized Professional	Requires a master's degree from a program accredited by CSWE.
Independent Professional	Requires an accredited MSW and at least two years of post-master's experience under appropriate professional supervision. (Requirements for the ACSW match this standard.)
Advanced Professional	Requires special theoretical, practice, administrative, or policy proficiency or ability to conduct advanced research or studies in social welfare, usually demonstrated through a doctoral degree in social work or a closely related social science discipline.

NASW's classification scheme has several benefits. First, it identifies and clari-
fies the practice levels existing in social work and, in general terms, spells out the
competencies that both clients and employers can expect from workers at each level.
Second, it describes a continuum of social work practice with several entry points
based on education and experience. Finally, it suggests a basis for job classification
that can increasingly distinguish among the various levels of social work competence
and assist agencies in selecting appropriately prepared social workers to fill their
positions.

THE SOCIAL WORKER'S KNOWLEDGE, VALUES, AND SKILLS

To practice social work effectively, specific knowledge and mastery of a variety of
intervention approaches are needed. The social worker not only must be able to

work directly with a client or clients, but also should be prepared to understand and work to change the environment of these clients. He or she must understand the culture in which the practice occurs, the background of the people served, and the functioning of the social agency where the services are provided. The social worker must also know what other services are available in the community, know the causes of the client's problems in social functioning, and have the means to effectively provide human services. It takes rigorous professional education to master the knowledge, values, and skills required for social work practice.

What basic competencies are fundamental to social work practice? Depending on the particular job, the type of agency where one works, client capabilities, problems being addressed, and resources available, the social worker will need to have differing competencies. Yet, any profession must have some common features in the tasks performed by its members. A comprehensive task analysis of social workers conducted by Teare and Sheafor has provided an empirically based description of the work of social workers and identifies competencies required to perform that work. This study is the basis for Chapter 8, which details a set of competencies required for social work practice. One finding of that study is that there are several tasks regularly performed by virtually all social workers. These tasks are related to interpersonal helping (i.e., basic interviewing and communication with clients), case planning and maintenance, professional competence development and workload planning, and the ongoing acquisition of knowledge about the human service delivery system.[17]

CHARACTERISTICS OF TODAY'S SOCIAL WORKERS

Who are the people who have elected a career in social work? It is difficult to accurately determine the characteristics of today's social workers because a single data source that includes all social workers does not exist. The U.S. Bureau of Labor Statistics (BLS) estimates that in 1996 there were 585,000 employed social workers in the United States who had completed a social work degree. Unfortunately, the BLS data provide little information about these social workers and it is necessary to examine only the characteristics of those social workers who are members of the National Association of Social Workers to gain more detail about the members of this profession. The NASW membership data are heavily skewed toward the specialized or independent, that is, the MSW-level workers (85.5%). For several reasons, such as the cost of NASW membership compared to salaries, the relative emphasis of NASW programs on the concerns of master's-level social workers, and the large portion of the BSW workers later going on to complete an MSW degree, only 9.9 percent of the NASW members are baccalaureate-level social workers.[18] Nevertheless, the NASW membership data summarized in Table 2-1 yield the most accurate depiction of social workers at bachelor's, master's, and doctoral educational levels that is currently available.

Although social work is highly committed to diversity, it is clear that the ranks of social workers are largely white females. It is evident from the NASW mem-

| TABLE 2-1 | Characteristics of Baccalaureate-, Master's-, and Doctoral-level Social Workers |

Social Worker Characteristic	BSW	MSW	DSW
Gender: Female	89.7%	78.5%	58.5%
Minority Group Member	13.7	11.3	13.6
Annual Income from Full-time Employment			
Less than $15,000	10.0	1.4	1.0
$15,000 to $19,999	20.1	2.6	0.4
$20,000 to $29,999	46.4	26.6	8.3
$30,000 to $39,999	16.6	38.0	25.5
$40,000 or more	6.8	31.5	64.7
Primary Employment Setting			
Social services agency	33.7	20.5	10.1
Health/mental health facility (hospital and outpatient)	26.6	38.9	20.0
Residential care facility	21.1	6.4	2.2
School (preschool through grade 12)	3.8	7.1	3.2
Private practice	3.1	20.2	24.1
Courts/justice system	2.6	3.9	0.6
College/university	2.6	2.6	37.2
Other	6.3	3.0	2.5
Primary Auspices of Employment			
Federal/state/local government	41.6	33.0	41.0
Private (nonprofit) agency	40.4	38.6	31.6
Private (for-profit) agency	18.1	28.3	27.5
Primary Practice Area			
Children-families	29.2	24.9	19.6
Mental health	18.3	39.6	40.7
Medical health	17.0	13.2	7.7
Aging	16.7	4.2	3.7
Schools	2.6	5.4	4.1
Criminal justice	2.5	1.1	1.1
Other	13.2	10.8	22.2
Primary Job Function			
Clinical/direct service	65.5	71.1	40.4
Administration/management	10.6	15.7	16.7
Teaching/training	5.9	2.8	32.1
Supervision	4.6	5.7	2.3
Other	13.5	4.2	8.4

Source: Margaret Gibelman and Philip H. Schervish, *Who We Are: A Second Look* (Washington, D.C.: NASW Press, 1997), pp. 54, 59, 71, 86, 103, 114, and 134.

bership data that the pay for social work is moderate with the median annual full-time employment income for BSW workers typically ranging from $20,000 to $30,000. Income increases about $10,000 per year for social workers practicing at the master's level, and for those at the doctoral level, it increases to well above $40,000 per year. Educational level is clearly the most significant factor influencing salary. However, other factors that are often associated with job access at the different educational levels also reflect substantial salary variations. For example, social workers working primarily with older people and children and youth (except for schools) are at the lowest pay levels, while those working in mental health, in business and industry, or at colleges and universities earn the most. Further, when auspices of the employing agency are considered, social workers employed by nonprofit agencies earn the least and those working for for-profit organizations earn considerably more. Finally, workers in direct practice (clinical) jobs average the least income, while those in administrative or management positions earn the most.[19]

Examination of the NASW membership data in Table 2-1 reveals substantial differences in the settings in which social workers are employed. Baccalaureate-level (or basic) social workers are most likely to be employed in social services agencies such as a public human services department or a small nonprofit community agency, followed by employment in a health/mental health agency, or a residential facility such as a group home or nursing home. Clearly the feature that distinguishes the basic social worker from the specialized or independent social worker is the concentration in practice positions working with older people and the relatively small proportion employed in mental health.

Master's-level workers, by contrast, are considerably more likely to work in mental health (particularly the for-profit agencies) or to maintain their own private practice in which they independently contract with their clients to provide services. The specialized- or independent-level social workers also report that they are somewhat more likely than basic workers to serve in administrative and management positions.

The doctoral-level social workers are most likely to be employed by a college or university, although about one-fourth of them are in private practice and another one-fifth are employed in health/mental health settings. Social workers at this advanced level are primarily direct service clinicians or social work faculty members and, to a lesser extent, agency administrators.

Concluding Comment

Since its inception more than a century ago, social work has emerged as a comprehensive helping profession. From the beginning, social workers sought that elusive common denominator that would depict this profession as clearly as possible and help social work form into a cohesive entity.

Recognition of the common mission of working simultaneously with both people and their environments to improve social functioning has consistently served as social work's primary mission and thus differentiates social work from the other helping professions. In addition to helping people deal with their environments, social workers also consider it their mission to bring about social change in order to prevent problems or to make social institutions more responsive to the needs of people—especially the most vulnerable members of the society. With this person and environment focus, social workers provide a combination of caring, curing, and changing activities that help people improve the quality of their lives and, therefore, help the society accomplish its goal of promoting the general welfare.

When carrying out their professional service activities, social workers are typically employed in public or nonprofit voluntary human service agencies that provide services ranging from child protection to family counseling to assisting the aged. An increasing number, particularly those with master's and doctorate degrees, are employed in for-profit agencies or as private practitioners where they contract directly with clients to provide services. Some are generalists and approach their practice in a manner like the physician who is a general practitioner, while others are specialists and provide in-depth services related to particular helping activities. As Chapter 8 will amplify, there is a core of competencies required of all social workers regardless of setting, educational level, practice area, or job function.

Social work has evolved a career ladder that recognizes professionals at four levels: basic, specialized, independent, and advanced. This classification scheme recognizes that at each of the four levels somewhat different job activities occur. The two entry levels (i.e., basic and specialized professional levels) require that the worker complete the requisite educational preparation represented in the accreditation standards of the Council on Social Work Education. At the latter two levels, additional practice experience and expertise and/or advanced education warrant the recognition.

KEY WORDS AND CONCEPTS

Natural and professional helping

Social betterment

Social functioning

Human diversity

Caring/Curing/Changing

"Working Definition" of social work

"NASW Definition" of social work

Dual focus on person and environment

Generalist social work practice

Advanced generalist social work practice

Specialist social work practice

Traditional practice methods

NASW classification of practice levels (basic, specialized, independent, advanced)

SUGGESTED READINGS

Bartlett, Harriet M. "Toward Clarification and Improvement of Social Work Practice," *Social Work* 3 (April 1958): 3–9.

Corey, Mariane Schneider, and Corey, Gerald. *Becoming a Helper*, 3rd Edition. Belmont, CA: Brooks/Cole, 1998.

Gordon, William E. "A Critique of the Working Definition," *Social Work* 7 (October 1992): 3–13.

National Association of Social Workers. *Social Work* 19 (September 1974); 22 (September 1977); and 26 (January 1981). (These three issues are devoted to conceptual frameworks for the profession.)

Reid, P. Nelson, and Popple, Philip R., eds. *The Moral Purposes of Social Work: The Character and Intentions of a Profession.* Chicago: Nelson-Hall, 1992.

Specht, Harry, and Courtney, Mark E. *Unfaithful Angels: How Social Work Has Abandoned Its Mission.* New York: Free Press, 1994.

Wagner, David. *The Quest for a Radical Profession: Social Service Careers and Political Ideology.* Lanham, MD: University Press of America, 1990.

ENDNOTES

1. Carol H. Meyer, "Social Work Purpose: Status by Choice or Coercion?" *Social Work* 26 (January 1981): 71–72.
2. For a brief description of a number of practice approaches, see Bradford W. Sheafor, Charles R. Horejsi, and Gloria A. Horejsi, *Techniques and Guidelines for Social Work Practice,* 5th Edition (Boston: Allyn and Bacon, 2000), Chapter 6.
3. American Association of Social Workers, *Social Casework: Generic and Specific: A Report of the Milford Conference* (New York: National Association of Social Workers, 1974), p. 11. (Original work published in 1929.)
4. Harriet M. Bartlett, "Towards Clarification and Improvement of Social Work Practice," *Social Work* 3 (April 1958): 5–7.
5. See *Social Work* 19 (September 1974); *Social Work* 22 (September 1977); and *Social Work* 26 (January 1981).
6. National Association of Social Workers, *Standards for Social Service Manpower* (Washington, D.C.: NASW, 1973), pp. 4–5.
7. Mary E. Richmond, *Social Diagnosis* (New York: Russell Sage Foundation, 1917).
8. Edith Abbott, "The Social Caseworker and the Enforcement of Industrial Legislation," in *Proceedings of the National Conference on Social Work, 1918* (Chicago: Rogers and Hall, 1919), p. 313.
9. Ernest V. Hollis and Alice L. Taylor, *Social Work Education in the United States* (New York: Columbia University Press, 1951).
10. Rosalie Balinsky, "Generic Practice in Graduate Social Work Curricula: A Study of Educators' Experiences and Attitudes," *Journal of Education for Social Work* 18 (Fall 1982): 47.
11. Mona S. Schatz, Lowell E. Jenkins, and Bradford W. Sheafor, "Milford Redefined: A Model of Initial and Advanced Generalist Social Work," *Journal of Social Work Education* 26 (Fall 1990): 217–231.
12. Council on Social Work Education, "Curriculum Policy Statement for Master's Degree Programs in Social Work Education" (Alexandria, VA: Council on Social Work Education, 1992), p. 10.
13. Todd N. Lennon, ed., *Statistics on Social Work Education in the United States: 1998* (Alexandria, VA: Council on Social Work Education, 1999), p. 45.
14. Ibid.
15. Ibid., p. 44.

16. Reprinted with permission from *NASW Standards for the Classification of Social Work Practice*, Policy Statement 4 (Silver Spring, MD: National Association of Social Workers, 1981), p. 9.

17. Robert J. Teare and Bradford W. Sheafor, *Practice-Sensitive Social Work Education: An Empirical Analysis of Social Work Practice and Practitioners* (Alexandria, VA: Council on Social Work Education, 1995).

18. Margaret Gibelman and Philip H. Schervish, *Who We Are: A Second Look* (Washington, D.C.: NASW Press, 1997), p. 23.

19. Ibid., pp. 134–145.

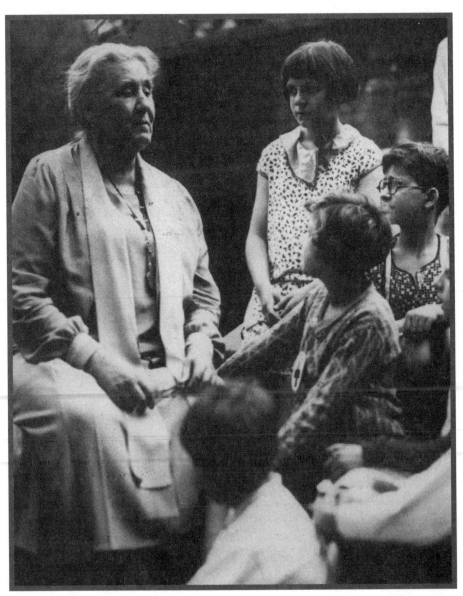

Social work pioneer Jane Addams visits with children at Chicago's Hull House.

CHAPTER 3

The Emergence
of Social Work as a Profession

**Prefatory
Comment**

In order to understand and appreciate social work more fully, it is useful to trace its emergence and identify key historical events and professional actions that have shaped the profession. While one could gain insight into the emergence of social work by examining the influence of external events, this chapter is guided by an examination of social work's efforts to become a recognized profession. It begins with a review of the nature of professions, particularly the helping professions, in U.S. society. It traces the emergence of social work during the past century, with emphasis on the choices made that affected its acceptance as a profession, and concludes with an analysis of its current professional status.

The growth and development of social work has not been a planned event. It just happened. It was a response to human suffering that began in several different parts of American society and eventually coalesced into a single, diverse profession.

Because its development has not been guided by a clear master plan, social work has been heavily influenced by a variety of factors. It has been pushed in one direction by forces such as periods of political and economic conservatism, the stress of wars and other major international events, and by competition from other emerging helping disciplines. At the same time, social work has been pulled in other directions by its own goals and aspirations, such as the need for a coherent concept of the profession that could incorporate its different roots and its intense desire to be recognized as a profession.

The Nature of Professions

A field of sociological inquiry is devoted to the definition and description of the nature of professions. One of the central figures in this field, Wilbert Moore, concluded that "to have one's occupational status accepted as professional or to have one's occupational conduct judged as professional is highly regarded in all post industrial societies and in at least the modernizing sectors of others."[1]

Professions are highly regarded, in part, because they have been granted sanction to perform essential services that ensure survival and help people enhance the quality of life. Professionals use specialized knowledge and skillfully provide services to people in need of assistance in sensitive areas of their lives. The knowledge and skills required exceed that expected of volunteers and other natural helpers. For individual members, being part of a profession is usually personally satisfying and financially rewarding, and yields high social status. From the client's point of view, the designation of professionalism signals those persons who are qualified to provide particular services and provides at least a minimum level of protection against incompetent and unethical behavior by practitioners. For the professions, this recognition is essential because it enhances the ability to recruit qualified people and ensures the respect of other professions and the general public. Recognition as professional, then, has been an important motivation driving many occupations.

How is it determined whether an occupation is a profession? One approach to the study of professions, known as the *absolute approach*, has been to examine the traditional professions of medicine, law, and higher education to isolate their fundamental elements. These studies revealed that professions could be characterized by such factors as their requirements for specialized skill and training, a specific base of knowledge, the formation of professional associations, and the development of codes of ethical behavior governing professional practice. Other occupations were then evaluated to determine whether they, too, contained these elements and could be considered professions. Using this approach, occupational groups were classified in one of two categories: professional or nonprofessional.

More recently, the prevalent approach to the study of professions has been to identify the key attributes common to professions and assess the degree to which any other occupational group possesses these attributes. This *relative approach* to professionalism allows for the placement of any occupational group along a continuum from nonprofessional to professional. Using this approach, Moore, for example, identifies the primary characteristics of a profession as a full-time occupation, commitment to a calling, identification with peers, specified training or education, a service orientation, and autonomy restrained by responsibility.[2] Using such criteria, it is possible to place each occupational group on a scale of professionalism relative to other occupations. The point at which an occupation sufficiently meets the criteria to be considered a profession is not absolute but determined by judgment.

As more has been learned about professions, three elements have been delineated to help explain the unique characteristics of the occupations that are considered to be professions. First, professionals must be free from constraints that might limit their ability to act in the best interests of their clients. The protection of this *professional autonomy* has been most successful in professions that contract directly with clients to provide services. In these situations few constraints are imposed on the manner in which practice is conducted. In agency-based professions, however, the organizations employ the professionals and contract with the clients to provide service. The agency's rules and regulations, intended to improve the organizations' efficiency and accountability, limit the professional's autonomy to exercise independent judgment regarding the manner in which services are provided.

Second, society has granted *professional authority* to a few people who have acquired the necessary knowledge and skills to provide the needed services in a given area of professional practice. Society grants this authority because it has, in effect, determined that it is inefficient, if not impossible, for every person to acquire all the knowledge and skill needed to meet complex human needs. Thus, these professionals are given the exclusive right to make judgments and give advice to their clients. In granting this professional authority, society, in essence, gives up the right to judge these professionals except in extreme cases of incompetent or unethical practice. Society depends on the members of that profession to determine the requisite entrance preparation and to be sure those who are practicing as members of that profession do so competently.

To be able to operate within the authority of a given profession, each member must master the knowledge and skills the profession has determined to be essential. Through the accreditation of its educational programs and the content of examinations that govern certification by a profession, the technical information and competencies fundamental to that profession are assured. However, human problems typically extend beyond the purview of any one profession. To be of maximum effectiveness, it is important that the professional not only has the technical training required for his or her profession, but also possesses a fund of general knowledge gained from the study of history, literature, philosophy, theater, and other fields that will help to provide a broad understanding of the human condition. In short, professionals must be both technically and generally educated.

Third, when the right to judge practice is relinquished by granting professional authority, the public becomes vulnerable and rightfully expects the professions to protect them from abuses that may accrue from the professional monopoly. Hughes indicates that the motto of the professions must be *credat emptor* ("buyer trust"), as opposed to the motto of the marketplace, *caveat emptor* ("buyer beware").[3] For example, where the layperson would rarely question the prescription of a physician, that same person might be very cautious when buying a used car and might have it thoroughly tested by an independent mechanic before making a purchase. To maintain this buyer trust, the professions must be accountable to the public that has granted them the sanction to perform these services. In order to establish and maintain this *professional responsibility,* professions develop codes that identify the expected ethical behavior of practitioners and establish mechanisms for policing their membership regarding unethical or incompetent practice.

In a sense, the professions and society struck a deal. In exchange for responsible service in sensitive areas of life, the professions were granted exclusive authority, that is, a professional monopoly, to offer these services.

Helping Professions: A Response to Human Need

All helping professions began as a response to unmet human need. As people experienced suffering or insufficient development in some aspect of life, when natural helping networks were not sufficient to meet the resulting needs, various forms of professional help emerged. Physicians, teachers, clergy, and other professional groups began to appear and to be given approval by the society to perform specific helping functions. The buyers', or clients', vulnerability was intensified in the area of helping services because they dealt in especially sensitive areas where unwitting persons could be harmed by the incompetent or improper actions of the professional. In addition to the codes of ethics and bodies established to investigate situations where abuses of this monopoly were alleged, the helping professions also characteristically have had external sources of client protection. For many professions, this additional protection has taken the form of licensing professional practice, while clients of agency-based professions are usually considered to have adequate supplemental protection through the monitoring of practice by the agencies and organizations.

It was soon realized that the effectiveness of these helpers was increased when their skills were supported by specific knowledge and values that could guide their interventions into the lives of clients or groups of clients. As this professional knowledge expanded through the development of theories and concepts, as well as through experience, trial and error, or practice wisdom, the professions expanded their technical knowledge requirements and their membership became increasingly exclusive. There was a time when each profession could respond to a number of human needs. However, the increasingly specialized knowledge necessary to provide effective helping services has led to a proliferation of helping professions, each with its own specializations.

What are these needs to which the helping professions have responded? Brill's description of needs helps to clarify the primary focus of the several helping professions as they exist today:[4]

- *Physical needs:* functioning of the physical structures and organic processes of the body (Physicians and Nurses)

- *Emotional needs:* feelings or affective aspects of the consciousness that are subjectively experienced (Psychologists)

- *Intellectual needs:* capacity for rational and intelligent thought (Teachers)

- *Spiritual needs:* desire for a meaning in life that transcends one's life on earth (Clergy)

- *Social needs:* capacity for satisfying relationships with others (Social Workers)

While the helping professions have tended to organize around a single need, there are exceptions, such as psychiatry, in which both emotional and physical needs—and their interaction—are the focus of professional service.

The increase of helping professions from few to many, and their overlap when providing services to people who experience more than one problem, has inevitably led to difficulty in defining professional boundaries. As professions like social work, occupational therapy, and music therapy have emerged, they have devoted considerable energy to staking out their professional boundaries. That activity is important because it identifies for each profession, the other professions, and the public the unique contribution made by each to meeting human needs. It also helps to focus their education and training programs, research activities, and the development of appropriate professional knowledge.

How a profession stakes out its professional boundaries has significant influence on that profession. The more elitist professions limit the people they claim as their target of service to those with narrowly defined problems, typically charging high fees to the few people who require that service. These professions usually require extensive and highly technical training and few people acquire the credentials to be recognized as part of that profession. This limited supply of professionals yields high prestige and financial reward for those who hold the proper qualifications. Other professions have been far more open in their membership requirements and more general in the type of issues for which they provide service. This lack of exclusiveness has at times been viewed as less professional and has resulted in lower prestige and less financial remuneration for the persons identified with these professions.

Two models of professionalism have developed in the United States. One is the *private model,* where the individual client contracts directly with the professional for service. Law and medicine are clear examples of professions that have followed this model. A second model, typified by teachers and city planners, is the *public model* in which the professionals primarily operate under the auspice of formal organizations and direct their services to the common good.

How, then, has social work emerged? Where does it fit among the helping professions?

Social Work as a Profession: A Historical Perspective

Social work did not evolve in a vacuum. A series of events affected its development and will continue to shape social work in the future. Some of those events are represented by major factors in the history of the United States such as settlement patterns, wars, international conditions, economic fluctuations, the philosophy of elected political leaders, and others. These events influenced decisions about the extent to which this society would respond to its members' social needs and, subsequently, to the social programs that would be supported.

Table 3-1 identifies some of the important events that affected the evolution of U.S. society's approach to the human services and shows selected mileposts in the development of social work. In columns 1 and 2 the table lists dates and events that identify a historical event that had a direct influence on a social program or social work such as the Civil War or the Great Depression. Column 3 identifies important historical events that shaped social programs (e.g., the Pierce Veto), and column 4 lists some critical events in the development of the social work profession—for example, publication of *Social Diagnosis* in 1917.

FROM VOLUNTEERS TO AN OCCUPATION (PRIOR TO 1915)

The roots of social work may be found in the extensive volunteer movement during the formative years of the United States. In the colonial period, for example, it was

▮ TABLE 3-1	**Timetable of Selected Events in Social Welfare and Social Work History**		
Approximate Date	**U.S. History Event**	**Social Welfare Event**	**Social Work Event**
Founding of United States	Agriculture-based society Open frontier	Family responsibility Mutual aid Puritan ethic Town meetings Orphan homes and first charitable societies First general hospital (Pennsylvania Hospital) Poorhouses First public mental hospital	
1776	Declaration of Independence Revolutionary War Act for the Gradual Abolition of Slavery (Pennsylvania)	Growth of voluntary social agencies based on special needs Society for Alleviating the Miseries of Public Prisons	
1789	George Washington inaugurated	Merchant philanthropists	
1800	United States prohibits importation of slaves War of 1812 Child labor laws Anti-Slavery Movement Treaty of Guadalupe–Hidalgo Chinese immigration began	Elizabeth Seton founds Sisters of Charity Mass. General Hospital Gallaudet School for Deaf Society for the Prevention of Pauperism NY House of Refuge (for juveniles)	Dorothea Dix begins crusade for improved conditions in "insane asylums"
1850	Emergence of industrial society Rise of cities and urbanization	Pierce Veto Children's Aid Societies Orphan Trains YMCA movement	
1863	Civil War Reconstruction Era	Freedman's aid societies Mass. Board of Charities Tenement (housing) reforms	U.S. Sanitary Commission (first paid social workers) National Conference on
1877	 Chinese Exclusion Act Dawes Act (Indian Land Allotment Act)	Buffalo Charity Aid Society	Charities and Correction Friendly visitors
1889	 Japanese immigration began	Hull House	Settlement workers
1898	Spanish-American War Immigration peaks	 First Juvenile Court	NY School of Philanthropy

Approximate Date	U.S. History Event	Social Welfare Event	Social Work Event
1910	World War I	White House Conference on Children	Introduction of medical social work
		U.S. Children's Bureau	Introduction of psychiatric social work
1915	Progressive Era	Community Chest (federated fund raising)	Introduction of school social work
		NAACP National Urban League	Flexner, "Is Social Work A Profession?" Richmond, *Social Diagnosis* National Social Workers Exchange Association of Training Schools for Prof. SW
1920	Women's Suffrage (19th Amendment)	County and state relief agencies Freudian influence Smith–Fess (Rehabilitation) Act	American Association of Social Workers Milford Conference
1930	Stock market crash The Great Depression "Great Migration" from Puerto Rico	American Public Welfare Association Indian Reorganization Act Federal Emergency Relief Act Civilian Conservation Corps (CCC)	American Association of Schools of Social Work
1935		Social Security Act Works Progress Administration (WPA)	American Association of Group Workers
1941	United States enters World War II Japanese relocation centers End of WW II Postwar recovery period	U.S.O. organized National Social Welfare Assembly	National Association of Schools of Social Administration Association for the Study of Community Organization Social Work Research Group Council on Social Work Education (merger of AASSW and NASSA)
1949		U.S. Department of Health, Education, and Welfare	
1952	Korean Conflict Civil Rights Movement	Indian Health Service	National Association of Social Workers (merger of six professional specialization groups and American Association of Social Workers)
1955			
	Women's Movement	Juvenile Delinquency Act	

(Continued)

| TABLE 3-1 | Timetable of Selected Events in Social Welfare and Social Work History (Continued) |

Approximate Date	U.S. History Event	Social Welfare Event	Social Work Event
1960	Kennedy administration	Herrington, *The Other America* Equal Pay Act	Greenwood, "Attributes of a Profession" NASW "Working Definition of Social Work Practice"
1963	Kennedy assassination Johnson administration Vietnam War	Community Mental Health Act Food Stamp Act Civil Rights Act of 1964 Economic Opportunity Act Appalachian Regional Development Act	NASW "Code of Ethics"
	Black Power Movement		
1965		Older American Act	Academy of Certified Social Workers (ACSW)
	Watts, Chicago, Detroit race riots Welfare Rights Movement Martin Luther King, Jr. assassination	Indian Civil Rights Act Immigration Act of 1965 Medicare Act Medicaid Narcotic Addict Rehabilitation Act	
	Nixon administration	Supplemental Security Income (SSI) approved	NASW recognition of baccalaureate social worker as professional
1970	East LA police riots; Stonewall "Riot" and Gay Liberation Movement		
1972		Child Abuse Prevention & Treatment Act	CSWE begins BSW accreditation process (generalist emphasis)
	Roe v. *Wade* decision		CSWE approves advanced standing for BSWs
1974	Watergate and Nixon resignation		
	Ford administration		NASW "Conceptual Frameworks" series
1977		Education of All Handicapped Children Act	
	Carter administration	Indian Child Welfare Act	
1980		Privatization of human services expanded	
	Reagan administration	Social Security Block Grant Act (decentralize some programs to states)	Expansion of private practice
		AIDS Epidemic Tax Equity and Fiscal Responsibility Act of 1982 (cutbacks in human service provisions by federal government) Equal Rights Amendment (ratification fails)	Expansion of doctoral social work education (GADE)

TABLE 3-1	(Continued)		

Approximate Date	U.S. History Event	Social Welfare Event	Social Work Event
1988	Bush administration		Academy of Certified Baccalaureate Social Workers (ACBSW)
	Persian Gulf War	Americans with Disabilities Act	
		Individuals with Disabilities Education Act	
1992	Clinton administration	Health care reform fails	Social workers licensed in all states, D.C., and some territories
	Los Angeles police riot (in the wake of the Rodney King verdict)		ACBSW terminated
	Republican "Contract for America"	Family and Medical Leave Act	
1996	Oklahoma City federal building bombing	Personal Responsibility and Work Opportunity Reconciliation Act	"Code of Ethics" revised
1999	Clinton impeachment Columbine High School gang massacre		

assumed that individuals and families would care for themselves, but if further difficulties existed, one could depend on *mutual aid*. Friends, neighbors, or other representatives of the community could be counted on to help out when needed. Volunteer activities involved interaction with the poor, the ill, and those experiencing other social problems. As social agencies began to develop, they soon learned how to train volunteers in constructive ways to relate to clients and improved their ability to be helpful.

Developing out of this background came social work as an *occupation*. The first paid social work-type positions in the country were jobs in the Special Relief Department of the United States Sanitary Commission. Beginning as a voluntary agency and then receiving public support as the Civil War progressed, the Special Relief Department and its agents served Union soldiers and their families experiencing social and health problems due to the war. Wartime needs temporarily opened the door to providing social services, and the outstanding performance of these workers helped pave the way for other positions in social work. Several women involved in the war effort performed important leadership roles in the development of human services. For example, Dorothea Dix (Superintendent of Nurses in the U.S. Sanitary Commission) previously had provided leadership in an attempt to secure federal government support for mental hospitals; Clara Barton later founded the American Red Cross; Josephine Shaw Lowell helped start the Charity Organization Society in New York City and also headed the Consumers' League, which worked to protect shopgirls from exploitation; Sojourner Truth gave leadership to the National Freedman's Relief Association; and Harriet Tubman, a central figure in the Underground Railroad, subsequently established a home for elderly African Americans. Following the war the Special Relief Department was closed.

Social work also appeared when the Massachusetts Board of Charities was established in 1863. Founded under the leadership of Samuel Gridley Howe, an advocate for the physically and mentally disabled, this agency coordinated services in almshouses, hospitals, and other institutions of the state. Although its powers were limited to inspection and advice, the Board gained wide acceptance under the leadership of Howe and its paid director, Frank B. Sanborn. The concept of boards overseeing state services spread to other states in the 1870s and became the forerunners to today's state departments of social services and institutions.

The Massachusetts Board of Charities also introduced social research into human service delivery. An 1893 report, for example, identified the causes of poverty as "first, physical degradation and inferiority; second, moral perversity; third, mental incapacity; fourth, accidents and infirmities; fifth, unjust and unwise laws, and the customs of society."[5] Although the approach was perhaps more moralistic than would be found in social work today, the report reflected the understanding that both personal and societal factors contribute to poverty.

Another significant development leading to the emergence of social work was the establishment of the Charity Organization Society (COS) of Buffalo, New York, in 1877. Modeled after an organization in London, charity organization societies sprang up in a number of communities with the dual purposes of finding means to help the poor and preventing the poor from taking advantage of the numerous uncoordinated social agencies that provided financial assistance. Leaders in social work from the COS movement included Mary Richmond, who helped identify a theory of practice in her books *Friendly Visiting Among the Poor* (1899) and *Social Diagnosis* (1917); Edward T. Devine, a founder of the New York School of Philanthropy in 1898 and its first director; and Porter Lee, who was instrumental in founding the American Association of Schools of Social Work in 1919.

Another important development that contributed to the emergence of social work was the Settlement House Movement initiated in 1886. Patterning settlement houses after London's Toynbee Hall, settlements were established in New York and Chicago. Within fifteen years, about one hundred settlement houses were operating in the United States. The settlements helped the poor learn skills required for urban living and simultaneously provided leadership in political action efforts to improve the social environment. Bremner sums up the impact of the settlement movement:

Where others thought of the people of the slums as miserable wretches deserving either pity or correction, settlement residents knew them as much entitled to respect as any other members of the community. Numerous young men and women who lived and worked in the settlements during the 1890s carried this attitude with them into later careers in social work, business, government service, and the arts.[6]

The residents of Chicago's Hull House are a good example. Its founder, Jane Addams, won the Nobel Peace Prize in 1931; Julia Lathrop became the first director of the U.S. Children's Bureau and was succeeded by other Hull House alumnae Katherine Lenroot and Grace Abbott, thus contributing to the protection of children and youth for several decades.

The efforts to integrate the African American population into the mainstream of U.S. society following the Civil War also contributed to the development of social work. George Haynes, the first African American graduate of the New York School of Philanthropy, for example, helped found the National Urban League, while Mary McLeod Bethune, who gave leadership to the education of African American women, was a founder of the National Council of Negro Women and was influential in making New Deal policies more equitable for the African American population.

Social work expanded into another setting in the early 1900s when Richard Cabot and Ida Cannon opened a social work program at the Massachusetts General Hospital. These social workers provided services for patients experiencing health-related social problems and also worked to strengthen the services of related health and welfare agencies throughout the community. Lubove identifies the significance of this development for the professionalization of social work:

> The enlistment of medical social workers marked an important stage in the development of professional social work. A casework limited to the charity organization and child welfare societies provided too narrow a base for professional development, associated as it was with problems of relief and economic dependency. Medical social work added an entirely new institutional setting in which to explore the implications of casework theory and practice.[7]

Medical social workers became interested in professional education as a means of moving beyond social work's "warm heart" image and into a more disciplined understanding of the psychic or social conditions as the base of patient distress. In 1912, with Ida Cannon's participation, a one-year training program in medical social work was established in the Boston School of Social Work.

Through these years, social work jobs were also springing up in other practice areas such as mental hygiene (mental health), prisons, employment and labor relations, and schools. Beginning in 1873 an organization designed to draw together members of this diverse occupation was formed, the National Conference on Charities. Later renamed the National Conference on Charities and Correction, this organization brought volunteer and professional staff members of social agencies together to exchange ideas about the provision of services, discuss social problems, and study the characteristics of effective practice. By the time World War I began social work was an established occupation distinguishable from the many volunteer groups and other occupations concerned with the well-being of the most vulnerable members of U.S. society.

PROFESSIONAL EMERGENCE (1915–1950)

With social work firmly established as an occupation, attention then turned to its development as a profession. At the 1915 meeting of the National Conference on Charities and Correction, Abraham Flexner addressed the subject, "Is Social Work a Profession?" Dr. Flexner, an authority on graduate education, had previously done a penetrating study that led to major changes in medical education. The organizers of this session of the National Conference apparently hoped Flexner would assure them that social work was, or was about to become, a full-fledged profession. However, that was not in the cards. Flexner, using an "absolute approach" to his study of professions, spelled out six criteria that an occupation must fully meet to be considered a profession:

1. Professions are essentially intellectual operations with large individual responsibility.
2. They derive their raw material from science and learning.
3. This material is worked up to a practical and clear-cut end.
4. Professions possess an educationally communicable technique.
5. They tend to self-organization.
6. They become increasingly altruistic in motivation.[8]

Based on these criteria Flexner concluded that social work had not yet made it into the professional elite. Following Flexner's admonition to "go forth and build thyself a profession," social workers busily attended to these functions over the next thirty-five years.

One effort was to develop a code of ethics. In 1921 Mary Richmond indicated that, "we need a code; something to abide by, or else we will have low social standing."[9] One code, the "Experimental Draft of a Code of Ethics for Social Case Workers," was discussed at the 1923 meeting of the National Conference on Social Welfare. Although this proposed code was never acted on, it represented a beginning effort at formulating a statement of professional ethics.

Probably the greatest amount of effort was devoted to self-organization. The National Social Workers Exchange was opened in 1917 to provide vocational counseling and placement and later became actively involved in the identification and definition of professional standards. In 1921 its functions were taken over by the broader American Association of Social Workers, which made significant efforts to develop a comprehensive professional association. This effort was later weakened by attempts of some specialties to develop their own professional organizations. A chronology of the development of these specialized groups follows:[10]

- 1918 American Association of Hospital Social Workers
- 1919 National Association of Visiting Teachers
- 1926 American Association of Psychiatric Social Workers

- 1936 American Association for the Study of Group Work

- 1946 Association for the Study of Community Organization

- 1949 Social Work Research Group

It was not clear whether social work was one or many professions.

Another development during this period concerned the required preparation to enter the social work profession. Social work education had begun as agency-based training, but a concerted effort was made during this period to transfer it to colleges and universities, where other professions had located their professional education. In 1919 the Association of Training Schools for Professional Social Workers was established with seventeen charter members—both agency and university affiliated schools. The purpose of that organization was to develop standards for all social work education. By 1927 considerable progress toward that purpose had been made, and the Association of Training Schools reorganized into the American Association of Schools of Social Work (AASSW). Although education programs had been offered in agencies, as well as at both undergraduate and graduate levels in colleges and universities, the AASSW determined that by 1939 only university affiliated programs with two-year graduate programs would be recognized as professional social work education.

That action led to a revolt by schools whose undergraduate programs prepared professionals to meet the staffing needs of the social agencies in their states. A second professional education organization was formed in 1942, the National Association of Schools of Social Administration, made up largely of public universities in the midwest that offered baccalaureate- and one-year graduate-level professional education programs. Harper described this development as "a protest movement against unrealistic and premature insistence upon graduate training and overemphasis upon professional casework as the major social work technique."[11]

With leadership from governmental and voluntary practice agencies, the two organizations were later merged (1952) into the Council on Social Work Education (CSWE) following the landmark Hollis–Taylor study of social work education.[12] The outcome of that decision favored the two-year master's program as the minimum educational requirement for full professional status. Undergraduate social work education temporarily faded from the scene.

Another important area of concern that was given only limited attention during this period was strengthening the knowledge and skill base of social work practice. Richmond's rich contribution, *Social Diagnosis,* was the first effort to formalize a communicable body of techniques applicable to the diverse settings in which social caseworkers were found.[13]

Momentum from this thrust, however, was lost as social work slipped into the grasp of the popular psychoanalytic approach. Cohen comments, "The search for a method occurred just at the time the impact of psychoanalysis was being felt. Did social work, in its haste for professional stature, reach out for a ready-made methodology for treating sick people, thus closing itself off from the influence of developments in the other sciences?"[14] This question must be answered in the affirmative. By adopting the helping methodology that was currently in vogue, social work embraced firmly, but perhaps inappropriately, the private model of professionalism. Writing in *Harper's Monthly* in 1957, Sanders accurately criticized social work for "floating with the ghost of Freud."[15] One might speculate about what would have happened if the model adopted had been the one for public education or public health.

CONSOLIDATING THE GAINS (1950–1970)

The move to consolidate the accrediting bodies for the schools of social work into the CSWE set an important precedent for the field and was part of a broad movement to treat social work as a single and unified profession. In 1950 the several specialized associations and the American Association of Social Workers agreed to form the Temporary Inter-Association Council of Social Work Membership Organizations (TIAC). The purpose behind the formation of TIAC was to bring these specialized groups into one central professional association. After considerable efforts by the specialties to maintain their identities, TIAC proposed a merger of the several groups in 1952. By 1955 this was accomplished, and the National Association of Social Workers (NASW) was formed.

NASW membership rose from 28,000 to 45,000 between 1961 and 1965, largely because of the formation of the Academy of Certified Social Workers (ACSW), which required both NASW membership and a two-year period of supervised experience. Many job descriptions were revised to require membership in the Academy, forcing social workers to join the NASW and obtain certification.

The late 1950s were a time of great introspection, and the professional journal, *Social Work,* was filled with articles such as "The Nature of Social Work,"[16] "How Social Will Social Work Be?"[17] and "A Changing Profession in a Changing World."[18] Perhaps the most significant work was Ernest Greenwood's classic article, "Attributes of a Profession," in 1957.[19] Greenwood, using the "relative approach" to the study of professions, identified five critical attributes of professions that, depending on the degree to which they have been accomplished, determine the degree of professionalism for any occupational group:

1. A systematic body of theory
2. Professional authority
3. Sanction of the community
4. A regulative code of ethics
5. A professional culture

He related the development of social work to each of these five criteria and concluded that social work was a profession. He observed:

> When we hold up social work against the model of the professions presented above, it does not take long to decide whether to classify it within the professional or nonprofessional occupations. Social work is already a profession; it has too many points of congruence with the model to be classifiable otherwise.[20]

To the credit of social workers, they were as stimulated by Greenwood's declaration that they had become a profession as they were by Flexner's conclusion that they were not yet in the select circle. In 1958 the NASW published the "Working Definition of Social Work Practice," a valuable beginning to the difficult task of identifying professional boundaries.[21] This was followed by Gordon's excellent critique, which helped strengthen and clarify some parts of the working definition, particularly in relation to knowledge, values, and practice methodology.[22] In 1960 the NASW adopted a Code of Ethics to serve as a guide for ethical professional practice,[23] thus completing the steps to become a fully recognized profession.

At what price has professional status been attained? Sanders pointedly noted that social work had become a profession but had lost a mission. She indicated that social work had avoided controversial issues to keep its image clean, had become rigid in efforts to control service provision, and had developed jargon to maintain exclusiveness.[24]

TURNING AWAY FROM THE ELITIST PROFESSIONAL MODEL (1970–PRESENT)

From the turn of the twentieth century to the late 1960s, social work displayed a pattern typical of an emerging profession. It created a single association to guide professional growth and development; adopted a code of ethical professional behavior; provided for graduate-level university-based professional schools and acquired recognition to accredit those educational programs; successfully obtained licensing for social work practice in some states; conducted public education campaigns to interpret social work to the public; achieved recognition for social work among the helping professions; and moved in the direction of other professions by increasing specialization and limiting access to the profession. Indeed, social work was on its way to carving its niche among the elite group of helping professions.

However, social work did not vigorously pursue the path that would lead to even greater professional status. Perhaps influenced by a renewed spirit of concern emanating from the Civil Rights, Welfare Rights, and Women's Rights movements, the development of social work as a profession during the 1970s and 1980s was marked by ambivalence over following the more traditional format of the established professions.

First, there was a resurgence of social change activity on the part of social workers. A legacy from Lyndon Johnson's Great Society programs was federal support, in the form of jobs and other resources, toward efforts to eliminate social problems and alleviate human suffering. Social work was already committed to those goals, and social workers were prepared to move away from their clinical orientation and onto the front lines of social action.

For social workers bent on achieving higher professional status, activist social workers were sometimes unpopular. Their somewhat controversial activities at times created an unwelcome public image of a profession characterized by activists on the front lines of social change. This change in the balance of activities performed by social workers, however, helped to bring social work back to its roots and reestablish the "change" orientation in its purposes of caring, curing, and changing the society. The more liberal political climate that supported social work activism was short-lived. Federal support for programs encouraging social change dwindled and was nearly nonexistent under the Reagan and Bush administrations.

Next, in 1970 NASW made a dramatic move by revising its membership requirements to give full membership privileges to anyone who had completed a baccalaureate degree in social work from an undergraduate program approved by CSWE. In opposition to the pattern of professions becoming more exclusive, social work opened its membership to more people, and a generalist approach to practice was embraced. Beginning in 1970, professional qualifications could be gained by obtaining professional education at the undergraduate level. However, social work has been uneasy about operating as a multilevel profession, and, although the NASW classification system is clear about the "basic social worker" being viewed as professional, the social worker at this level has never been fully accepted by many MSW social workers. Some advocates for the baccalaureate social worker contend that NASW has not devoted sufficient attention to this practice level and that its program priorities in the 1980s "centered too much on licensing, vendor payments, private practice and other issues that were not sufficiently relevant to the baccalaureate worker."[25] NASW's creation of the Academy of Certified Baccalaureate Social Workers in the early 1990s represented movement away from that overemphasis on the interests of master's-level social workers, but the discontinuance of that certification in 1996 was a retreat from that position.

With NASW's formal recognition of baccalaureate social work as fully professional, in 1974 the Council on Social Work Education began accrediting baccalaureate social work education (BSW) programs. Initially, 135 schools met the undergraduate accreditation requirements, and by 1999 that number had increased to 415 schools in the United States and Puerto Rico with another 31 schools in candidacy for accreditation.[26] Of particular importance was the accessibility of these programs to persons wishing to become social workers. Whereas most MSW programs were located in urban areas, undergraduate programs were located in both urban and rural communities. A study of BSW practitioners in 1989 found that 43.9 percent of the "basic social workers" worked in communities of 40,000 or fewer (as compared to approximately 22% of the U.S. population), and 16.7 percent were employed in communities of 10,000 or fewer.[27] These data suggest that the professionalization of baccalaureate social work opened educational opportunities to people who could not attend schools in urban areas and who have enriched the provision of services in smaller communities by filling human service jobs in these areas.

Similarly, the emergence of professionally sanctioned baccalaureate-level social work education increased the opportunity for members from minority and lower socioeconomic backgrounds to enter social work, as they could complete the requisite education preparation without needing both baccalaureate and master's degrees. To illustrate, in 1998, 33.6 percent of the 35,816 full-time baccalaureate majors were of minority background, as compared to 25.5 percent of the 20,409 full-time MSW students.[28]

The return of a conservative political climate in the United States during the 1980s created a perception that few jobs would be available in social work when the Reagan Administration completed its objective of dismantling the Great Society programs. When it became evident that such mass destruction of human service programs was not going to occur, interest in careers in social work revived and social work education programs experienced a resurgence of student interest. After peaking at nearly 28,000 undergraduate social work majors in the late 1970s, that number declined by more than one-fourth in 1983, returned to the 28,000 level in 1990, and increased to nearly 36,000 in 1998. For the MSW programs a similar pattern occurred. Full-time enrollment declined by one-fifth between 1978 and 1983, but increased to nearly 20,500 in 1998.[29]

Concluding Comment

In the past century, social work has developed in a manner that meets the generally accepted criteria for professions. Consensus about its unique purpose among the professions has been reached, and social work has achieved sanction as the appropriate profession to help people resolve problems in their interaction with their environments. Social workers have been granted the professional authority to provide the necessary helping services for people in need, although they are constrained by the fact that most are employed in social agencies that sometimes limit their professional autonomy. Increasingly, they are entering private practice where the constraints are less severe.

Social work has taken its authority to provide these professional services seriously. Its national professional organization, the National Association of Social Workers, has worked through the decades to clarify social work's knowledge, value, and skill base. Social work has developed educational programs that prepare new people to enter this profession and has established a process for accrediting the programs that meet qualitative educational standards at both the baccalaureate and master's levels. Accredited programs exist in more than 442 colleges and universities and enroll approximately 74,000 full- and part-time students each year.[30]

Social work has also adopted a comprehensive Code of Ethics and has established procedures for dealing with social workers who might violate that code. A process has been established through the National Association of Social Workers that allows the profession to carry out its professional responsibility to protect clients and the general public from abuses that might arise from the monopoly it has achieved.

One might expect social workers to feel satisfied with these accomplishments. Yet, within this profession of many faces, there are inevitably varied opinions. While most social workers believe the progress made in becoming a recognized profession is desirable, some believe that it has become too elitist and is targeting its services too much to the white middle class. Others believe that it has lowered professional standards by opening its membership to those with less than graduate-level credentials. Some believe it should become more entrepreneurial like the private professions, and still others believe it should more fully embrace the agency-based model of the public professions where the most vulnerable members of the society are likely to be served. Some also believe that social work's unique role in interprofessional practice should be that of the case manager who orchestrates or coordinates the client services provided by several disciplines, while others view social work's role as providing more specialized social treatment services on a parallel with the other helping professions as they respond to clients' physical, emotional, spiritual, and intellectual needs. These issues must continue to be on social work's agenda.

KEY WORDS AND CONCEPTS

Profession

Relative vs. absolute professions

Professional autonomy

Professional authority

Professional responsibility

Public vs. private professions

U.S. Sanitary Commission

State boards of charities

Charity organization societies

Settlement houses

Social Diagnosis

Council on Social Work Education

National Association of Social Workers

SUGGESTED READINGS

Brieland, Donald. "History and Evolution of Social Work Practice," in Anne Minahan, ed., *Encyclopedia of Social Work,* 18th Edition. Silver Spring, MD: National Association of Social Workers, 1987, pp. 739–754.

Greenwood, Ernest. "Attributes of a Profession," *Social Work* 2 (July 1957): 45–55.

Howe, Elizabeth. "Public Professions and the Private Model of Professionalism," *Social Work* 25 (May 1980): 179–191.

Leigninger, Leslie. *Social Work: Search for Identity.* Westport, CT: Greenwood, 1987.

Lowe, Gary R. "Social Work's Professional Mistake: Confusing Status for Control and Losing Both," *Journal of Sociology and Social Welfare* 14 (June 1987): 187–206.

Lubove, Roy. *The Professional Altruist.* Cambridge, MA: Harvard University Press, 1989.

Trolander, Judith Ann. *Professionalism and Social Change: From the Settlement House to Neighborhood Centers, 1886 to the Present.* New York: Columbia University Press, 1987.

ENDNOTES

1. Wilbert E. Moore, *The Professions: Roles and Rules* (New York: Russell Sage Foundation, 1970), p. 3.
2. Ibid., pp. 5–6.
3. Everett C. Hughes, "Professions," *Daedalus* (Fall 1963): 657.
4. Naomi I. Brill, *Working with People. The Helping Process,* 3rd Edition (New York: Longman, 1985), pp. 24–28.
5. Cited in Ralph E. Pumphrey and Muriel W. Pumphrey, eds., *The Heritage of American Social Work* (New York: Columbia University Press, 1961), p. 12.
6. Robert H. Bremner, *From the Depths* (New York: New York University Press, 1956), p. 66.
7. Roy Lubove, *The Professional Altruist* (Cambridge, MA: Harvard University Press, 1965), p. 32.
8. Abraham Flexner, "Is Social Work a Profession?" in *Proceedings of the National Conference on Charities and Correction, 1915* (Chicago: National Conference on Charities and Correction, 1916): 576–590.
9. Pumphrey and Pumphrey, *Heritage,* p. 310.
10. John C. Kidneigh, "History of American Social Work," in Harry L. Lurie, ed., *Encyclopedia of Social Work,* 15th Edition (New York: National Association of Social Workers, 1965), pp. 13–14.

11. Herbert Bisno, "The Place of Undergraduate Curriculum in Social Work Education," in Werner W. Boehm, ed., *A Report of the Curriculum Study* Vol. II (New York: Council on Social Work Education, 1959), p. 8.

12. Ernest V. Hollis and Alice L. Taylor, *Social Work Education in the United States* (New York: Columbia University Press, 1951).

13. Mary E. Richmond, *Social Diagnosis* (New York: Russell Sage Foundation, 1917).

14. Nathan E. Cohen, *Social Work in the American Tradition* (New York: Holt, Rinehart, & Winston, 1958), pp. 120–121.

15. Marion K. Sanders, "Social Work: A Profession Chasing Its Tail," *Harper's Monthly* 214 (March 1957): 56–62.

16. Werner W. Boehm, "The Nature of Social Work," *Social Work* 3 (April 1958): 10–18.

17. Herbert Bisno, "How Social Will Social Work Be?" *Social Work* 1 (April 1956): 12–18.

18. Nathan E. Cohen, "A Changing Profession in a Changing World," *Social Work* 1 (October 1956): 12–19.

19. Ernest Greenwood, "Attributes of a Profession," *Social Work* 2 (July 1957): 45–55.

20. Ibid., p. 54.

21. Harriet M. Bartlett, "Towards Clarification and Improvement of Social Work Practice," *Social Work* 3 (April 1958): 5–7.

22. William E. Gordon, "Critique of the Working Definition," *Social Work* 7 (October 1962): 3–13; and "Knowledge and Values: Their Distinction and Relationship in Clarifying Social Work Practice," *Social Work* 10 (July 1965): 32–39.

23. National Association of Social Workers, *Code of Ethics* (Washington, D.C.: The Association, 1960).

24. Sanders, pp. 56–62.

25. Bradford W. Sheafor and Barbara W. Shank, *Undergraduate Social Work Education: A Survivor in a Changing Profession* (Austin: University of Texas School of Social Work, 1986), Social Work Education Monograph Series 3, p. 25.

26. Nancy Randolph, "Report of the Division of Accreditation," *The Social Work Education Reporter* (Spring 1999): 22.

27. Robert J. Teare and Bradford W. Sheafor, *Practice-Sensitive Social Work Education: An Empirical Analysis of Social Work Practice and Practitioners* (Alexandria, VA: Council on Social Work Education, 1995), p. 35.

28. Todd N. Lennon, ed., *Statistics on Social Work Education in the United States, 1998* (Alexandria, VA: Council on Social Work Education, 1999), pp. 44–45.

29. Ibid.

30. Ibid.

TWO

Social Work Career Options

In Part One we identified two characteristics of Western societies. One is the tendency to create programs to meet the basic social needs of its citizens. The second is the tendency to create professions to deliver those programs to the people in need. Within that framework social work has emerged during the past century as a central feature of U.S. society. Its emergence has been uneven and confusing because, in fact, social work is an umbrella profession that includes many and varied practice activities.

For the person entering social work, the vagueness about social work's focus is offset by the flexibility it permits. Compared to the schoolteacher, for example, who has relatively few career options within the education profession, the social worker has many choices. One can practice as a professional social worker at the baccalaureate, master's, or doctoral level. A social worker's potential fields of practice include working with older people, addressing physical or mental health problems, practicing in schools or the correctional system, or even being part of the staff of a major corporation. Although increasingly social workers independently open an office and engage in their own private practice, most are employed by some form of human service organization ranging, for example, from public welfare agencies to safehouses for battered women.

Each social worker must make certain decisions that will affect his or her career path in social work. One important decision concerns one's level of educational preparation. Chapter 4 summarizes a considerable amount of data about social workers at different educational levels and highlights the employment opportunities at each. In essence, the baccalaureate-level social worker works in direct services with clients and is most likely to serve either children and youth or older people. The master's-level social worker, in contrast, has much more job flexibility. Many hold administrative and supervisory positions, and those in direct service positions are most likely to address medical, mental health, and school-related issues with the breadwinning adult population, their most frequent clients. Some doctoral-level social workers can be found scattered throughout advanced administrative and direct practice jobs, but the majority are concentrated in teaching positions.

A second decision concerns the practice area one chooses to enter. Chapter 5 surveys thirteen unique fields in which social workers apply their trade. The potential practice areas from which a social worker might select vary from social work with children to social work in business and industry, from corrections to mental health, and from hospitals to residential treatment centers. Despite the differences in these fields of practice, a basic pattern emerges of the social workers helping people interact more effectively with the world around them.

Finally, a social worker must decide if he or she is to work in a human service organization or engage in private practice. Chapter 6 examines those public and private human service agencies where most social workers are employed. Factors affecting agency structure and functioning are discussed, with special attention given to the inherent conflicts that exist between the professional practice model and the bureaucratic model of organization usually found in social agencies. In addition, this chapter addresses the fact that some social workers have adopted an entrepreneurial approach to their work and have opted for private practice. Private practice presents a different set of problems than are experienced by those social workers employed in human service organizations.

By understanding the various career options in social work and the issues surrounding each, the prospective social worker can make informed decisions about important career choices. There are fundamental values and competencies, as Part Three will identify, that are transferable among the various expressions of social work. Thus, the social worker has considerable job mobility and any career choice can be altered.

CHAPTER 4

Entry to the Social
Work Profession

**Prefatory
Comment**

Selecting a career is one of the most important decisions a person must make. Whether that decision is to become a homemaker, physician, salesperson, teacher, chemist, or social worker, it should be based on a thorough understanding of the physical, emotional, and intellectual demands of the field and a close look at one's own suitability for that type of work. Whatever the choice, it will dictate how a person spends a major part of each day. It will also spill over into other aspects of life, including lifestyle, general satisfaction with self, and quality of life.

The decision to enter a particular profession does not lock a person into that occupation for a lifetime, but it does represent a substantial commitment of time, energy, and resources to prepare for professional practice and obtain the requisite credentials. After entering a profession, a person's job consumes a major part of his or her daily activity, and, if that was a good career choice, one's job can be an exhilarating and stimulating experience. However, if there is a poor fit between a person and their chosen occupation, work can be frustrating and unrewarding. If the career choice is one of the professions, the work will not typically result in an 8:00 AM to 5:00 PM job that is left at the office when the workday ends. Rather, the calling to the profession requires a commitment to clients and concern about their welfare that cannot readily be turned off when one goes home. Further, the complexity of human situations requiring professional assistance and the growing knowledge about effective helping obligates the professional to a career of continued learning and skill development. Unless a person is willing to make such a commitment, a professional career should not be pursued.

For the person considering the social work profession, it is useful to have a clear perception of the career opportunities this profession affords. Social work has evolved a four-level career ladder that has two entry points (i.e., the basic and specialized social worker) and two additional levels based on more advanced experience and education. Determining one's niche in social work requires careful investigation. This chapter describes the educational preparation and practice experience required for each practice level and identifies factors that shaped the evolution of social work practice at those levels.

Making a career choice is difficult because of the wide range of careers to choose from but, more importantly, because of the problems an outsider experiences in gaining an adequate and accurate understanding of a career. Too often, only after a person has made substantial commitments in time, energy, and money or has cut off other opportunities by taking steps to enter a career does he or she find that it is not what was expected or wanted. Another difficulty lies in having a clear perception of one's own needs, interests, and abilities. Personal introspection, occupational preference testing, guidance counseling, and experience in activities related to the career are all resources for making this choice.

The person contemplating a career in social work must consider a number of factors.[1] It is evident that social work is extremely broad in scope—ranging from social action to individual therapy—and is constantly changing, with a knowledge base that is far from stable or well developed. Thus, explicit guidelines for social work practice do not exist, leaving the social worker with the responsibility for exercising a great deal of individual judgment. Furthermore, the skills demanded of the social worker vary widely and require a flexible, creative, and introspective person to practice them. The pressures of a social work job create a degree of stress because the outcome of the work is critically important to the clients. In addition, social workers are regularly criticized by both clients and the general public, frequently in regard to programs social workers administer but over which they have little policy-making influence.

If a person can tolerate the ambiguity, responsibility, pressures, and criticism that are a part of social work; if the values, skills, and interests required of social workers are compatible; and if it is rewarding to work constructively to help people improve their level of social functioning, social work offers a rich and satisfying career. Before selecting social work as a career, one needs a general knowledge of this profession. In addition, volunteer experience, summer or part-time jobs in social agencies, and personal interaction with social workers may also help to determine one's suitability for a career in social work. The information contained in this chapter provides an orientation to a social work career.

Issues in Social Work Preparation and Employment

Membership in any profession requires that the persons aspiring to enter it acquire the specified qualifications. The very act of defining professional membership is inherently elitist in that whenever qualifications are established, some persons who operate with similar knowledge and values but lack the identified qualifications will be excluded. In social work, for example, completion of the education and practice experience specified by the National Association of Social Workers (NASW) in its membership qualifications is necessary to gain professional recognition. However, social workers are cognizant that many other helping people with different educations and experiences make important contributions to the delivery of human services. For the person entering social work, or considering becoming a member of this profession, it is important to be aware of several issues that relate to professional qualifications.

EDUCATION AND ACCREDITATION

The social work profession contends that a person must have a formal social work education; that is, either a baccalaureate degree with a major in social work or a master's degree in social work (MSW) from an accredited social work education program, as a minimum for professional recognition. The *accreditation* process is administered by the Council on Social Work Education (CSWE) and has become a significant factor in social work because the graduate of the accredited program is assumed to be prepared to enter practice as a beginning-level professional social worker—ready to apply the appropriate knowledge, values, and skills in the service of clients. For all practical purposes, education is the primary gatekeeper of the profession. This does not mean that all graduates are equally prepared to enter practice, that some people who do not have all the required social work courses are unable to perform many tasks of the social worker, or even that all schools offer the same opportunity for learning the essentials of social work. Rather, accreditation attests to the fact that the public can have confidence that graduates are at least minimally prepared for beginning-level social work practice because they have completed an instructional program that is soundly designed and taught by competent faculty.

PROFESSIONAL CERTIFICATION

The National Association of Social Workers provides confirmation to clientele and employing human services agencies that some social workers have demonstrated the requisite knowledge and competence to engage in practice, that is, *professional certification*. Where accreditation is testimony to the quality of an educational program, certification is the profession's testimony regarding the individual's knowledge, values, and skills.

In 1960 NASW initiated its first professional certification by creating the Academy of Certified Social Workers (ACSW). This credential was intended to recognize the "independent" social worker who had completed an MSW degree from an accredited college or university, had practiced a minimum of two years under the supervision of an ACSW social worker, had earned a satisfactory score on a national examination, and had received favorable evaluation of practice competence by peers. Today, the ACSW is a required credential for many social work jobs and 60,000 social workers are members of the Academy.[2]

In 1990 NASW created a similar credential for the baccalaureate-level social worker, the Academy of Certified Baccalaureate Social Workers (ACBSW). However, few agencies required the ACBSW as a job credential, and thus relatively few workers sought this professional credential. As a result, the ACBSW was discontinued in 1996.

Three other professional certifications created by NASW, however, have succeeded: the Qualified Clinical Social Worker (QCSW), Diplomate in Clinical Social Work, and the School Social Work Specialist. Each requires graduation from an accredited master's program in social work, adherence to NASW's Code of Ethics, and two or more years of post-master's practice experience. The Diplomate further requires an additional three years of full-time clinical social work experience. The two clinical certifications are designed to interface with the ACSW and/or state licensing requirements. These credentials are designed to serve as indicators of competence for specialized positions in schools and social agencies or as evidence to clients and insurance companies that offer reimbursement for social workers' services that these workers have the profession's stamp of approval.

LICENSING OR STATE REGULATION OF SOCIAL WORK PRACTICE

The social work profession, through the Council on Social Work Education, has shaped its educational programs through accreditation requirements and, through NASW, has sought to identify its competent and experienced practitioners by creating its certification programs. However, over the past two decades perhaps the most dominant issue on NASW's agenda has been to encourage the licensing of social workers throughout the United States.

As described by the American Association of State Social Work Boards, *licensing* is:

> . . . a process by which an agency of state government or other jurisdiction acting upon legislative mandate grants permission to individuals to engage in the practice of a particular profession or vocation and prohibits all others from legally doing so. By ensuring a level of safe practice, the licensure process protects the general public. Those who are licensed are permitted by the state to use a specific title and perform activities because they have demonstrated to the state's satisfaction that they have reached an acceptable level of practice.[3]

The intent of licensing is to have neutral sources, that is, state governments, identify those social workers who are properly prepared through professional education and experience to provide client services. Both consumers of service (particularly in private practice settings) and health insurance companies that reimburse for the cost of social work services have looked to licensing as a desirable way to determine a social worker's practice competence. In order to attract clients and to be eligible for payments from insurance companies, social workers have embraced state licensing for social work. All fifty states, the District of Columbia, Puerto Rico, and the Virgin Islands license (or certify) social workers. Thirty-four offer specialized forms of certification to experienced MSWs and thirty-three recognize the basic social worker.[4] Where professional certification is national in scope, licensing is conducted on a state-by-state basis with each state having somewhat unique standards and requirements. Because of these differences, a license from one state may not be accepted by another.

PROFESSIONAL STANDARDS

A profession is required by society to protect the public from those members who abuse the professional monopoly. To conduct this self-policing, every profession must establish standards and develop procedures for evaluating complaints and imposing negative sanctions if a member engages in incompetent or unethical practice. State licensing, too, performs this client protection function by withdrawing the legal right to practice as a social worker if such violations occur.

NASW has been granted authority by the social work profession to establish appropriate standards of conduct and maintain a process to ensure the public that recognized professional social workers meet those standards. The standards for social workers are embodied in NASW's *Code of Ethics*. The Code spells out in some detail the social worker's ethical responsibilities to clients, colleagues, practice settings, other professionals, the profession of social work, and the broader society.[5] When a social worker becomes a member of NASW, he or she must profess willingness to practice within the guidelines prescribed by the Code of Ethics, and the Code, in turn, becomes the baseline for evaluating the professional behavior of social workers.

Because social work is primarily an agency-based profession, NASW has also established standards for appropriate personnel practices in agencies that employ social workers. These guidelines describe personnel standards and practices that uphold the fair treatment of social workers in the hiring process, assure necessary working conditions for social work practice, and identify proper procedures for the termination of a social worker's employment.[6] These standards serve as the basis for judging the validity of claims by social workers that they have been wrongfully treated by their employers.

The process established for complaints begins with the local chapter of NASW. An individual or organization may lodge a formal complaint about the practice of a social worker or the personnel practices of an agency. A committee of the chapter will then conduct an investigation of the complaint and make a determination that the complaint is or is not substantiated. Either party has the right to appeal to the NASW National Committee on Inquiry, which reviews the charges and makes a final judgment. If the Committee on Inquiry concludes that standards have been violated, a plan to correct the behavior through training or treatment may be developed or the individual's membership in NASW may be suspended. Action taken against either an individual or agency is published in the *NASW News*. The sanctions remain in effect until the terms established by the Committee on Inquiry are satisfied.

Options for Human Service Practice

Addressing complex human needs requires a range of service providers equipped with a variety of knowledge and skills. The human services, therefore, are made up of many people—from volunteers to members of related disciplines—who provide many different forms of helping. The person considering a career in a helping profession should carefully compare social work with other human service providers to determine if serving as a social worker would be the most satisfying way to spend one's work life.

VOLUNTEERS

One cannot fully examine the human services without recognizing the important role played by volunteers. For many people who have other vocations, one way to be involved with human services is to volunteer. The willingness to give of oneself, without monetary reward, in order to help others is characteristic of human societies and is expressed in the activity of millions of people who give their time, energy, and talents to make this a better world. It was from efforts to prepare volunteers to provide more effective human services that social work became a paid occupation and, later, a significant helping profession.

Today, social workers work closely with volunteers in many agencies. Their jobs often include the recruitment, selection, training, and supervision of volunteers. Although most commonly found in youth-serving agencies, such as scouting organizations or the YMCA, volunteers also serve on the boards of, or in a direct working capacity in, every human service agency imaginable—from nursing homes to crisis hotlines to mental hospitals.

The qualifications of volunteers vary from activity to activity. At times professionals volunteer their services beyond their jobs in their own agencies or to help in other agencies. These volunteer activities may use their professional abilities but may also require skills unrelated to professional training. Like any other good citizen, the social worker has an obligation to donate his or her talents in order to improve social conditions.

NONPROFESSIONAL SERVICE PROVIDERS

Not all human service practice requires the competencies of a social worker or someone with related professional skills. Many important services can be provided by persons who bring to the helping situation the perspective of the client population. These people have been referred to in the literature as *indigenous workers*. They may be clients, former clients, or others who have rapport with low-income or other client groups based on having similar experiences to the client population. At times indigenous workers can build relationships with clients when professionals have difficulty establishing rapport. Indigenous workers can be found in human service organizations ranging from neighborhood centers to welfare agencies. His or her life experience and knowledge of the individuals or groups being served are the most important qualifications.

Another important source of nonprofessional personnel for human service agencies are *graduates of community colleges*. These Associate of Arts (AA) degree programs vary considerably from school to school but focus on preparing for very specific human service jobs with titles such as mental health technician, community service aide, case aide, or eligibility worker. The AA degree programs usually include the study of human growth and behavior, social problems, the social service delivery system, personal values and self-awareness, and basic communication skills. These programs may provide field experiences so students have an opportunity to apply knowledge acquired in the classroom. The tasks the AA graduate can be expected to perform are very concrete and require limited individual judgment. They include such activities as fact finding relative to specific cases, interviewing to obtain data, locating sources of assistance, organizing community groups around specific issues, making social provisions (e.g., money, food stamps, and housing) available to people, and screening applicants for service.

OTHER BACCALAUREATE-LEVEL DISCIPLINES

Several disciplines offer majors in colleges and universities that are closely related to social work. Completing these degrees can serve as helpful preparation for some human service jobs and can also be good preparation for a subsequent degree in social work. However, these programs of study should not be confused with social work degree programs that, if accredited, carry professional recognition.

SOCIAL SCIENCE DISCIPLINES. Social work has traditionally had a close relationship with the social science disciplines for two reasons. First, social work has drawn on basic knowledge from the disciplines of psychology, sociology, anthropology, economics, and political science, while developing its theoretical base for understanding the individual, family, group, organization, community, and the impact of culture on all these. Second, in higher education, social work has had close administrative ties with these disciplines at the baccalaureate level. It is not uncommon to find a baccalaureate-level social work education program housed in a sociology department or in a multidisciplinary social science department.

Most positions for social scientists involve research or teaching, and, thus, a Ph.D. is necessary to be competitive in the job market. With the exception of the small branch of applied sociology, social scientists do not typically engage in the provision of human services. Their purpose is to develop and test theories that will increase understanding of the people or places they study, but they do not intend to intervene to help people or social institutions change.

RELATED HELPING PROFESSIONS. When making a career choice within the helping services, a person should examine a range of helping professions that might fit his or her individual talents and interests. The more established professions are medicine, law, nursing, teaching, dentistry, and psychology. Other helping professions, such as physical therapy, music therapy, speech pathology and audiology, occupational therapy, recreation therapy, urban planning, and school counseling, also offer challenging and rewarding careers.

Each of these is an established profession and has prescribed and accredited educational programs a person must complete to be recognized as a member of that profession. Like social work, these professions identify standards for competent and ethical practice and take responsibility for policing the membership for compliance with these standards. The clientele of these professions, then, have some protection from the possible misuse of professional authority. Employment opportunities in these professions vary considerably, but most jobs are defined as requiring the requisite professional education for entry.

It is instructive to compare estimates of the demand for social workers with that of other helping professions. Table 4-1 provides a comparison of selected helping professions based on the projections of the U.S. Bureau of Labor Statistics (BLS). The supply estimate is derived from BLS data reporting the number of persons who completed professional preparation for that discipline. In social work, for example, graduates of BSW and MSW programs are compared to the number of social workers needed to fill new positions and replace workers who are permanently leaving the labor market. These data overstate the supply of "new" social workers by about 10 percent[7] because some who have completed a BSW return to school for a master's education and therefore are not new social workers. It is clear from these data that social work's supply and demand are about equal.

| TABLE 4-1 | Employment Projections among the Helping Professions: 1996–2006 |

Profession	Estimated Workers, 1996[a]	Estimated Annual Growth Rate[i] %[a]	Total New and Replacement Workers Needed Annually[a]	Estimated Annual Supply[b]	Annual Supply as % of Demand
Lawyers	622,000	1.9	29,000	41,067[c]	141.6
Occupational Therapists	57,000	6.6	4,400	3,641[d]	82.8
Physical Therapists	115,000	7.1	9,400	6,320[d]	67.2
Physicians	560,000	2.1	19,700	15,786[c]	80.1
Psychologists	143,000	0.8	2,500	4,027[e]	116.1
Registered Nurses	1,971,000	2.1	68,300	96,893[f]	141.9
Social Workers	585,000	3.2	27,700	28,888[d]	104.3
Speech Pathology/Audiology	87,000	5.1	5,400	4,670[g]	86.5
Teachers					
Administrators	386,000	1.6	14,600	13,335[d]	91.3
Preschool and Kindergarten	499,000	2.0	19,000	9,373[h]	49.3
Elementary	1,491,000	1.0	43,800	60,984[d]	139.2
Secondary	1,406,000	2.2	73,000	67,645[d]	92.7
Special Education	407,000	5.9	29,900	20,621[d]	69.0
School Counselors	175,000	1.9	7,300	12,288[g]	168.3
Urban and Regional Planners	29,000	0.5	600	1,806[d]	301.0

[a]George T. Silvestri, "Occupational Employment to 2006," *Monthly Labor Review* 120 (November 1997), pp. 58–67.

[b]Bureau of Labor Statistics, *Occupational Projections and Training Data, 1998–99 Edition* (Washington, D.C.: U.S. Department of Labor, 1998), pp. 37–51.

[c]Includes professional degree (e.g., law, medicine) only.

[d]Includes bachelor's and master's degrees.

[e]Includes doctoral degree only (an increase of master's-level jobs is developing in psychology).

[f]Includes associate and bachelor's degrees.

[g]Includes master's degree only.

[h]Includes associate, bachelor's and master's degrees.

[i]Growth Rate Definitions

  Increase 3.6% or more = grow much faster than average

  Increase 2.1% to 3.5% = grow faster than average

  Increase 1.0% to 2.0% = grow about as fast as average

  Increase 0% to .9% = grow more slowly than average

EMERGING HUMAN SERVICE OCCUPATIONS. During the 1970s a new occupational group began to emerge, known generally as *human services* or *human development.* The human services occupations differ from the helping professions we have reviewed because they intend to be nonprofessional. Most people giving leadership to these occupations are professionally trained in other disciplines and have been largely involved in corrections and mental health services—although they branch into every aspect of the social services.

The development of the human services field was stimulated by dissatisfaction with the service delivery system. Fundamental to the philosophy behind this field are two viewpoints.[8] First, the human services have been fragmented into problem areas (e.g., public welfare, corrections, mental health) that create barriers to good service because many clients experience complex problems and must deal with multiple agencies, programs, and service providers. Second, the integration of services into "umbrella agencies" and the creation of a broad discipline that can provide a wide range of services is preferable to the more focused professional orientation.

Social workers would agree that the fragmented methods of delivering social services often make it difficult for clients to locate help. However, the profession does not regard service integration as a solution (division lines can exist just as rigidly within one large agency as in several smaller ones) and believe that the professional model, with all its limitations, continues to be the most valid means of identifying the people who are prepared with the knowledge, values, and skills to respond to specific human needs. Social work would argue that clients are better served through greater efforts at *interdisciplinary practice,* rather than the emergence of new human service disciplines that have no clear service focus or practice approach, no established standards for ethical conduct, no professional responsibility for quality control, and no standardized educational preparation subject to professional accreditation.

Professional Social Work Practice

Social work's evolution as a profession has been uneven, and the career paths one might follow as a social worker can be confusing. Figure 4-1 portrays the various career options available to the professional social worker. It recognizes that before a person decides to begin the educational preparation required to become a professional social worker, he or she will typically have had some positive experiences that have motivated this decision. This future social worker will typically have been a good natural helper or volunteer, the client of a social worker who received useful services, or perhaps a human services provider who did not have professional preparation. If he or she has not already completed a bachelor's degree, the most likely place to begin would be in a BSW program. However, if this is a person who has a degree in another discipline, a second entry point is available—an MSW program.

To make appropriate career development decisions, it is useful for the potential social worker to understand what is expected of a social worker at each of the four practice levels and how that practice level has emerged historically. The following materials, based on NASW's classification system,[9] briefly describe each level, identify the qualifications, and trace the manner in which its central characteristics have emerged.

THE BASIC PROFESSIONAL

Description: Practice as a basic social worker requires professional practice skills, theoretical knowledge, and values not normally obtainable in day-to-day experience

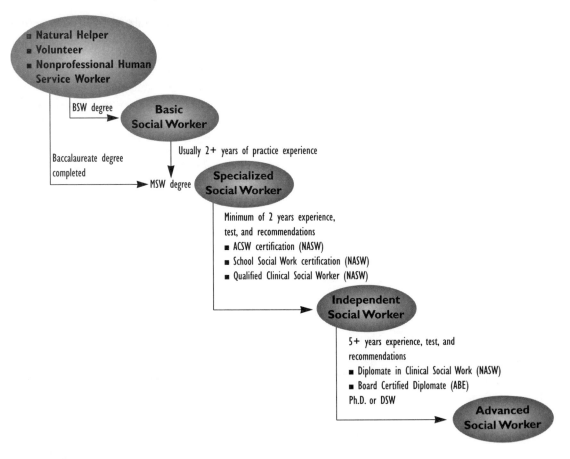

FIGURE 4-1   Career Options for the Professional Social Worker

but that are obtainable through formal social work education. This knowledge is distinguished from experiential learning by being based on conceptual and theoretical knowledge of personal and social interaction and by training in the disciplined use of self in relationship with clients.

Qualifications: Requires a baccalaureate degree from a social work program accredited by the Council on Social Work Education.

Characteristics: Practice at this first level has been formally recognized as professional only since 1970, when the NASW first admitted to full membership persons with a BA or BSW from a social work program approved by the Council on Social Work Education. This recognition not only reflected a movement away from professional elitism but also increased the quantity and quality of undergraduate social work programs.

A few schools offered baccalaureate-level social work courses as early as the 1920s.[10] However, the thrust of social work was toward graduate education. In 1932 the American Association of Schools of Social Work (AASSW) declared that, to be recognized as professional, a social worker must graduate from a four-year college and complete at least one year of graduate education. In 1937 this position was revised to establish two years of graduate education as the minimum level for professional practice.

In response to the AASSW policy, in 1942 several schools created a competing organization, the National Association of Schools of Social Administration (NASSA), for the purpose of having undergraduate programs recognized as professional preparation. After several years of conflict over the legitimacy of undergraduate education, thirteen organizations interested in the resolution of this issue and in the overall enhancement of social work education formed the National Council on Social Work Education. As an initial activity of this organization, the Hollis–Taylor study of social work education was commissioned.

The Hollis–Taylor report, released in 1951, urged that undergraduate education maintain a broad focus and avoid teaching social work skills or preparing students for social work practice on graduation.[11] However, the process by which this study was conducted created harmony between the AASSW and the NASSA, which then merged with the National Council to create what is now the single accrediting body for social work education: the Council on Social Work Education (CSWE).

The CSWE offered membership to both undergraduate and graduate schools and undertook a thirteen-volume curriculum study of social work education at both levels. One volume of this study recommended establishment of professional social work education at the undergraduate level with a continuum developed from undergraduate to graduate programs.[12] This recommendation was initially rejected by the CSWE. During most of the 1960s, undergraduate programs operated under CSWE guidelines that might best be described as a traditional liberal arts education oriented toward social welfare.[13] They were usually taught in departments of psychology or sociology, offered no more than three or four social work courses, and sometimes had no social workers as faculty. With little independent identity on their campuses, and with the failure of both employers and graduate social work programs to give preference or credit for completion of these programs, they were not popular—even among students who planned to enter social work.

Disenchantment of students, employers, and professional social workers with undergraduate education contributed to the establishment of a joint CSWE–NASW Ad Hoc Committee on Manpower Issues in 1968. The Committee's recommendations contributed to concurrent actions in 1970 by NASW members to grant full membership to graduates of approved undergraduate programs and by the CSWE to establish standards for approval of these programs. The first standards adopted were essentially structural: they contributed to the visibility of social work programs, required that social workers be included in faculty, and demanded specification of educational objectives.[14]

CSWE "approval" was granted to 220 schools by 1973, but was at best a limited and informal type of accreditation. Its primary concern was that the schools have an adequate structure for the growth and development of a baccalaureate program.

Specification of curriculum content was slower to develop because a workable division between baccalaureate- and master's-level education had not yet evolved.

In 1973 CSWE took the second step to complete legitimate accreditation: it adopted much more substantial standards for baccalaureate degree programs, placing the primary focus on preparation for professional social work practice. Some previously "approved" programs could not meet the new standards, but most were able to secure the necessary resources to upgrade their programs and achieve accredited status. The number of BSW programs gradually increased, and by 1980 a total of 261 met the accreditation requirements.[15]

In 1984 another significant step to upgrade the quality of baccalaureate social work education was taken when the CSWE operationalized a new set of accreditation standards and a much more substantive Curriculum Policy Statement. These standards spelled out the expectations for each program relative to its purpose, structure, and resources, and also required that each school's curriculum be consistent with the Curriculum Policy Statement.[16] While the standards did not dictate how a school should organize its curriculum, they were considerably more explicit than the 1974 accreditation standards about the content of the student's learning experience. Rigorous application of the accreditation standards did not deter colleges and universities of all sizes in all states from building and maintaining undergraduate social work education programs. As of 1999, 446 colleges and universities had BSW programs that were fully accredited or in candidacy status.[17]

With NASW recognition came the gradual acceptance of baccalaureate-level social work, both by employers as preparation for practice and by the graduate programs as preparation for advanced standing. Increasingly, jobs were defined to recognize the competence and abilities of social workers who had completed this type of educational program, and salary and work assignments were differentiated from those without this preparation. Furthermore, in 1972 CSWE granted approval for graduate schools to accept up to one year's credit for special groups of students. By 1998, 85 percent of the graduate programs offered some form of *advanced standing* to graduates of accredited programs that typically amounted to waiving one to two terms of graduate work.[18]

Clearly, the developments in the 1970s and 1980s enhance the conclusion that the social worker who has completed an accredited undergraduate social work program should be prepared with the competencies for the level of professional practice. Perhaps the most valid test of the acceptance of baccalaureate or basic social workers is whether they find employment as social workers. One study of 5,228 graduates of BSW programs found that 71.4 percent found their first job in social work; 86.8 percent secured employment within six months after graduation. Over time 84.3 percent of the BSW graduates were employed as social workers. These data suggest that the human service agencies found baccalaureate-level social workers attractive, especially in direct service positions, in which 90.2 percent were employed in their first social work job.[19]

THE SPECIALIZED PROFESSIONAL

Description: Practice at this level requires the specific and demonstrated mastery of therapeutic techniques in at least one knowledge and skill method, as well as general knowledge of human personality as influenced by social factors. Specialized practice also requires the disciplined use of self in treatment relationships with individuals or groups, or a broad conceptual knowledge of research, administration, or planning methods and social problems.

Qualifications: Requires a master's degree (MSW) from a social work program accredited by the CSWE.

Characteristics: Prior to the reemergence of baccalaureate-level social work education and the basic social worker, the generally accepted level of preparation for social work practice was that of the specialized social worker. Although it is expected that the MSW social worker, too, will make use of professional supervision, he or she should have sufficient competence to appropriately exercise independent judgment and initiative.

Historically, master's-level social work education began much like the more sophisticated in-service training programs of today. The first formal education program, known as the New York School of Philanthropy (now the Columbia University School of Social Work), was a six-week course offered under the auspices of the New York Charity Organization Society in 1898. The early curricula of the evolving schools incorporated preparation for a range of services, from individual helping approaches to economic and reform theory. They included a heavy investment in internships or field experiences as tools for learning practice skills and tended to be organized around practice settings, such as hospital social work and school social work. The MSW programs' greatest emphasis was on preparation for the services offered by private social agencies, and they tended to neglect the growing demand for social workers in the public social services.

By the 1940s the two-year MSW had become the minimum requirement for professional practice, although a few schools with strong undergraduate programs were resisting that requirement. The two-year programs were typically organized around what was known as the "Basic Eight," in reference to what at that time were considered the eight primary divisions of social work practice: public welfare, social casework, social group work, community organization, medical information, social research, psychiatry, and social welfare administration.

The period from 1950 through 1965 was one of rapid growth in the number of MSW programs and the relative standardization of these programs. By 1965 there were sixty-seven accredited graduate schools and nearly 9,000 students.[20] The schools had largely abandoned programs structured on the basis of practice setting and instead organized curricula around the practice methods of casework, group work, community organization, administration, and research.

Three factors have significantly influenced social work education at the graduate level in the past quarter-century. First, the reemergence of baccalaureate-level social work forced some reorientation of master's education; it was necessary to adapt to the student who entered the MSW program with a substantial social work education already completed. For this student, provision was made for advanced standing in the graduate-level program, which typically meant waiving or testing out of up to one year of graduate work. A continuum of education between the baccalaureate and master's programs began to emerge.

Second, the Council on Social Work Education's Standards for Accreditation and Curriculum Policy Statement allowed individual schools increased flexibility in determining curriculum content. As the typical two-year MSW program evolved, it offered a general orientation to social work practice during the first year and then provided more specialized content based on population served, social problem addressed, practice intervention approach, or client group served during the second year. Prior to that development, students attending MSW programs could expect pretty much the same basic curriculum regardless of which school they attended. Today, this selection is based on the specialization the student desires to develop and the interests and capacity of the school's faculty. In a real sense, graduate social work education has become what traditionally was the expectation of graduate-level work; that is, it is more substantive and specialized than that which one would find at the baccalaureate level.

Finally, the conservative philosophy that dominated the United States during the 1980s initially eliminated some social work jobs and created a tighter job market in the human services. Student interest shifted toward the clinical aspects of social work, and particularly to private practice, where one could avoid the risks of employment in an agency that might lose its funding as a result of a conservative administration. The data on applications for first-year and advanced standing admission to MSW programs provide clear evidence of potential students' fears that the human services would be diminished. In 1979, for example, the number of applications had peaked at 33,978 and 59.9 percent of these students were accepted to admission. Applications then dropped precipitously until 1984 when there were only 22,158 applications of which 78.9 percent were accepted. After hitting bottom in 1984, the applications began to increase and by 1990 the losses were recouped. In 1994 an all-time high of 51,668 applications for the first year of study or advanced standing were received by the graduate programs and an all-time low percentage (46.7%) were accepted for admission.[21] By adjusting acceptance rates, the schools avoid a decline in the number of new social workers being prepared at the master's level, which would create a shortfall when the market for social workers rebounded.

How do basic and specialized social workers differ in the expected abilities they bring to their jobs? The 1992 revisions to the CSWE's Curriculum Policy Statement provide guidelines that social work education programs must follow when preparing students at the two entry levels of social work practice. Table 4-2 compares these two levels and indicates that, while many of the same abilities are expected at both levels, there are uniquenesses that reinforce the perception of the master's-level graduate as a specialized practitioner (i.e., one who has a particular area of concentration) and the basic social worker as one who functions under the supervision of an experienced worker. The social worker with the more advanced degree, according to the Curriculum Policy Statement, is also expected to have greater ability to synthesize and analyze knowledge, to influence policy formulation, and to engage in empirical practice research.

The Basic Social Worker	The Specialized Social Worker
Graduates of a baccalaureate social work program will be able to:	Graduates of a master's social work program are advanced practitioners who can analyze, intervene, and evaluate in ways that are highly differentiated, discriminating, and self-critical. They must synthesize and apply a broad range of knowledge as well as practice with a high degree of autonomy and skill. They must be able to refine and advance the quality of their practice as well as that of the larger social work profession. These advanced competencies must be appropriately integrated and reflected in all aspects of their social work practice, including their ability to:
1. Apply critical-thinking skills within the context of professional social work practice.	1. Apply critical thinking within professional contexts, **including synthesizing and applying appropriate theories and knowledge to practice interventions.**
2. Practice within the values and ethics of the social work profession and within an understanding of and respect for the positive value of diversity.	2. Same as BSW standard.
3. Demonstrate the professional use of self.	3. Same as BSW standard.
4. Understand the forms and mechanisms of oppression and discrimination and apply the strategies and skills of change that advance social and economic justice.	4. Same as BSW standard.
5. Understand the history of the social work profession and its current structures and issues.	5. Understand **and interpret** the history of the social work profession and its current structures and issues.
6. Apply the knowledge and skills of generalist social work to practice with systems of all sizes.	6a. Apply the knowledge and skills of **a generalist perspective** to practice with systems of all sizes. 6b. **Apply the knowledge and skills of advanced social work practice in an area of concentration.**
7. Apply knowledge of bio-psycho-social variables that affect individual development and behavior, and use theoretical frameworks to understand the interactions among individuals and between individuals and social systems (i.e., families, groups, organizations, and communities).	7. **Critically analyze** and apply knowledge of bio-psycho-social variables that affect individual development and behavior, and use theoretical frameworks among individuals and between individuals and social systems (i.e., families, groups, organizations, and communities).
8. Analyze the impact of social policies on client systems, workers, and agencies.	8. Analyze the impact of social policies on client systems, workers, and agencies **and demonstrate skills for influencing policy formulation and change.**
9. Evaluate research studies and apply findings to practice, and, **under supervision,** evaluate their own practice interventions and those of other relevant systems.	9a. Evaluate research studies and apply findings to practice, **and demonstrate skills in quantitative and qualitative research design, data analysis, and knowledge dissemination.** 9b. **Conduct empirical evaluations** of their own practice interventions and those of other relevant systems.
10. Use communication skills differentially with a variety of client populations, colleagues, and members of the community.	10. Same as BSW standard.
11. Use supervision appropriate to **generalist** practice.	11. Use supervision **and consultation** appropriate to **advanced practice in an area of concentration.**
12. Function within the structure of organizations and service delivery systems and, **under supervision,** seek necessary organizational change.	12. Function within the structure of organizations and service delivery systems and seek necessary organizational change.

Source: Council on Social Work Education, *Handbook of Accreditation Standards and Procedures* (Alexandria, VA: CSWE, 1994), pp. 99, 138.

THE INDEPENDENT PROFESSIONAL

Description: The independent practice level is based on appropriate specialized training beyond the MSW and continued professional development under supervision that is sufficient to ensure dependable, regular use of professional skills in independent private practice. A minimum of two years post-master's experience is required to demonstrate this direct practice, administration, or training competence.

Qualifications: Requires an accredited MSW and at least two years of post-master's experience under appropriate professional supervision.

Characteristics: The independent social worker is expected to have developed and integrated the knowledge, values, and skills of social work in at least one practice area. From this experience, he or she should be able to develop sufficient expertise in that field to function independently and skillfully in sensitive situations and should be prepared to practice outside the auspices of a social agency. Furthermore, the independent social worker should be able to provide leadership in at least one practice arena and to supervise and consult with other social workers.

One indicator of reaching the independent professional level is membership in the *Academy of Certified Social Workers* (ACSW). The ACSW was established in 1960 to protect clients from the abuses and incompetence of inadequately prepared practitioners. The Academy also was intended to establish a more favorable public image, to obtain societal sanction, and to increase confidence and understanding in social work. Requirements for becoming a member of the Academy include maintaining membership in NASW, having a minimum of two years full-time practice experience, providing reference letters from professional peers, and achieving a sufficient score on the ACSW exam (a multiple-choice test).

As Figure 4-1 further indicates, NASW has developed two other certification programs intended to certify that workers are prepared to practice independently in specialized areas. To earn the *Qualified Clinical Social Worker* credential, a social worker must have had at least two years of post-MSW clinical practice experience in an agency that was supervised by an experienced clinical social worker. In addition, he or she must hold either the ACSW or a state license and receive favorable references from social work colleagues. The *School Social Work Specialist* must meet similar qualifications and achieve a passing score on the School Social Worker Specialty Area Test, which is a specialty area of the National Teacher's Examination.

THE ADVANCED PROFESSIONAL

Description: Practice at the advanced level is that which carries major social and organizational responsibility for professional development, analysis, research, or policy implementation, or is achieved by personal professional growth demonstrated through advanced conceptual contributions to professional knowledge.

Qualifications: This level requires proficiency in a special theoretical, practice, administration, or policy area, or the ability to conduct advanced research studies in social welfare; usually demonstrated through a doctoral degree in social work or another discipline—in addition to the MSW.

Characteristics: This classification is reserved for the most highly experienced practitioners as well as for social workers who have obtained a doctoral in social work or a related field. In contrast to many professions, relatively few social workers seek or achieve the advanced professional level.

For direct service or clinical practitioners who aspire to the advanced level, two indicators have been developed that provide national identification of the person's competence. One is the *Diplomate in Clinical Social Work* (DCSW) offered by NASW. To be recognized as a diplomate in clinical social work, a person must have completed an accredited MSW program, possess an advanced or clinical state license, have a minimum of five years of post-master's clinical experience, perform satisfactorily on a case-based essay examination, and receive a favorable comprehensive supervisory evaluation. A similar recognition with similar requirements, the *Board Certified Diplomate,* is offered by the independent American Board of Examiners in Clinical Social Work (ABE).

Doctoral education represents the second route to the advanced social work level. The purposes for doctoral degrees (DSW or Ph.D.) in social work have not followed a consistent pattern. Most devote their efforts to preparing the researcher and teacher, but increasingly there as been some focus on preparation for the advanced practitioner. Since the doctorate is not viewed as an entry degree for the social work profession and it is not accredited by the profession, the doctoral programs receive their sanction only from their universities. Therefore, the schools have considerable flexibility to determine the focus of their curricula and have taken on unique identities. By the late 1990s, sixty-two doctoral programs in social work were available throughout the United States enrolling about 1,000 full-time and slightly fewer part-time students. In 1998, 266 doctoral degrees in social work were awarded.[22] These numbers do not, however, reflect the total number of social workers completing doctoral degrees because some complete doctoral work in related fields such as sociology, psychology, higher education, and public administration.

At this time the advanced social worker represents a very small part of social work and is rarely recognized in job-classification schemes or state licensing provisions. This level might best be viewed as a means of holding a classification title for this gradually developing aspect of social work.

Concluding Comment

Through the years of its emergence, social work has gradually evolved four distinct practice levels. The professional membership association, the National Association of Social Workers, has codified these levels into a classification system with expectations for the practitioner at each level defined and education and experience qualifications specified. This classification system embraces two problems in terminology—both created by the acceptance of the concept of an advanced generalist social worker (see Chapter 2). First, the MSW graduate prepared as an advanced generalist is qualified under the classification system as a "Specialized Social Worker." Can one be a specialized generalist? Also, an advanced generalist social worker is not the same as an Advanced Social Worker in NASW's classification system. Persons new to social work should be aware of this confusing terminology.

Nevertheless, the NASW classification of social work practice levels is a useful tool for both social agencies wanting to match workers with job demands and for persons considering a career in social work. For the latter, the selection of a particular practice level as a career goal requires that one assess his or her desire to provide the particular types of service for which that level offers the necessary preparation and the ability to arrange one's personal life to acquire the requisite professional education and experiences. In social work, in contrast to some of the other helping professions, one can change directions after entering the profession. A person might enter social work in a particular field of practice, such as providing services to the aged or developmentally disabled, and later transfer the skills used in that job to employment in mental health or corrections. Or the direct service worker (usually with a master's degree) might transfer into a job involving agency administration or move away from agency-based practice and into autonomous or private practice.

KEY WORDS AND CONCEPTS

Accreditation (of educational programs)

Professional certification

Academy of Certified Social Workers

Licensing (state regulation of practice)

Volunteers

Indigenous workers

Social science professions

American Association of Schools of Social Work

National Association of Schools of Social Administration

Advanced standing

Basic social worker

Specialized social worker

Independent social worker

Advanced social worker

SUGGESTED READINGS

Biggerstaff, Marilyn A. "Licensing, Regulation, and Certification." In Richard L. Edwards, ed., *Encyclopedia of Social Work,* 19th Edition. Washington, D.C.: NASW Press, 1995, pp. 1616–1624.

Gibelman, Margaret, and Schervish, Phillip H. *Who We Are: A Second Look.* Washington, D.C.: NASW Press, 1996.

Teare, Robert J., and Sheafor, Bradford W. *Practice-Sensitive Social Work Education: An Empirical Analysis of Social Work Practice and Practitioners.* Alexandria, VA: Council on Social Work Education, 1995.

ENDNOTES

1. For suggestions of issues one might examine when considering social work as a career choice, see Bradford W. Sheafor, Charles R. Horejsi, and Gloria A. Horejsi, *Techniques and Guidelines for Social Work Practice,* 5th Edition (Boston: Allyn and Bacon, 2000), Chapter 2.

2. Ruth R. Middleman, *A Study Guide for ACSW Certification,* 4th Edition (Washington, D.C.: NASW Press, 1996), p. v.

3. Robert R. Wohlgemuth and Thomas Samph, *Summary Report: Content Validity Study in Support of the Licensure Examination Program of the American Association of State Social Work Boards* (Oak Park, IL: The Association, 1983), p. 2.

4. Donna DeAngelis, *State Comparison of Laws Regulating Social Work* (Washington, D.C.: National Association of Social Workers, 1993).

5. *NASW News* 42 (January 1996): 19–22.

6. National Association of Social Workers, *Standards for Social Work Personnel Practices: Policy Statement No. 2* (Washington, D.C.: The Association, 1971).

7. Todd M. Lennon, *Statistics for Social Work Education in the United States: 1994* (Alexandria, VA: Council on Social Work Education, 1995), p. 30.

8. Joseph Mehr, *Human Services: Concepts and Intervention Strategies,* 6th Edition (Boston: Allyn and Bacon, 1995), pp. 11–20.

9. National Association of Social Workers, *NASW Standards for the Classification of Social Work Practice* (Washington, D.C.: The Association, 1981).

10. A comprehensive analysis of the evolution of baccalaureate-level social work can be found in Bradford W. Sheafor and Barbara W. Shank, *Undergraduate Social Work Education: A Survivor in a Changing Profession* (Austin: University of Texas at Austin School of Social Work, 1986).

11. Ernest V. Hollis and Alice L. Taylor, *Social Work Education in the United States* (New York: Columbia University Press, 1951).

12. Herbert Bisno, *The Place of Undergraduate Curriculum in Social Work Education,* Social Work Curriculum Study Vol. 2 (New York: Council on Social Work Education, 1959).

13. Council on Social Work Education, *Social Welfare Content in Undergraduate Education* (New York: The Council, 1962), pp. 3–4.

14. Council on Social Work Education, *Undergraduate Programs in Social Work* (New York: The Council, 1971).

15. Allen Rubin, *Statistics on Social Work Education in the United States: 1980* (New York: Council on Social Work Education, 1981), p. 1.

16. Council on Social Work Education, *Handbook of Accreditation Standards and Procedures* (Washington, D.C.: The Council, 1984).

17. Nancy Randolph, "Report from the Division of Standards and Accreditation," *The Social Work Education Reporter* 49 (Spring–Summer 1999): 22.

18. Council on Social Work Education, *Summary Information on Master of Social Work Programs: 1997–98* (Alexandria, VA: Council on Social Work Education, 1998).

19. Robert J. Teare, Barbara W. Shank, and Bradford W. Sheafor, "Career Patterns of the BSW Social Worker." Unpublished manuscript, Colorado State University, Fort Collins.

20. Raymond DeVera, ed., *Statistics on Social Work Education, 1965–66* (New York: Council on Social Work Education, 1966), p. 6.

21. Allen Rubin, *Statistics on Social Work Education in the United States: 1983* (New York: Council on Social Work Education, 1984), p. 49; Elaine C. Spaulding, *Statistics on Social Work Education in the United States: 1987* (Washington, D.C.: Council on Social Work Education, 1988), p. 36; and Todd M. Lennon, *Statistics on Social Work Education in the United States: 1998* (Alexandria, VA: Council on Social Work Education, 1999), p. 45.

22. Lennon, *Statistics,* 1999, pp. 1, 45.

CHAPTER 5

Fields of Social
Work Practice

One factor that makes social work different from many other professions is the opportunity to help people deal with a wide range of human problems without needing to obtain specialized professional credentials for each area of practice. During his or her lifetime, for example, one social worker might organize and lead self-help groups in a hospital, deal with cases of abuse and neglect, develop release plans for persons in a correctional facility, plan demonstrations protesting racist or sexist injustices, arrange for foster homes and adoptions for children, secure nursing home placements for older people, supervise new social workers, and serve as executive director of a human service agency. Regardless of the type of work performed, the social worker always has the same fundamental purpose—to draw on basic knowledge, values, and skills in order to help achieve desired change to improve the quality of life for the persons involved.

Although there are similarities in the tasks performed by social workers regardless of the nature of the services provided, there are also unique aspects of their practice with each population group. For example, services to children and youth differ from services to the elderly, the needs of a disabled adult differ from those of a person about to be released from a correctional facility, or the assistance required by a pregnant teenager differs from that needed by a teenager engaged in gang activity or substance abuse. Each of these fields of practice typically uses at least some specialized language, emphasizes specific helping approaches and techniques, or may be affected by different laws or social programs. Therefore, what a social worker does and needs to know will vary to some extent from field to field.

The human services system is indeed complex, and the layperson cannot be expected to negotiate this system alone. As the profession with the primary responsibility for helping people in need to gain access to the services in a community, the social worker must not only know what services are available, but must also be prepared to interpret them to their clients and help these clients gain access to the resources they need. To reduce the client's sense of "getting the runaround" in securing services, and perhaps reduce the chance of the client becoming discouraged and not getting to needed help, the social worker must carefully check that the referral is to an appropriate resource. In addition, the professional, at times, may need to provide a variety of supports, such as encouragement, telephone numbers, names of individuals to contact, or even transportation to facilitate the client's getting to the correct resources. Thus, the social worker must not only work within a single practice field but should also be prepared to help clients negotiate services among practice fields.

This chapter identifies some of the features of the primary fields of social work practice to familiarize the beginning worker with the range of places where a social worker might be employed. *Field of social work practice* is a phrase used to describe a group of practice settings that deal with similar client problems. Each field may include a number of different agencies or other organized ways of providing services. For example, in any community, the social agencies concerned with crime and delinquency might include a juvenile court, a residential center or halfway house, a community corrections agency, a probation office for adult offenders, and/or a correctional facility where offenders are incarcerated. All fields work with people who have come to the attention of the legal system and would be considered part of the practice field of corrections. Although the fields discussed in the remainder of this chapter do not exhaust the full range where social workers might practice, those identified suggest the great variety of settings in which the social worker is prepared to provide services.

Below, when each of the thirteen selected fields of social work practice is described, data are presented in a table that reports percentage of BSW and MSW social workers who are employed in that field, that is, their *primary practice area*. In addition, where data are available, information is included in the table that indicates the percentages of social workers who consider the client problems in this field one of the three most prevalent client needs they address in their practice—even if addressing that need is not their primary practice activity.* For example, as reported in the following section, 16.5 percent of the basic social workers report that their primary practice area is providing services to aged persons. However, 23.6 percent indicate that one of the three most dominant client needs they address in their work relates to some problem associated with aging. Thus, in addition to those who consider aging their primary practice area, another 7.1 percent of the basic social workers also work extensively with the aging population.

---

*All data reported in this chapter are from Robert J. Teare and Bradford W. Sheafor, "National Task Analysis of Social Work Practice." A description of the method of data collection appears in Robert J. Teare and Bradford W. Sheafor, *Practice Sensitive Social Work Education: An Empirical Analysis of Social Work Practice and Practitioners* (Alexandria, VA: Council on Social Work Education, 1995).

Aging

	Primary Practice Area	Prevalent Client Need
Basic Social Worker	16.5%	23.6%
Specialist/Independent Social Worker	3.7	10.2

Many social workers provide services to older people, both those requiring support to remain in their own homes and those residing in long-term care facilities such as nursing homes and congregate-care centers. Basic social workers are the primary service providers for older people, although many workers at the specialized and independent levels also regularly serve older people as part of their social work practice.

With increased industrialization and technological development in U.S. society, meaningful roles for older people have decreased. Improved medical care that extends life and inflation that reduces the buying power of savings and retirement funds have made the elderly a vulnerable population. Today more than 12.7 percent of the U.S. population (34.1 million people) are age sixty-five or over, and nearly four million of these older persons are over age eighty-five—an age at which it is estimated that approximately one-half need assistance with everyday living activities.[1] Those who are able to remain in their homes or the homes of family members experience more physical and social problems than the general population. For example, 3.4 million older people live in poverty, 6 percent live in housing with severe physical problems, 37 percent deal with one or more chronic illness, many are lonely due to the loss of a mate (42.3% of the women are widows and 15% of the men are widowers), and many find it difficult to adapt to a changing life style caused by retirement or a health condition.[2]

A number of programs are available to help older people remain in their own homes as long as doing so is a safe and satisfying experience. Social workers help older people make links to community programs that bring health care, meals, and homemaker services into their homes; provide transportation services; and offer day care or recreation programs. Increasingly, when older people are faced with a terminal illness, social workers help them deal with their impending death through counseling or referral to a hospice program.

For approximately 4 percent (1.4M) of the older people, some form of long-term care in a nursing home or other group living facility becomes a necessity. Social workers frequently help the individual and/or family select the facility and make moving arrangements; some are even staff members of the facility.

While much attention in a long-term care facility is directed toward meeting the basic physical and medical needs of the residents, social workers in these facilities contribute to the quality of life for residents by helping them maintain contact with their families and friends when possible, develop meaningful relationships with other people within the facility, and engage in a variety of activities both within and outside the facility. They also facilitate access to other social services when needed and help residents secure arrangements that protect their personal rights and ensure quality care while living in the long-term care facility.

Alcohol and Substance Abuse

	Primary Practice Area	Prevalent Client Need
Basic Social Worker	3.2%	20.1%
Specialist/Independent Social Worker	2.2	14.8

Considering the size and scope of alcohol and drug problems in U.S. society, relatively few social workers have this field as their primary practice area. Those who do are primarily employed in alcohol and drug treatment centers or are engaged in private practice. However, the interrelationship between substance abuse and other social problems is evident in the fact that these problems were prevalent in the work of between 15 and 20 percent of all social workers. Social workers employed by virtually every type of human service organization, from mental health and correctional facilities to schools and hospitals, deal with the effects of substance abuse on social functioning. Between nine and twelve million individuals in the United States are alcoholics or drug abusers, and each individual usually affects at least four other persons in some negative, unhealthy, or destructive manner.[3] The social implications of alcohol and substance abuse are significant as they are highly correlated with murders, suicides, accidents, health problems, and domestic violence.

In recent years social workers have increasingly found success in working with alcohol and substance abusers. Much of the credit for this success has come as social workers and other professionals have moved from viewing alcoholism not "as a moral weakness, requiring only a strong will and determination to 'reform,' "[4] toward viewing it as a disease. This has been beneficial not only for enlisting an alcoholic in his or her own recovery but also for approaching the problem from a sounder scientific basis.

Using current scientific understanding of these problems, Lawson and Lawson have identified three primary factors that should be considered in treating and preventing alcoholism and substance abuse. First, they recognize that physiological factors such as physical addiction, disease or physical disorders, medical problems, inherited risk, and/or mental disorders with physiological causes may contribute to the problem. Second, Lawson and Lawson identify several sociological factors, such as ethnic and cultural differences, family background, education, employment, and peer relationships, as also related to alcoholism and substance abuse. Finally, they note that psychological factors, including social skills, emotional level, self-image, attitude toward life, defense mechanisms, mental obsessions, judgment, and decision-making skills all can be contributors to this disease.[5] Growing understanding of these associated and interrelated factors has provided the helping professions with an opportunity to apply their knowledge and skills to helping clients prevent and resolve their problems. Social work plays a particularly important role, as the addictions inevitably have a significant effect on family, friends, coworkers, and others who are in contact with the person experiencing the addiction. Both the person and the environment must be helped to change when this disease is treated.

Children and Youth

	Primary Practice Area	Prevalent Client Need
Basic Social Worker	18.8%	63.6%
Specialist/Independent Social Worker	13.1	66.1

From work in the almshouses in the 1800s to work with street gangs today, social workers have devoted a major part of their effort to creating conditions that improve the quality of life for children and youth. This work is the largest primary practice area for basic social workers and follows only mental health and family services among the specialist and independent social workers. Further, nearly two-thirds of both groups work with children and youth as a primary part of their social work practice.

The U.S. society has entrusted the family with full responsibility for the care and nurturing of children. Law and custom mandate that other social institutions must not interfere with the rights and responsibilities of the family to care for its children. Historically, it has been assumed that parents would make choices that were in the best interest of both themselves and their children. For example, if parents thought it more important for children to work in a factory or to help with farm work than to attend school or have time for play, that decision was honored. That authority, however, left children vulnerable. Legislation permitting other social institutions (e.g., child protective services, police, and courts) to intervene in family situations that were potentially harmful to children was reluctantly adopted. Today, children and youth continue to be somewhat hidden within families with only limited protection when abusive situations are present.

In most situations social workers seek to work with both the parents and children. Children can often be helped most if parents are assisted in obtaining needed resources and/or developing effective ways to raise their offspring. In addition, social workers have not only provided services directly to parents and children but have also actively promoted laws, programs, and public understanding of the needs of children and youth. Examples of some of the practice areas in which social workers serve children and youth follow.

ADOPTION AND SERVICES TO UNMARRIED PARENTS

The adoption process begins with the expectant mother, often unmarried, who faces the difficult decision of whether to keep her baby or place the child for adoption. A few of the factors to be considered in this decision include the mother's plans for the future, such as continuing school or securing employment and child care, the attitudes of the mother's family about the pregnancy, the feelings of the father and the mother's relationship with him, and where the mother will live while pregnant and after the baby arrives. Social workers use both individual and group counseling to help women consider the implications of their decisions. They also, at times, offer counseling to unmarried fathers to help them deal with this situation.

If the decision is made to place the child for adoption, the social worker must screen and select adoptive parents carefully. Matching parents and children is a difficult task that requires considerable knowledge and skill. To gain the best information possible on which to base these decisions, the social worker might conduct group orientation meetings and develop thorough social histories of the prospective adoptive parents. Detailed information on the child's background and even special interests of the natural mother for the child's future (religious affiliation, for example) become part of the basis for final adoptive placement.

There has always been an abundance of prospective adoptive homes, and recent trends making it more socially acceptable for single parents to raise children have reduced the supply of infants available for adoptive placement. However, it continues to be difficult to secure satisfactory adoptive homes for older children or those who are physically or mentally disabled. An important function of the social worker is to recruit parents for these hard-to-place children.

FOSTER CARE

At times children may need to be removed from their own homes, but it is not possible, nor desirable, to permanently sever the relationship with their natural parents, as in placing them for adoption. In these cases, temporary (sometimes long-term) foster care is required. The social worker must work with the parents, the child, and the courts to obtain a decision to remove a child from his or her own home and make a foster home placement. This process involves a careful assessment and a plan whereby the child can return home if conditions improve.

The social worker is also responsible for developing a pool of good quality foster homes. He or she must recruit, select, train, and monitor those families that are entrusted with the care of foster children. The placement of a child in a foster home often creates severe stress on the child, the natural parents, and the foster parents. Considerable practice skill by the social worker is required if he or she is to help resolve these problems.

RESIDENTIAL CARE

At times the appropriate placement for a child is a residential care facility, that is, a group home or a residential treatment center. These facilities are most likely to be chosen when the child exhibits antisocial behavior or requires intensive treatment to change behaviors that may create problems for him- or herself or others.

In these situations, one role of the social worker is to select an appropriate residential care facility, which involves working with the child, the family, and, often, the courts. In addition, other social workers are usually staff members of such a facility, providing care and treatment for the children who are placed there. They are especially involved in helping maintain positive contact between the child and the family and in making plans for the child to return home when appropriate. The fact that these residential care facilities require licensing creates another role for the social worker—evaluating facilities for the purpose of licensing.

SUPPORT IN OWN HOME

Much work with children and youth involves providing support services in order to keep children in their own homes. These support services can take the form of counseling or linking clients with outside resources.

Counseling may involve one-to-one consultation with a parent or child to resolve a particular problem with the child–parent relationship. It may also involve family consultation in which all the family members work with the social worker in an attempt to improve some aspect of their functioning. Family members may also participate in group counseling with other parents or children experiencing similar problems. The social worker guides the participants as they address the issues relevant to their problems.

In work with children and youth, the most common outside resources are day care and homemaker services. Day care centers can provide a stimulating environment for children and relieve parents of the stress created by the child's continual presence in the home. The social worker must know the strengths and limitations of various day care centers and match children with appropriate resources. Homemaker services help parents learn homemaking skills and reduce the pressures of caring for the children and the household.

PROTECTIVE SERVICES

Some children are abused or neglected by one or both parents. Abuse, whether it is physical, sexual, or emotional, is an active mistreatment or exploitation of the child. Neglect is a more passive mistreatment of the child but can be just as damaging. It can take the form of inadequate food and shelter, unwholesome conditions, failure to have the child attend school, or inadequate provision of medical care.

The social worker, as an agent of society, seeks to protect the child without infringing on the rights of the parents. When a referral is received, the social worker must determine if the child is in immediate danger, assess the ability of the parents to resolve the problem, and make a judgment about the risks of working with the family while keeping the child in the home. If the child is removed from the home (with approval of the courts), the social worker continues to work with the family in an effort to eliminate the difficulties that led to the referral. This process may involve individual, family, or group counseling; the provision of support services; or education of family members in the areas of their incompetence.

YOUTH SERVICES

Very early in U.S. history a number of human service programs were developed to provide educational and recreational opportunities for people of all social classes. These services were aimed at character-building among youth, with organizations such as the YMCA, YWCA, Boys and Girls Clubs, and various scouting groups developing. Later, with the growth of settlement houses, programs were broadened to serve other age groups. Although other disciplines also provide staff for these organizations, this field of practice continues to be a small but important area of social work.

These services seek to enhance the growth and development of all interested participants, from the poor to the well-to-do. Through the use of such activities as crafts, sports, camping, friendship groups, drama, music, informal counseling, and other forms of group participation, the members are guided toward personal development. The role of the social worker might be to administer these agencies, to lead the group process, or to provide individual counseling.

Community/Neighborhood

	Primary Practice Area	Prevalent Client Need
Basic Social Worker	0.5%	No data
Specialist/Independent Social Worker	1.5	No data

Relatively few social work jobs are primarily related to helping communities improve their functioning. These data suggest that neighborhood and community change activity, when it does occur, is most likely to be a secondary part of a social work job. As Chapter 8 indicates, analysis of the tasks performed by social workers in all fields of practice does not support the conclusion that they do, in fact, engage in a substantial amount of social action or community change activity. These data raise a question about the degree to which social workers are fulfilling their mission of addressing issues of *both* person and environment.

Beginning with the Charity Organization Societies and the Settlement House Movement in the late 1800s, social workers clearly saw the need both to coordinate the multiple human services that existed in a community and to stimulate change in these communities to make them more responsive to the needs of people or change patterns of operation that have negative effects on people. When social workers do provide neighborhood or community services today, three forms of intervention are typically applied: community organization, community planning, and community development.

COMMUNITY ORGANIZATION

A traditional practice area for social work has been working within the network of human services to increase their effectiveness in meeting human needs. This activity involves collecting and analyzing data related to the delivery of services, matching that information with data on population distribution, securing funds to maintain and enhance the quality of services, coordinating the efforts of existing agencies, and educating the general public about these services. The principal agencies in which social workers are employed to do this type of work are community planning councils, United Way agencies, and other federations of agencies under the auspices of religious groups, such as the Jewish Welfare Federation.

COMMUNITY PLANNING

A few social workers with specialized training join physical, economic, and health planners in the long-range planning of communities. This work requires the ability to apply planning technology in order to project and plan the growth and development of communities. The special contribution of the social worker is to analyze the needs for human services as towns, cities, or regions undergo change. These contributions might range from anticipating "boom-town" developments in energy-impacted areas of Colorado or Wyoming to helping an urban ghetto plan for an increase in human service needs brought about by businesses moving to the suburbs, leaving the central city with an eroding tax base.

COMMUNITY DEVELOPMENT

Social work joins a number of disciplines in giving assistance to people in communities as they seek to improve conditions. This approach is based on a self-help philosophy that encourages members of the community to mobilize their resources in order to study their problems and seek solutions. In rural areas, the social worker contributes to this "grass roots" approach by guiding those involved toward a sound process that maximizes the participation of many concerned citizens. The social worker or other professional also serves as a resource for obtaining technical consultation in areas where there is not expertise among the community members. In urban areas this process, sometimes known as an "asphalt roots" approach, is used to help neighborhoods or special population groups (such as the poor, minorities, or older people) work together to improve the quality of their lives.

Corrections/Criminal Justice

	Primary Practice Area	*Prevalent Client Need*
Basic Social Worker	2.7%	6.4%
Specialist/Independent Social Worker	1.3	4.0

Another small but important part of social work practice occurs in the area of corrections and criminal justice. Correctional social workers are employed in courts, parole and probation offices, and correctional facilities. Social workers often find corrections a perplexing field of practice because the structure of services is usually based on punishment and taking custody of the lives of offenders, which conflicts with many social work values and principles. Yet, because the nature of the problems experienced by persons who come to the attention of professionals in this field are basically those of social functioning, the social worker has a valuable contribution to make.

The corrections field embraces offenders from all aspects of society—youth and adults, males and females, rich and poor, members of dominant population groups and minorities, and even former politicians. In correctional settings, the poor, especially minorities, are very much overrepresented. The social worker's involvement with the criminal justice system can begin at the time of arrest and terminate at the person's release. Some social workers serve as, or work with, juvenile officers in diversionary programs, where they provide crisis intervention or referral services at the time of arrest. These programs divert people from the criminal justice system and into more appropriate community services. Social workers also prepare social histories and make psychosocial assessments of individuals charged with crimes as part of the data a judge uses in making decisions about a case. If the person is placed on probation, a social worker might be the probation officer providing individual, family, or group counseling and helping the convicted person make changes in behavior that will satisfy the terms of probation and prevent additional problems from developing.

Social workers are also found in correctional facilities. In these facilities they provide counseling and serve as a link to the outside world, which encompasses the family, potential employers, and the community service network that will provide support to that person at the time of release. If parole is granted, a social worker might serve as the parole officer or work in a halfway house where the person may live prior to a completely independent re-entry to the community.

Disabilities (Physical/Mental)

	Primary Practice Area	Prevalent Client Need
Basic Social Worker	10.4%	33.4%
Specialist/Independent Social Worker	4.1	34.0

Assisting persons with physical, mental, and developmental disabilities is a field of practice in which basic social workers are most likely to be the primary service providers. Yet helping people deal with disabling conditions affects most fields of social work. Social workers are concerned with such disabling conditions as mental retardation, visual and hearing impairment, communication disability, learning disability, and cerebral palsy, which affect not only the person's physical and intellectual functioning but also interaction with others, that is, social functioning. The special role of social work is to help these persons and their families learn to live as successfully as possible in a society structured for the more fully functioning individual.

Disabling conditions are about equally divided among mental retardation, behavioral disorders, and sensory and/or physical disorders. In addition, some persons experience more than one form of disability with a few experiencing the "dual diagnosis" of both a developmental disability and emotional illness.

What is a *developmental disability?* The term has evolved to include a rather broad range of disabling conditions that affect the physical, social, and intellectual development of a person. The Developmental Disabilities Assistance and Bill of

Rights Act (Public Law 95-602) provides the following definition of a developmental disability:

> . . . a severe chronic disability of a person which: a) is attributable to a mental or physical impairment or combination of mental or physical impairments; b) is manifested before the person attains age 22; c) is likely to continue indefinitely; d) results in substantial functional limitations in three or more of the following areas of major life activity, including self-care, receptive/expressive language, learning, mobility, self-direction, capacity for independent living, and economic self-sufficiency; and e) reflects the person's need for a combination and sequence of special, interdisciplinary, or generic care, treatment, or other services which are individually planned and coordinated.[6]

While the definition of a disabled person contained in PL 95-602 does not include all physically and intellectually disabled people, it does encompass a large share of the most seriously disabled. In an effort to enhance the quality of life for all people, social workers serve clients who experience both mild and severe disabilities. To accomplish this goal, social workers help people find suitable living arrangements (either with their families or in community facilities), assist in the alleviation of problems associated with the disability, contribute to public education efforts about the causes and society's responses to these disabilities, and help individuals gain access to needed services.

Education and Training

	Primary Practice Area	Prevalent Client Need
Basic Social Worker	0.3%	10.5%
Specialist/Independent Social Worker	3.4	9.8

Some social work practice does not involve directly serving clients, but rather teaches others to provide services needed by individuals, families, groups, organizations, and communities. Most of these social workers are employed by colleges and universities, while others provide training programs for volunteers or employees of human service organizations. Rarely is education or training the primary function of either a basic or specialized social worker. This function is usually performed by advanced workers.[7] However, it is noteworthy that about 10 percent of all social workers devote a part of their practice to various education and training activities.

Education and training require a wide range of skills. Much of the work involves classroom, workshop, or seminar formats for providing instruction. However, training also involves more individualized forms of instruction found in the direct observation and coaching of volunteers, students, professionals, or other staff members of social agencies. The communication skills and group interaction skills used in many aspects of social work practice have made social workers particularly effective in conducting education and training activities.

Family Services

	Primary Practice Area	Prevalent Client Need
Basic Social Worker	13.7%	38.3%
Specialist/Independent Social Worker	13.7	45.1

Social workers at all levels are likely to be involved in helping families address issues in their social functioning, both as their primary practice area and as a client need they frequently address when employed in other fields of practice. Why are family services such a substantial part of social work practice? Changing marital arrangements, child-rearing practices, and patterns of employment in the United States have placed considerable strain on the nuclear family. A growing number of single-parent families, reconstituted families (often involving her children, his children, and their children), duo-breadwinner families, and gay/lesbian households, for example, have dramatically affected social structures that were established for the older family pattern of a mom, a dad, and their children. Social workers have a key role in helping society address these changes and in assisting individual families and households to adapt to these newer conditions or resolve problems associated with them. Three broad service areas capture the bulk of the activities in which social workers engage: family counseling, education, and planning.

FAMILY COUNSELING

Social work employs three approaches to family counseling in an effort to help the family adjust to its changing role and deal with the problems it experiences. One is *family casework*. This approach emphasizes helping individual members of the family change their behaviors in order to make them more productive contributors to the family. It draws on techniques used in individual casework and is strongly influenced by psychosocial treatment approaches and a problem-solving orientation.

A second approach is termed *family group work*. Recognizing that the family is a special form of a small group, this approach incorporates much of the theory of social work practice with groups. It emphasizes the process by which the family examines its relationships. The social worker helps family members work together to resolve their problems.

The third approach is *family therapy*. This approach seeks to change the structure of the family to make it more supportive of its members. The family, then, is regarded as a unit that can contribute to the well-being of its individual members and is encouraged to perform this function. Family therapy requires advanced skills and training to prepare properly for this therapeutic activity.

FAMILY LIFE EDUCATION

The quality of family life can sometimes be strengthened through activities that fall under the label of family life education. This social work practice activity recognizes that all families face certain kinds of stress, and it seeks to prevent family breakdown by educating family members to cope with anticipated problems. It teaches about interpersonal, family, and sex relationships to help people to have more satisfactory and fulfilling lives. Family life education is a preventive approach to human services that has the potential for reaching a large number of people.

FAMILY PLANNING

Social workers have long been sensitive to the fact that both an unwanted child and his or her parents often experience problems. Adequately carrying out the responsibilities of raising a child is difficult under the best of circumstances, and an unwanted pregnancy makes it even more difficult. Most social workers contend that each child should have the right to begin life as a wanted person. Helping families to plan the number, spacing, and timing of the births of children to fit with their needs improves the chance of achieving the goal of bearing wanted children.

Family planning does not imply that there should be a minimum or maximum number of children in a family or that any specific birth control method should be used. Rather, from the social work perspective, the family is helped to make decisions about their patterns of reproduction in order to maximize the quality of life for all family members.

The social worker does not have medical training and cannot replace the important role of physicians and nurses in teaching the physiological aspects of family planning. However, he or she must have a minimal understanding of human reproduction, contraception, and abortion to help families with the decisions they must make. Because the issue of family planning can arise in many counseling situations, social workers in hospitals, public welfare agencies, mental health clinics, family services, health departments, schools, family planning clinics, and private practice must be prepared to help clients when the need for family planning decisions arise.

Income Maintenance

	Primary Practice Area	*Prevalent Client Need*
Basic Social Worker	3.1%	14.9%
Specialist/Independent Social Worker	1.5	7.1

Once the primary discipline engaged in income maintenance, today relatively few social workers report employment in public assistance positions. Many more, however, indicate that financial issues are one of the most common problems experienced by their clients. Therefore, it is important for social workers to be knowledgeable about poverty and the various income maintenance programs available to assist poor people.

Social workers have learned that living in poverty is much more than just not having a sufficient supply of cash. Poverty is much more complex and insidious. It is associated with the quality of housing in which one lives, the safety of the neighborhood, the quality of meals, the person's health and thus regularity of school and work attendance, and many other factors. Experience indicates that financial assistance, at least at the levels U.S. society has been willing to make available, will not, in itself, break the cycle of poverty. Yet, sufficient income is a prerequisite for addressing many other problems in social functioning.

Despite the many factors that contribute to poverty, lack of income is an unmet need that brings poor people to the attention of the social worker. A number of government-sponsored and voluntary social programs have been developed to provide assistance to, or reduce financial demands on, the poor. The two dominant areas of the income maintenance field are public assistance and social insurance programs, although there are other programs that serve this area of human need.

The reasons that people require financial assistance vary, and so do the programs designed to meet these needs. For some, help with the purchase of food is enough, and providing families with *food stamps* is adequate to reduce hunger. For others, the federal government provides funds through *Temporary Assistance for Needy Families (TANF)*, which offers more substantial financial aid that will help to pay for housing, clothing, and other daily living costs. Some of these families may also receive food stamps to supplement the TANF income. States supplement these programs from their revenues by providing *general assistance* to give temporary support to people who, for varying reasons, are not eligible for other financial aid programs. A more specialized program is *Social Security Income (SSI)*, which is intended to provide a minimum level of income for some of the most vulnerable members of the society—the aged, blind, and disabled. Finally, the *Medicaid* program provides for hospital and medical care for the poor in an effort to minimize the financial impact of a serious illness on people who cannot afford medical insurance. These programs reflect the "safety net" concept of human services, requiring that the recipient experience serious problems before the services become available.

Other basic social services are provided through individual and employer contributions to a specific program, rather than through direct tax revenues. These *social insurance* programs are "universal" because they are available without the stigma of demeaning eligibility tests. Assistance is viewed as a right, not charity. The major social insurance program is *Old Age, Survivors, Disability, and Health Insurance (OASDHI)*, better known as Social Security. It provides income and other benefits to the worker, worker's spouse, and dependent children of a retired or disabled worker. *Medicare* is a federal health insurance program directed at persons over age sixty-five, who are especially vulnerable to serious illnesses that can quickly deplete financial resources and place them permanently in need of public assistance. Other important social insurance programs are *Unemployment Insurance* and *Worker's Compensation Insurance*. The former provides temporary benefits to eligible persons who have lost their jobs, and the latter furnishes income and medical expenses to people who have been injured on their jobs.

Finally, a wide range of cash and in-kind benefits is also provided through a variety of private sources in people's own communities. Local churches and social agencies usually have small amounts of emergency support funds, food banks, food kitchens, and other resources from which the poor can obtain help in meeting their basic needs. These resources are so indigenous to local areas that local human resources directories or local experts on the services such as social workers must be consulted to locate needed sources for assistance.

Medical and Health Care

	Primary Practice Area	*Prevalent Client Need*
Basic Social Worker	12.8%	26.8%
Specialist/Independent Social Worker	13.5	18.3

Medical social work was initiated in the early 1900s, with social workers playing a peripheral role to physicians and nurses in health and medical settings. With increased understanding that illnesses can be caused or exacerbated by social factors, social workers gained a more central role in providing medical and health care. Today, social work in hospitals, outpatient clinics, and other health-related organizations is one of the largest practice fields for both basic and specialist/independent social workers.

A primary place for social work practice in this field is in hospitals. In these settings, for example, social workers address social and psychological factors that are either contributing causes of medical ailments or are side effects of a medical condition that must be dealt with to facilitate recovery and prevent occurrences of nonfunctional dependence. Social workers help to link patients, perhaps with changed levels of functioning due to a medical problem, with their environments by providing individual, group, and family counseling; serving as patient advocates; and working with self-help groups of patients experiencing similar medical or social problems. Social workers also might be engaged in counseling terminally ill patients and their families.

In addition, social workers are involved in other health and medical care facilities besides hospitals. They work in public health clinics and private physicians' offices providing counseling and referral services to people who have sought medical treatment related to family planning, prenatal care, child growth and development, venereal disease, and physical disability, for example. They have also taken an active role in health maintenance and disease prevention programs in local communities. With the skyrocketing costs of medical care, it is even more important that these efforts be continued by the social work profession.

Mental Health and Illness

	Primary Practice Area	*Prevalent Client Need*
Basic Social Worker	9.9%	No data
Specialist/Independent Social Worker	28.3	No data

It has long been recognized that one's mental health and capacity for social functioning are highly correlated. A person who is depressed, hyperactive, hallucinating, or experiencing any of the other symptoms of mental illness is likely at some time to become the client of a social worker. It is estimated that 15 percent of the general population experience emotional disturbance at any one time, creating a high demand for social workers in this field. In fact, social workers are twice as prevalent as psychologists and psychiatrists in the mental health field. Most social workers serving mentally ill persons are at the specialist or independent social worker level; however, 15 to 20 percent of the BSWs report dealing extensively with mental health problems such as anxiety and depression, interpersonal relations, character or behavior disorders, and, more generally, mental illness.

Social workers in mental health settings work with people experiencing these difficulties by treating those who have the potential for change. They help them learn to cope with problems in their social functioning and, at the same time, work to change factors in their environment to promote better mental health or eliminate social conditions that have a negative effect on their functioning. There are three practice settings where social workers are most likely to engage in psychiatric social work, outpatient mental heath clinics, inpatient psychiatric hospitals, and in private practice.

About 8.7 percent of the BSW and 17.9 percent of the MSW workers provide mental health services on an outpatient basis in a mental health center, sheltered workshop, or counseling center. They provide clinical or therapeutic services to individuals and families or to small groups of clients. They may also consult with a variety of organizations, such as group homes, or work with the mass media, in an effort to create an environment that is conducive to the health, growth, and development of all people—both clients and the public.

A much smaller number of social workers (4.4% of the BSW and 2.9% of the MSW workers) provide mental health services on an inpatient basis in psychiatric hospitals. These services are given to people of all ages experiencing severe mental health problems requiring the full-time care and structure available at a hospital or other living situation. Whereas the MSW workers may provide a variety of treatment activities, the BSW workers are more likely to serve as liaisons to the patient's outside world and help the patient and family or friends maintain contact while the person is hospitalized. The social worker might also assess the impact of family, friends, employer, school, and so forth on the client's situation and offer assistance in helping these significant others change in ways that will benefit the client. Finally, when patients are ready to return to the community, social workers become the key professional people helping them to make arrangements for returning to school or work, securing an appropriate living situation, connecting with support programs in local human service agencies, and developing and maintaining needed social relationships

Occupational Social Work

	Primary Practice Area	Prevalent Client Need
Basic Social Worker	0.6%	8.1%
Specialist/Independent Social Worker	1.1	12.4

Social work has been practiced in business and industrial settings since the late 1800s. Social workers have been employed both by management and labor unions to offer services and provide consultation through employee assistance programs. In recent years, with businesses increasingly realizing that worker productivity is closely related to the workers' general satisfaction with the quality of their lives, an investment in helping employees resolve problems in social functioning is seen as simply good business. This perspective has created a small but growing field of practice known as occupational or industrial social work. With more than 131 million people in the civilian labor force,[8] the workplace is an opportune setting in which to identify social problems and provide needed services. Often, early intervention at the location of one's employment can prevent more serious problems from developing later.

Shank and Jorve identify three models of social work practice in business and industry: the employee service model, the consumer service model, and the corporate social responsibility model.[9] An explanation of each follows.

The *employee service model* of occupational social work focuses on activities that provide direct service to the employees of a business or industry. The social worker using this model might develop and implement employee assistance programs and various supervisory training programs. In addition, the social worker might provide counseling to individuals or families in relation to marital, family, substance abuse, aging, health, and retirement problems; offer referral to other community agencies or self-help groups such as Alcoholics Anonymous; and consult with management on individual problems. Typical problems the social worker might also address would be the identification of job-related factors such as boredom or stress, an employee's desire to find resources to upgrade his or her job skills, the need for preretirement planning, or a linkage to Worker's Compensation or unemployment insurance programs.

The occupational social worker following the *consumer service model* might serve as the company's representative to various consumer groups and focus on identifying consumer needs and methods of meeting them. Typically found in banks, public utilities, and government agencies, these social workers help to provide a liaison between consumer groups and social service agencies, develop outreach programs, and provide counseling to customers to meet unique needs.

The third model of practice, the *corporate social responsibility model,* places the social worker in the role of assisting corporations and businesses to make a commitment to the social and economic well-being of the communities in which they are located. The social workers consult with management on their policies concerning human resources, their donations to nonprofit organizations, and social legislation they may wish to support. In addition, social workers may administer health and welfare benefit programs for employees, represent the company in research and community development activities, and provide linkage between social service, social policy, and corporate interests.

Schools

	Primary Practice Area	Prevalent Client Need
Basic Social Worker	1.4%	8.4%
Specialist/Independent Social Worker	6.3	13.6

Just as places of employment are important locations for identifying and addressing problems of social functioning for the employed population, schools are an important place to serve children and youth. Although individual and family problems directly affect a child's ability to learn, relatively few school social workers are employed to help parents, teachers, and the children themselves address these complex issues. Most of these social workers are prepared at the specialist or independent worker level.

The traditional approach of social workers in schools has been to counsel the child and confer with the family. They have depended on the cooperation of teachers to make referrals when problems are evident and have had varying degrees of effectiveness, depending on the willingness of teachers and school systems to use them as a resource. Problems of truancy, suspected child abuse, inadequate nutrition, substance abuse, parental neglect, and inappropriate behavior are often referred to the social worker.

Recently this practice field has undergone a marked change with the school being approached as a primary setting where social problems should be identified and addressed. Social workers have, under this approach, become more aggressive in their practice activities, serving as a link between school, family, and community. Some activities that school social workers typically perform include offering counseling to children, their families, and teachers related to factors that affect the child's performance at school; serving as an advocate for children with school administrators and community agencies when specialized services are needed; organizing parent and community groups to strengthen school and community relationships; and coordinating teams that draw on different disciplines' expertise and parent's interests to assess a child and develop a plan to assist a child's development.

Concluding Comment

For the person considering a career in social work, it is important to have an understanding of the many different fields of practice open to the social worker. It is evident that the attention social workers give to helping people and their environments interact more favorably makes an important contribution to resolving social problems or enhancing social functioning in many areas.

The most current data about social work practitioners indicate there are some practice areas where substantial numbers of both basic and specialist/independent social workers are employed, and this includes such areas as work with children and youth, families, and health care. BSW-level workers are much more likely than their MSW counterparts to be engaged in providing services to the aged and working in the disabilities area, while the primary practice area for the MSWs, by a substantial margin, is mental health.

A clear picture of client needs addressed by social workers emerges from data presented in this chapter. Helping clients resolve problems in family functioning stands well above all others. A second and often interrelated tier of issues are those of client functioning that have been affected by mental illness or retardation, character disorders or behavior problems, health-related matters, anxiety or depression, difficulties in interpersonal relations, and problems associated with alcohol and substance abuse.

The knowledge and skills acquired when obtaining a baccalaureate or master's degree in social work are intended to prepare one to engage in social work practice in any of these practice fields. The ability to transfer these competencies from field to field gives the social worker considerable flexibility in selecting where he or she will work and what type of client issues will be the focus of practice. This job flexibility has long been an attractive feature of social work.

KEY WORDS AND CONCEPTS

Field of practice	Community development
Primary practice area	Developmental disability
Prevalent client need	Occupational or industrial social work
Community organization	Public assistance
Community planning	Social insurance

SUGGESTED READINGS

Literally hundreds of books and articles are published each year on the various fields of practice described in this chapter. The two books listed below are recommended as resources for beginning the process of acquiring additional information about these and other fields of social work. One book, the 2,600-page *Encyclopedia of Social Work,* is a valuable resource for investigating most topics relevant to social workers. The author(s) of each chapter is selected by the *Encyclopedia*'s editorial board as highly respected experts on the subject matter. These authors, then, provide a "state-of-the-art" summary of the topic and a bibliography of the seminal literature on that subject. In the second recommended book, Gibelman provides another useful way to examine social work. Her book, *What Social Workers Do,* is packed with short chapters describing more than fifty different examples of social work practice. Each contains a short case vignette that helps the reader gain insight into what the social worker actually does when serving clients.

Edwards, Richard L., editor-in-chief. *Encyclopedia of Social Work,* 19th Edition. Washington, D.C.: NASW Press, 1995. (Available in hardcopy and CD-ROM versions.)
Gibelman, Margaret. *What Social Workers Do.* Washington, D.C.: NASW Press, 1995.

ENDNOTES

1. U.S. Bureau of the Census, "Profile of Older Americans: 1998." (http://www.aoa.dhhs.gov/aoa/stats/profile/default.htm#older)
2. Ibid.
3. Ronald E. Herrington, George R. Jacobson, and David G. Benzer, eds., *Alcohol and Drug Abuse Handbook* (St. Louis: Warren H. Green, 1987), p. xiii.
4. David Cook, Christine Fewell, and John Riolo, eds., *Social Work Treatment of Alcohol Problems* (New Brunswick, NJ: Rutgers School of Alcohol Studies, 1983), p. xiii.
5. Gary W. Lawson and Ann W. Lawson, *Alcoholism and Substance Abuse in Special Populations* (Rockville, MD: Aspen Publishers, 1989), pp. 5–7.
6. Robert L. Schalock, *Services for Developmentally Disabled Adults* (Baltimore: University Park Press, 1982), p. 12.
7. Robert J. Teare and Bradford W. Sheafor, *Practice-Sensitive Social Work Education: An Analysis of Social Work Practice and Practitioners* (Alexandria, VA: Council on Social Work Education, 1995).
8. U.S. Bureau of the Census, "USA Statistics in Brief." [http://www.census.gov/ftp/pub/statab/USAbrief/part2.txt]
9. Barbara W. Shank and Beth K. Jorve, "Industrial Social Work: A New Arena for the BSW." Paper presented at the National Symposium of Social Workers, Washington, D.C., 1983, p. 14.

CHAPTER 6

Settings for Social Work Practice

Prefatory Comment

Our society's commitment to the welfare of its members is played out through an extensive array of social programs that are delivered by several different helping professions—including social work. For people to gain access to these programs and professionals, there must be some form of organizational structure that serves as a vehicle for delivering human services. Usually that is a formal organization that operates under the auspices of a federal, state, or local government, or it is a private human services agency that is structured as either a nonprofit or for-profit agency. Increasingly these services are also offered by social workers who are private practitioners, that is, social workers who contract directly with their clients for services in the same manner as the private physician or attorney contracts with his or her clients.

These differing practice settings influence the nature of the problems a social worker addresses, the clients served, the amount of red tape and paperwork required, the salary earned, and many other factors that affect one's work activity and job satisfaction. This chapter examines the advantages and disadvantages for both social workers and their clients in the different practice settings.

Throughout its history, social work has been an agency-based profession. Like teaching, nursing, and the clergy, social work practice emerged primarily within organizations, and today, as in the past, most social workers are employed in some form of human service organization. Accreditation standards require that all students complete a substantial learning experience in a social agency, and the profession does not consider social workers ready for the independent level of practice, that is, private practice, until they have a period of supervised work in an agency after completing the MSW.

In recent years there has been a shift in the employment patterns of social workers. Where once virtually all social workers were employed in either government or nonprofit human services agencies, a whole new sector of employment has opened for social workers today. As indicated in Table 6-1, the public or *government sector* is the largest employer of basic social workers and encompasses nearly one-third of the master's-level social workers. The basic and specialist/independent social workers are about evenly divided in the *voluntary sector* with nearly 40 percent of both groups working in nonprofit agencies. However, a substantial portion of the MSW-level social workers (28.3%) work in the *business sector* where they are employed in for-profit agencies or are engaged in private practice. This chapter examines the practice conditions and issues social workers typically face when working in each of these three primary sectors of the society.

Characteristics of Practice Settings

When social programs are created, a decision must be made about how the program will be delivered. Whether it offers a direct benefit, such as food stamps, or depends on a third-party payment, such as Medicare, the program must be provided under the auspices of a human service organization or by an independent practitioner.

When programs are provided by human service organizations, the agencies establish the necessary policies and supply the administrative structure to make the program available to recipients. Clients then contract with that agency to provide the needed service and the agency employs staff to deliver the program. The organization is responsible for determining who is eligible for service and how that service will be performed, for screening and selecting its staff, assigning the work to various staff members, monitoring the quality of the work, and securing funds to pay the costs of providing the service.

TABLE 6-1   **Sector of Primary Employment for NASW Members: 1995**

Employment Sector	Basic	Specialist/Independent
Government Sector	41.6%	33.0%
Local	21.4	17.3
State	16.8	12.1
Federal	2.7	2.7
Military	0.7	0.9
Voluntary (nonprofit) Sector	40.4%	38.6%
Business (for-profit) Sector	18.1%	28.3%

Source: Margaret Gibelman and Philip H. Schervish, *Who We Are: A Second Look* (Washington, D.C.: NASW Press, 1997), p. 71.

When the service is delivered by a social worker in private practice, the client contracts directly with the social worker or the private practice group with which the worker is associated. The client then pays directly for the service or draws on insurance, Medicare, or other funds to pay for the service. Certification and licensing help the clients or companies paying for this service to determine if the practitioner is qualified to perform this service. One reason NASW requires two years of supervised practice experience beyond the MSW in order to be recognized as an "independent social worker" (see Chapter 4) is that the person engaged in private practice does not have an agency structure to monitor the quality of service given, and, NASW has concluded, this requirement provides greater protection to clients against the possibility of contracting with an inexperienced or incompetent worker.

The type of practice setting, whether agency or private practice, partially determines who will be clients, how clients will be protected against incompetent practice, and the degree of flexibility the worker has in providing services to clients. Thus, it is useful to examine the several types of organizational structures that serve as the settings for social work practice.

GOVERNMENT SECTOR SETTINGS

Government organizations are established and funded by the general public with the intent to provide services that preserve and protect the well-being of all people in the community. These agencies reflect city, county, state, and federal governmental efforts to respond to human needs and are limited by the provisions of the laws under which they were established.

Most government sector social programs are created by lawmakers in Washington, D.C., or a state capital. These policy makers are usually geographically distant from the clients and service providers alike and, too often, are unfamiliar with the issues that arise when these laws are implemented by local agencies. For this reason social workers often find their practice in government agencies frustrating. There is inherent inflexibility in these settings because laws are difficult to change, budgeting and auditing systems are highly structured, cumbersome civil service or personnel systems are mandated, and coordination among the different governmental levels is difficult. Further, these organizations are subject to political manipulation, and financial support and program development can be significantly influenced by a changing political climate. Except through substantial political action efforts, those who must carry out these programs have limited opportunity to influence their structure and funding.

On the positive side, although sometimes client fees are required, public agencies are financed almost completely by taxes, and the regular flow of tax money offers some stability to the programs. Legislative bodies are authorized to levy taxes so human needs can be met, and, in times of economic difficulty when voluntary contributions may be reduced, legislators have the power to tax and, therefore, maintain the services. Also, the larger amounts of money potentially available to public agencies allow for experimentation with various methods of service provision. Research and demonstration grants sponsored by government agencies have, in recent years, been the most significant factor in developing new and creative approaches to meeting human needs.

It should be recognized that government sector agencies provide services that are likely to meet the most basic human needs such as food, clothing, and shelter. It simply is not possible to adequately respond to the fundamental needs of the poor, homeless, disabled, aged, and others through voluntary and for-profit human services.

VOLUNTARY (NONPROFIT) SECTOR SETTINGS

Out of the history of providing assistance for persons needing help, a number of *mutual aid organizations* have been created to facilitate members of a group providing services for other members of that group. Churches, labor unions, and civic clubs are examples of this type of voluntary organization. Although civic and fraternal organizations such as Rotary, Soroptimist, and Kiwanis Clubs and various Masonic and ethnic group-focused organizations support some human service programs, they rarely employ professional staff.

Religious groups, however, have created *sectarian programs* staffed by social workers and limited to members of that denomination or faith. A substantial amount of human services from counseling to social provisions are provided to group members by synagogues and various denominational groups on a daily basis. Most of this service is not documented and largely goes unrecognized. These church-sponsored human service agencies that restrict their services to members, however, are only a small part of the social programs supported by religious groups. Many organized religions believe that a part of their responsibility is to serve persons in need, whether a member of that faith or not. Most human service programs sponsored by religious organizations (e.g., hospitals, group homes, retirement centers, and family counseling agencies), therefore, are *nonsectarian*. As such, they are designed to fulfill a religion's responsibility to serve the whole community.

Labor unions represent another mutual aid setting where social workers might be found. Although relatively few social workers are employed by labor unions, they have expanded their social services in recent years. Unions historically have been successful in organizing workers who are underpaid and undervalued by management. Like social workers employed in business and industry, the labor union setting presents an exceptional opportunity to intervene with people at the place they work, and therefore improve the likelihood of resolving problems before they reach a crisis level. Social workers in these settings typically help union members with such work-related problems as finding child care, dealing with family problems related to work schedules, and addressing stress created by changed family roles when both spouses are employed.

A second type of practice setting in the voluntary sector of human services is the *private nonprofit agency*. Private agencies traditionally have depended on voluntary individual and corporate support for their operation. Their sources of funds have included gifts and bequests, door-to-door solicitations, membership dues, fees for service, and participation in federated campaigns such as a United Way or a Jewish Welfare Federation. More recently, however, private agencies have begun receiving a substantial share of their funding through contracts with government agencies to provide specific direct services, conduct research and demonstration projects, or to support their programs through block grants or revenue sharing. Government agencies have increasingly found this a desirable arrangement because it has allowed them to bypass much of the rigidity of the large bureaucratic organizations in favor of the more flexible private agency structures.

Although there has been an intermingling of taxes and donated funds in the budgets of these private agencies, they are classified as part of the voluntary sector because they operate with policies established by a governing board made up of community volunteers. In the structure of their governance, then, nonprofits differ dramatically from government agencies that have elected officials responsible for making basic policy decisions. In most instances, these agencies have the advantage of being small and primarily concerned with the provision of local services. Thus, the board members are able to become directly exposed to the agency and are more capable of responding to changing conditions and needs for services in a local community.

A board, however, does not have complete autonomy in developing policies and programs for the agency. Many nonprofit agencies receive a part of their funding from a local United Way, and that participation as part of a federation of agencies inevitably requires some loss of autonomy. Also, some agencies are affiliated with a national organization such as the Child Welfare League of America or the Family Service Association of America, which may impose some limitations on agency functioning.

The term *nonprofit* indicates that if the agency should end a year with any funds remaining, those resources are allocated to enhance the agency's operation and not paid to staff, board, or any other parties. Since no one profits financially from the operation of the agency and it serves the public good, the Internal Revenue Service has created a process to approve agencies [Section 501 (c) (3) of the Internal Revenue Code] as nonprofit organizations. With this designation, persons who donate funds to support the agency can deduct the contribution from their income taxes. In this way, the government is underwriting the voluntary sector human services.

BUSINESS SECTOR SETTINGS

The most rapidly growing setting for social work practice is the for-profit or business sector. This category of practice includes both private practice and employment in large organizations that exist to earn a profit for their owners.

The term *private practice* is used to indicate a practice situation where a contract for the provision of service is made directly between the worker and the clients. Usually this term is applied in reference to social workers who provide clinical services, but sometimes private practice involves nonclinical activities such as consulting, conducting workshops or training programs, or contracting to perform research or other professional service for a fee.

With direct client–worker contracts, the practitioners have considerable autonomy in determining how the practice situation will be addressed and what intervention approaches will be used. However, without the monitoring of services that human services agencies provide, clients are more vulnerable to incompetent or unethical practitioners. It is fundamentally for client information and protection that all 50 states license or certify social workers and the NASW has created credentialing processes for workers at the independent level.

For some social workers, private practice is an attractive alternative to agency-based practice. Usually there is less paperwork to manage, more flexibility in scheduling, and, often, the elimination of unnecessary supervision. In addition, private practice is among the highest-paying settings for social workers. The downside of private practice is that it is a small business and, like many small businesses, is difficult to sustain. A practice must attract a sufficient number of clients who can pay high fees to support the ongoing operating costs (e.g., space, utilities, clerical staff) and also provide a wage for the social worker. For this reason, many social workers engage in private practice on a part-time basis and maintain their primary employment in a human services agency.

Another emerging entrepreneurial setting for social work is in *for-profit organizations*. During the past decade there has been a transformation in the funding of human service programs. From the 1930s through the 1970s a pattern emerged in which legislative bodies allocated substantial funds for government agencies to provide services directly to clients. Therefore, a relatively large public sector developed. Later, that pattern shifted to purchase-of-service agreements with nonprofit agencies rather than governmental agencies providing these services themselves. A second, and perhaps even more dramatic, shift known as *privatization* is now occurring. Governmental agencies have begun to invest a substantial amount of their funds in the purchase of service from for-profit organizations that are owned and operated as any other business. In fact, many are owned and operated by large corporations.

Several fields of practice have rapidly increased their reliance on these businesses to provide human services. For example, a national study of child welfare services found that proprietary firms were used as vendors for services for 51 percent of all residential treatment, 49 percent of institutional care, and 58 percent of the services provided in group homes.[1] To a lesser degree public agencies rely on contracts with proprietary organizations to provide day care, day treatment services, nursing home care, correctional facilities, and health care.

Social work, as well as other professions, is uneasy about the growing amount of for-profit practice. The trend toward the privatization of human services threatens to replace the service orientation of professions with the profit motive. Privatization risks making the bottom line the amount of return to the shareholder, rather than the quality of service to the client. When the shareholder is also the professional, serious ethical issues arise that can erode public trust in the professions.

One development that has affected all social workers in the business sector, whether in private practice or employed by for-profit organizations, is the evolution of *managed care*—or perhaps more accurately, managed costs. Stimulated by the escalating cost of health and mental health services, a variety of plans have been developed to provide health care consumers with needed services at controlled costs.[2] On the positive side, these plans require greater accountability for the quality of services offered, which ultimately should enhance the services clients receive. However, analysts of managed health care programs conclude that many decisions about the nature and extent of services provided are being shifted from the professionals and clients to the managers of the insurance companies. These are not typically people with the qualifications to determine an individual's need for professional services. Although social workers continue to provide a substantial part of the direct services delivered under managed care plans, they increasingly play an, active role as advocates with insurance companies or government agencies for clients who do not receive the services they require.

Social workers have a central role to play in all three sectors of the economy—government, voluntary, and business. The ability of these professionals to perform their function depends at least partially on their ability to effectively work within a human services organization or manage a private practice. Understanding several issues typically experienced in each of these settings can help future social workers anticipate difficulties they may face and be prepared to deal with them head on.

Issues Affecting Agency-Based Practice

When considering a social work job, it is important to address issues that are likely to be experienced when working in a formal organization. Potential employing agencies should be examined in relation to their relative compatibility with professional values and standards and the autonomy workers have to exercise their professional judgment in performing the job tasks. The manner in which a human service organization deals with the following issues will affect the work of its professional staff, and they are, therefore, useful to recognize.

ACCOMMODATING HORIZONTAL AND VERTICAL INFLUENCES

Social workers employed in most human service organizations, as well as those in private practice, often find they cannot successfully work in isolation from other agencies. Clients' needs are not necessarily experienced in the same way as social agencies identify their mission, and often clients must address multiple issues simultaneously—some extending beyond the programs offered in any one agency.

At the local level, social workers often lead efforts to coordinate the services provided to clients by the full array of social agencies in that community. This coordination requires that interagency networks, or *horizontal affiliations,* are developed among the agencies. The form of these horizontal networks may range from informal discussions among agency representatives regarding human service programs to the formal creation of human resources planning organizations that study the local service network, encourage efforts to fill gaps in the services, and facilitate cooperation among the agencies. The ability of a social worker to effectively perform his or her professional tasks is enhanced when there is a strong interagency network in a community and the social worker's employing agency supports his or her participation in these activities.

Social agencies and social workers are also influenced by *vertical affiliations,* that is, those organizations external to the community that have the authority to at least partially shape the services or operating procedures of a local agency. Voluntary agencies, for example, might affiliate as chapters or members of a national organization, which can immediately give the agency name recognition, provide the community with some assurance that at least minimum standards acceptable in that practice field are being met, make staff development opportunities available through national meetings, and sometimes help secure financial resources. At the same time, these agencies give up some local autonomy as they are committed to operate within the guidelines of the national organization. Vertical affiliation with the American Red Cross, Boy or Girl Scouts of America, the YWCA or YMCA, the American Heart Association, the Salvation Army, or the Family Service Association of America are typical examples of such affiliations. Further, many local voluntary agencies must meet state licensing requirements or other state standards if they are vendors of services to public agencies. This also limits their discretion.

Public agencies typically have more direct and formal vertical relationships. A local governmental agency may be implementing programs that have been created and partially funded at the federal level, further defined and partially funded at the state level, and finally modified and also funded by county government. Thus, a county social services department, for example, is constrained by requirements imposed by federal, state, and county governments. Although these vertical affiliations add considerably to the complexity of tailoring service programs to local needs, they have the advantage of fostering greater equality in the benefits and services provided to people throughout a region and the nation. In addition, vertical affiliation creates a larger geographic area for securing funds to support the services, making it possible to more adequately meet needs in a local or regional area that lacks its own resources.

BALANCING EFFICIENCY AND EFFECTIVENESS

A fundamental goal of all human service agencies, whether they are public or private, is to use the scarce resources available to provide the most and best service possible. To achieve this goal agencies must operate both efficiently and effectively. An agency that leans too far in favoring one over the other ultimately creates problems for the staff members employed in that agency.

Efficiency represents the efforts of the agency to achieve the maximum output of services with a minimum input of resources. The goal of efficiency places the emphasis on the quantity of services provided and often attracts most of the attention of lawmakers, governing boards, and local media. Yet, quantity must be related to quality if an agency is to find a balance that represents the maximum level of service. The qualitative aspects of service are represented in an agency's *effectiveness,* or the degree to which the agency achieves its goals.

The governance of most social agencies has been dominated, in both the public and voluntary sectors, by people who have given leadership to thriving business and industrial enterprises. They often bring a strong bias toward efficiency; and, although some degree of effectiveness in producing goods was necessary, low cost-per-unit production was clearly the most valued goal. That orientation is especially evident in managed care and the for-profit human service organizations. Thus, the social worker considering agency employment should carefully examine the agency's effectiveness orientation lest the quality of his or her work be seriously compromised in favor of overemphasis on efficiency.

How can efficiency be attained in human service organizations? Successful managers from business and industry have transferred one proven tool in their work to the human services—bureaucratic structure. And why not? Bureaucracy had worked to build automobiles and appliances at a fraction of the cost of handmade products. Weber created the clearest statement of bureaucratic theory. His "ideal-type" description of the characteristics of a bureaucratic organization was intended to reflect a pure, but extreme, statement of the characteristics of a bureaucracy:[3]

1. *Division of Labor.* Each person in the organization has a clearly defined and specialized assignment in the organization.
2. *Hierarchy.* Specific lines of authority exist in which every person in the administrative structure is not only responsible for his or her own assignments but is also responsible for the performance of subordinates.
3. *Consistent System of Rules.* Every task in the organization is governed by an explicit set of rules which specify the standards of performance and the relationships among tasks.
4. *Spirit of Impersonality.* Work is to be performed without favoritism or prejudice entering official decisions.
5. *Employment Constitutes a Career.* Persons are employed only on the basis of technical qualifications required by the organization, with rewards provided to encourage loyalty and offer opportunity for a career in that organization.

With some modifications, when applied to the assembly line that produces automobiles in Detroit or toasters in New Jersey, bureaucratic principles led to a high degree of organizational efficiency. This model yielded good results when the product was made from standardized parts. In fact, the greater the standardization, the more effective the bureaucratic organization becomes. A person could quickly be trained to perform a very specific function, for example, installing a fuel pump as an automobile passes on the assembly line. With a line supervisor to check for quality control and enforce the rules established for efficiency (the worker cannot be taking a break when the engine arrives for a fuel pump), the company usually produced a good-quality product. Under this system there could be no allowance for the worker's personal problems, nor could the boss play favorites. Bureaucratic theory assumes that the rewards of seniority, salary increases, and promotion are sufficient to keep the successful employee satisfied with the organization.

When these principles are applied to human services agencies, social workers and other professionals often find that bureaucratization has both positive and negative consequences. Indeed, the application of bureaucratic principles can ensure equity for both clients and workers, facilitate efficiency in operation, and enhance public support of the organization.

Accommodating the Professional Model

Rigid application of bureaucratic principles, however, is in direct conflict with the very nature of professions. As opposed to manufacturing products, in human services the parts being worked with are people who are constantly changing, and the product (attaining maximum client well-being) differs to some degree in each situation. It is simply not realistic to provide narrow technical training, to create highly specialized assignments, or to establish an inflexible system of rules that a staff must follow regardless of the uniqueness of the client or practice situation.

When the professional model (see Chapter 3) is compared to the bureaucratic model, inherent conflicts emerge. These conflicts have been identified by Scott as: (1) the professional's resistance to bureaucratic rules; (2) the professional's rejection of bureaucratic standards; (3) the professional's resistance to bureaucratic supervision; and (4) the professional's conditional loyalty to the bureaucratic organization.[4] These conflicts are present in varying degrees in any organization where the professional social worker, or any other professional, is employed.

Bureaucratic rules present a constant dilemma for professionals. When a division of labor exists, each person provides only a part of the work for the agency. Procedures, or rules, must then be established to facilitate interaction among the workers and coordinate their activities. Those rules are inherently arbitrary and somewhat inflexible, making it difficult for professionals to respond to unique client needs, thus limiting their autonomy in delivering client services.

Bureaucratic standards also present difficulties for the professional. Standards are ordinarily based on a perception of the "typical client," but in reality, clients present great variability and require services that may not fit the profile that was followed when a social program was created. The professional model suggests that social workers will serve clients as long as service is needed, but bureaucratic standards such as agency eligibility requirements, limits on length of service, access to specialized services, and so on may limit the ability of the professional to fulfill the professional obligation to provide needed services.

In bureaucratic systems, authority is assigned to a position. Conversely, professional authority is generated from competence as judged by one's peers. It is no wonder that professionals resist *bureaucratic supervision*, which is based on authority derived from a person's place in the organization. By definition a professional is considered competent to perform his or her job without the requirement of someone constantly monitoring that performance—particularly when the person monitoring may be from another profession or an administrator with no professional preparation at all.

Finally, professionals typically display a *conditional loyalty*, rather than a strong commitment to the employing organization. Professionals are prepared with general competencies that are transferable from one organization to another, making it relatively easy to leave an unsatisfactory work environment. A professionally educated social worker, for example, can move from juvenile court to a hospital without additional educational preparation. Any additional knowledge about the specific setting or field of practice can be obtained by reviewing the literature on the subject, through supervision, and by attending various workshops and seminars. People wedded to a bureaucratic organization, however, do not have that degree of flexibility and can experience job mobility primarily by moving up in the organization. At times, the person who is too dependent on the organization must compromise service to clients, as well as professional integrity, in order to succeed as a member of the organization and receive the rewards (e.g., salary increases, promotions) the organization offers its employees.

DETERMINING THE STATUS OF SOCIAL WORK

One final factor to consider when selecting a place of employment is the centrality of social work to the mission of that particular setting. The status of social work in an agency influences the manner in which a social worker spends much of his or her time and affects the opportunity of clients to have the full benefit of the perspective that social work brings to the helping situation. When the policies and procedures of the organization are designed to maximize social work services, social workers can most effectively serve their clientele. However, in a practice setting where another discipline is dominant, social workers often spend considerable effort educating others about the contributions social work can make to the agency's clientele.

In some practice settings social work is the *primary discipline.* The primary services provided call for social work expertise, most key jobs require social work training, and social workers hold the major administrative jobs. In practice fields such as child welfare, family services, and income maintenance, social work has traditionally been the primary discipline. In these settings other disciplines may be involved to provide specialized expertise or consultation, but the services are organized to maximize the contributions of the social worker.

In other practice settings the social worker is an *equal partner* along with members of one or more other disciplines. The services are organized to maximize interdisciplinary cooperation, and a member of any of the disciplines might provide administrative leadership to the agency. The fields of aging, mental health and retardation, and community and neighborhood services are examples of practice fields that are shared by several disciplines.

In still other settings social work might provide supporting services to another profession. As the *secondary discipline* in these agencies, social work is, in one sense, a guest of the primary discipline. The agency is organized to allow the primary discipline to work as effectively as possible, and the needs of social work or other professions receive lower priority. The role of the social worker in a medical setting illustrates social work as a secondary discipline. Hospitals, a setting for medical practice, are geared to the needs of the physician. Social services are provided at the physician's referral and are organized so they do not compete with the schedule and work of the medical profession. A similar role would be assumed by the social worker in corrections, school, and industrial settings.

SUCCEEDING AS A SOCIAL WORKER IN AN AGENCY STRUCTURE

Clearly, an employee is obligated to work within the legitimate requirements of his or her employer, and a social worker cannot ethically ignore the rules and regulations of the agency. However, it is not sufficient to be merely a passive employee who unquestioningly accepts and carries out the rules and regulations of the agency. Client services can be compromised if social workers do not actively work to promote agency flexibility in service provision and, when warranted, be willing to challenge the agency's methods of operating. At times, this may mean taking some risks that may affect one's evaluations, pay increases, or even employment in the agency. Thus the successful agency-based social worker must be smart about organizational change efforts.

Many times constricting agency rules and regulations do not need to be changed. Creative interpretations that stretch the rules to fit client needs are often possible and frequently can be applied with the full support of one's supervisor. Some regulations, however, may not lend themselves to this flexibility, and it may be necessary to attempt to initiate a process to change these rules. Change, especially in large public agencies, takes considerable time and effort. The social worker who has attempted to bring about such change can identify with the adage, "The change agent must have the time sense of a geologist." With skill, patience, and perseverance, such change can be accomplished and the professional obligation of the worker to provide the best services possible fulfilled. If this effort fails, however, the worker must either learn to live with the existing regulations or make the decision to seek employment elsewhere.

Assuming that satisfactory conditions exist in an agency for performing social work practice, it becomes important for the worker to discover ways to be responsible to the agency and at the same time maximize the ability to provide services to clients. Pruger suggests four helpful tactics that a worker might employ.[5] First, it is important to understand the agency's (or supervisor's) legitimate authority. Within the guidelines of responsible behavior, the social worker seeks to discover the limits of the discretion that a worker has in providing services to clients. Second, because organizations often present demands (e.g., paperwork, staff meetings) that divert the worker's time and energy from the work of providing services, the worker should be cautious about overcommitting to these activities that are of secondary importance. Third, the worker should develop supplemental competencies that are needed by the agency. Professional work involves more than carrying out the routine job duties. It involves making a commitment to expand one's contributions by learning, for example, new practice techniques, skills in grant writing, knowledge of computer applications in practice, or methods of interpreting the agency and its services to the public. Finally, the worker should not yield unnecessarily to agency requirements established for administrative convenience. For instance, it may be convenient to have clients come to the worker's office to receive services so that back-to-back interviews can be scheduled and the worker's time used efficiently. However, for some clients the requirement of arranging transportation, leaving work, or the unfamiliarity with the agency may discourage them from keeping the appointment. In such a case, a home visit by the worker may be far more successful. Although challenging unproductive regulations may not help the social worker win popularity contests, this action can be a valuable contribution to the organization's effectiveness.

Another contribution that a social worker can make to an employing agency is to prepare to move into a supervisory role or to assume an executive or high-level administrative position in the agency. Making such a transition is difficult. A study (reported in more detail in Chapter 8) that compared the tasks performed by social workers in direct practice positions and administrative positions revealed two very different sets of activities, although some skills overlapped the two job functions.[6] As compared to direct service practitioners, the social workers who were administrators were much more involved in activities such as making staff assignments and conducting evaluations of their work, representing the agency and helping to build the service delivery system in the community, engaging in program development, and carrying various tasks (e.g., budget development, expense approval, staff coordination) that help to maintain the organization's daily operations.

Finally, a worker should be prepared to engage in teamwork and interprofessional practice. Agency practice typically draws together persons from varying professions who have their own unique areas of expertise, volunteers with their basic talents, and other staff members in an effort to respond to human needs. In theory the unique roles and capacities of each discipline appear clear and workers need only coordinate their efforts. In reality, however, there is considerable blurring of lines between the various helping disciplines. Turf problems inevitably emerge that, if not resolved, can jeopardize good client service. Thus, interprofessional collaboration and teamwork are essential.

Human services agencies continue to seek means of improving interprofessional cooperation through various administrative structures, team approaches to case situations, the development of protocols that spell out the functions to be performed by each discipline, and the use of case managers charged with coordinating the services an individual or family might require. Social workers, with their mission to facilitate the interface of clients with their environments, have a particularly important leadership role to perform in facilitating interprofessional collaboration.

ADVANTAGES OF AGENCY-BASED PRACTICE

Given the complexities of agency practice, why does social work continue to function as an agency-based profession? Why not adopt the private practice model of other successful professions? Most social workers recognize that agency-based practice offers several advantages.

First, it makes the services more visible and, therefore, more accessible to all persons in need. The existence of agencies in a community over time and the attendant publicity about their operations typically make both their programs and their locations familiar to all members of the community. As opposed to nonagency practice, which caters to those who can pay the full cost of services, public and private human service agencies are more likely to have as clients the most vulnerable members of society. For the social worker committed to serving the part of the population experiencing the most serious social problems, agency practice is the only game in town.

Second, agencies survive because they have received the sanction, or approval, of the community for the services they provide. Clients approach the helping situation with a greater trust in the quality of services they will receive because of the agency's implied responsibility to ensure that quality services are delivered. In private practice situations the client must place full trust in the individual practitioner to perform high-quality practice.

Third, clients have the benefit of an extra layer of protection against possible misuse of professional authority in social agencies. Clients in any setting are protected by both the professional ethics of the workers and, in many cases, the legal regulation or licensing of that practice. In agencies, however, they are also protected by the agency's selection of staff and ongoing monitoring of the quality of services.

Fourth, human service agencies tend to have a broad scope and often employ persons from several different professions, which provide clients with ready access to the competencies of multiple professions and give the worker the opportunity for interdisciplinary practice activities. In addition, as opposed to the more limited service focus found in private practice, agencies typically offer a broad range of services, from direct practice to social action. Thus, they provide the social worker with the stimulation of engaging in a range of different practice activities and make it possible to change the focus of one's practice area or move into supervisory or management positions without changing employers.

Fifth, most agencies offer staff development opportunities that stimulate professional growth among workers. Characteristically, social agencies employ a large enough number of staff members that workers do not feel isolated and, in fact, typically carry out programs that contribute to the continued professional growth and development of other members. The rapidly changing knowledge and skill base of the helping professions makes continuing professional development important to the services the clients receive and adds to the intellectual stimulation of the staff.

Last, agencies have the ability to raise funds from the community, whether from taxes or voluntary contributions, and to offer a stable salary to employees. Agencies do not face as great a risk of a fluctuating income as is experienced by persons in private practice settings.

Issues in Private Practice

The principal alternative to agency-based practice for the social worker is private practice. The remarkable expansion of this setting in the past decade is an important feature of social work today. It is useful for future social workers to be aware of the issues that surround this practice setting.

Why is private practice gaining such popularity among social workers? From the vantage point of the social worker, private practice is attractive partially because of the greater opportunity for financial gain, but more importantly, for the freedom to exercise professional autonomy in the conduct of social work practice. The bureaucratic constraints of many human service agencies have placed restrictions on practice activities that compromise the ability of social workers to effectively use their professional competencies for the benefit of clients. Thus, some social workers have actively sought a different practice setting that would not restrict their work.

Although private practice avoids many of the limitations that accrue from practice within a bureaucratic structure, it also places greater responsibility on the social worker to follow the ethical guidelines of the profession. There is no professional monitoring of private practice, although complaints can be filed with a state licensing board or the local NASW chapter. NASW has rightfully been concerned about establishing guidelines that will identify for the public those social workers who have the requisite preparation and experience to conduct autonomous practice.

THE ORGANIZATION OF PRIVATE PRACTICE

What does a social worker do in private practice? In his study of clinically oriented private practice, Wallace found that the average for these social workers was "63 percent of private practice time in individual treatment, 19 percent devoted to work with marital couples, 8 percent to group therapy, 7 percent to family treatment, and 2 percent to joint interviews with clients other than married couples."[7] For the delivery of these clinical services, three organizational approaches are used.

In the first approach, the social worker engages in multidisciplinary practice. In this arrangement the social worker participates with members of other disciplines (for example, psychiatry and psychology) to provide a *group practice* that can meet a broad range of client needs. The social worker is an equal partner with the other disciplines and, in fact, is a co-owner of the business.

In the second form of private practice, the social worker provides a *supportive practice* for a member of another profession. For example, some physicians are hiring social workers to help patients deal with social problems related to specific illnesses. The social worker might also provide more general services in the physician's office such as educating expectant parents about child development, counseling families that need help with child-rearing practices, or referring people to appropriate community resources for help with other problems.

In the third form, social workers are the *sole owners* of their private practice. Sole ownership involves securing office space, hiring staff, advertising services, making contacts to acquire referrals, overseeing the determination and collection of fees, and doing everything related to the management of a small business. Like any other business, private practice is a "sink or swim" proposition with no guarantee of income equivalent to expenses. The main problems for full-time private practitioners are generating sufficient referrals to be able to keep the business solvent, handling the business details including securing payment from third-party vendors, obtaining competent consultation, minimizing the inherent isolation, arranging for backup in managing crisis situations, and protecting practitioners against their vulnerable position if there should be malpractice charges.

It is estimated that two to three times as many social workers are engaged in part-time as are in full-time private practice. Many of these social workers are employed by a social agency but maintain a small private practice as well. Kelley and Alexander identify four groups of social workers who elect to engage in part-time private practice:[8]

1. Agency practitioners who welcome the independence and additional income,
2. Social workers in supervisory or administrative positions who wish to maintain client contact and clinical skills,
3. Educators who wish to have sufficient practice activity to remain sufficiently current with a practice to effectively teach clinical courses, and
4. Social workers who are parents of young children and need to control their hours of work.

Part-time private practitioners experience many of the same problems as those in full-time practice. Kelley and Alexander's study of part-time private practitioners indicates that the most serious problems they face in getting a practice started are generating referrals and handling the practical business issues such as locating office space, securing financing, keeping records, and the like. Although these matters continue to be problems, they are somewhat transitional and become less consuming once a practice is established. Later, and particularly unique to the person in part-time private practice, time management problems become the most difficult part.[9]

Some social workers in private practice provide indirect services such as consultation. Consultation might be provided to another social worker or to a member of another helping profession concerning the handling of a case. For example, a social worker might consult with a lawyer about a divorce or child custody case. He or she might also be involved in working with a social agency, such as helping a nursing home with staff–patient relations, administrative procedures, or program development.

Another form of indirect private practice involves the training of social workers, or members of other disciplines, in special skills. The increasing demand for experienced social workers to provide workshops, seminars, or other forms of training is contributing to the growing demand for private practice.

CONCERNS RELATED TO PRIVATE PRACTICE

The private practice approach represents a substantial departure from social work's historical agency orientation. It has not been without controversy in the profession and has experienced problems in becoming accepted and appreciated in the general community. Four issues have emerged concerning this practice mode.

First, private clients do not have an agency monitoring system to provide protection against incompetence or abuses of the professional monopoly. Therefore, social work has been careful to specify more extensive education and experience as minimum preparation for the private practitioner than for the agency-based practitioner. The standards established by NASW call for completion of a master's degree in social work from an accredited school of social work, two years of full-time or 3,000 hours of part-time practice experience, and successfully passing the examination required for membership in the Academy of Certified Social Workers (ACSW). To be listed in both the *National Registry of Health Care Providers in Clinical Social Work* and NASW's *Register of Clinical Social Workers*, a social worker is required to have completed at least two years of full-time, post-master's employment as a social worker.

Second, because many private practitioners work on a part-time basis, some agencies are concerned that private practice will detract from agency practice. They fear the social worker will place self-interest above the needs of the agency. A study of twenty voluntary agencies yielded the following common concerns about private practice.[10]

1. That the worker will not do justice to his or her agency responsibilities because of the amount of time and energy that may go into private practice.
2. That the worker may take clients from the agency or gain clients in the community who may otherwise have gone to the agency.

3. That the staff person will become more his or her own agent instead of being an enabler for the agency.
4. That the staff person may not meet the minimum standards set by the National Association of Social Workers for private practice.

On the other side of this issue, it is argued that private practice offers different professional stimulation than is found in agency practice and also provides a supplemental income to agency salaries that keeps workers satisfied with their agency employment. Some agencies even encourage social workers to engage in some part-time private practice by allowing them to use their agency offices in the evenings or by arranging schedules to allow a day off each week for this purpose. Such arrangements, however, are ripe for conflict of interest issues.

Finally, some critics have accused private practitioners of diverting social work from its mission of serving the most vulnerable members of society. There is little argument that clinical private practice represents a deviation from social work's philanthropic roots. Barker states, "Undoubtedly, the major dilemma is that private practice services are less accessible to the very people who have historically been social work's traditional clientele—the disadvantaged."[11] Moreover, private practice has been accused of failing to perform the social action responsibilities that are central to social work's mission of person and environment change. Teare and Sheafor confirmed this accusation, but additionally found that most other direct service practitioners also failed to engage in social change activities.[12]

ADVANTAGES OF PRIVATE PRACTICE

There are also arguments in favor of social work's movement toward private practice. First, in most human service agencies clients have little opportunity to exercise individual choice in regard to which professionals will provide services. Clients typically cannot select their individual social workers nor can they fire them if unsatisfied with the services received. Clients exercise considerably more control in a private setting.

Second, from the social worker's perspective, agency rules and regulations place constraints on the worker's ability to conduct a practice in the manner he or she believes would be most effective. Professional autonomy is inherently compromised. For example, agency-based social workers cannot choose their clients; are not completely free to determine the amount and type of service to be given; and are almost always supervised, at times by one who interferes with the professional judgment of the worker.

Third, agency salaries tend to be lower than those of the private practitioner. Further, as opposed to the market-driven income of the private practitioner that is, at least theoretically, based on competence, agency salaries are based to a greater degree on seniority and position within the agency.

Last, few agencies avoid the pitfalls that plague most bureaucratic organizations, in which workers find that a disproportionate share of their time is devoted to meetings and paperwork. The less elaborate mechanisms required for accountability in private practice free the worker from much of the less people-oriented activity found in agency practice.

For both clients and social workers, there are gains and losses from both agency and private practice. These factors influence the nature and quality of services provided as well as the social worker's satisfaction with his or her employment.

Concluding Comment

Social work practice has permeated U.S. society to the extent that it occurs in every sector of society: government, voluntary, and business. Although the roots of social work are in agency-based practice, where public concerns for people in need took the form of creating human service agencies, social work now is offered through both agency and private practice modes.

Most social workers continue to be employed in agency settings, and thus they must be able to work effectively within agency structures if they are to maximize their ability to serve clients. Understanding the principles on which agencies are organized and the problems social workers commonly experience in matching their professional orientation with agency requirements is, therefore, important for providing quality services.

An increasing number of social workers have entered private practice to avoid some of the problems experienced by the agency-based practitioner and to increase potential income. However, private practice is certainly not trouble-free. Social work is beginning to address the important issues related to private practice: adequate preparation for the responsibilities of independent practice, the lessening quality of agency practice, the move away from the social work mission of focusing services on the poor and other vulnerable population groups, and public sanction and client protection for this relatively new method of service delivery.

It appears, at this point in history, that the trend in social work is toward an increasingly entrepreneurial approach to practice. However, it is clear that some critical social programs can never be made available through the mutual benefit organizations and entrepreneurial human services in sufficient quantity to meet the needs of the most vulnerable members of this society. Thus, it is reasonable to conclude that social work will continue to be primarily an agency-based profession and that social workers must continue to devote attention to making these organizations more responsive to the requirements for effective professional practice.

KEY WORDS AND CONCEPTS

Government sector	Managed care
Voluntary sector	Horizontal/vertical influences
Business sector	Efficiency vs. effectiveness
Mutual aid organization	Bureaucracy
Nonprofit agencies	Bureaucratic vs. professional model
For-profit organizations	Interprofessional teamwork
Private practice	Social work as: primary discipline, equal
Privatization	partner, secondary discipline

SUGGESTED READINGS

Barker, Robert L. *Social Work in Private Practice: Principles, Issues, Dilemmas,* 2nd Edition. Washington, D.C.: NASW Press, 1991.

Kamerman, Sheila, and Kahn, Alfred J., eds. *Privatization and the Welfare State.* Princeton, NJ: Princeton University Press, 1989.

O'Looney, John. *Redesigning the Work of Human Services.* Westport, CT: Quorum Books, 1996.

Salamon, Lester M. *Partners in Public Service: Government-Nonprofit Relations in the Modern Welfare State.* Baltimore: Johns Hopkins University Press, 1995.

ENDNOTES

1. Catherine E. Born, "Proprietary Firms and Child Welfare Services: Patterns and Implications," *Child Welfare* 62 (March–April 1983): 112.

2. Golda M. Edinburg and Joan M. Cotter, "Managed Care," in Richard L. Edwards, ed., *Encyclopedia of Social Work,* 19th Edition (Washington, D.C.: NASW Press, 1995), *The Social Work Reference Library* (CD-ROM).

3. Peter M. Blau and Marshall W. Meyer, *Bureaucracy in Modern Society,* 2nd Edition (New York: Random House, 1973), pp. 18–23.

4. W. Richard Scott, "Professionals in Bureaucracies—Areas of Conflict," in Howard M. Vollmer and Donald L. Mills, eds., *Professionalization* (Englewood Cliffs, NJ: Prentice-Hall, 1966), pp. 264–275.

5. Robert Pruger, "The Good Bureaucrat," *Social Work* 18 (July 1973): 26–27.

6. Robert J. Teare and Bradford W. Sheafor, *Practice-Sensitive Social Work Education: An Analysis of Social work Practice and Practitioners* (Alexandria, VA: Council on Social Work Education, 1995), pp. 180–182.

7. Marquis Earl Wallace, "Private Practice: A Nationwide Study," *Social Work* 27 (May 1983): 265.

8. Patricia Kelly and Paul Alexander, "Part-Time Private Practice: Practical and Ethical Considerations," *Social Work* 30 (May–June 1985): 254.

9. Ibid., p. 255.

10. Janice Proshaska, "Private Practice May Benefit Voluntary Agencies," *Social Casework* 59 (July 1978): 374.

11. Robert Barker, "Private Practice Primer for Social Work," *NASW News* 28 (October 1983): 13.

12. Teare and Sheafor, Ibid., p. 117.

THREE

The Practice of Social Work

The payoff in social work is in the services rendered to clients or improvements made to problematic social conditions in society that affect the quality of life for some or all people. That activity is commonly referred to as social work *practice*. In order to most effectively carry out the practice of social work, the social worker must know *what* he or she is doing, *why* it is done, and *how* to do it. Parts One and Two of this book addressed the what and the why. In Part Three we turn to how.

It has long been recognized that social work practice requires attention to *values* (what we believe ought to be), *knowledge* (our perception of how things are), and *skills* (our ability to use knowledge and intervention techniques effectively in our practice). It is the latter part of social work practice that is most visible to clients. The competence with which the worker draws together his or her professional knowledge, values, and skills and joins them to his or her personal practice style directly affects the quality of services the client receives.

Chapter 7 examines the value base of social work. The profession of social work is founded upon adherence to certain values. Central among these values are beliefs that all people are inherently worthy of being treated with respect and should be assisted in meeting their social needs; that people have a need to belong and should be helped to have meaningful interaction with others; that people are interdependent and must take responsibility for providing for

themselves, for assisting their fellow human beings, and for improving the society; and that the society has a responsibility for helping its members lead fulfilling lives. Without adhering to those values, the social work profession would be unable to perform its role in U.S. society. Additionally, social workers must be highly ethical in their work, as they are involved with highly personal and sensitive aspects of the lives of vulnerable people. Attention is given in this chapter to the NASW Code of Ethics and its important place in shaping how a social worker practices.

Chapter 8 describes the basic competencies required of most social workers. The chapter is organized around the tasks most frequently performed by social workers as identified in the National Task Analysis Study of Social Work Practice. Eighteen clusters of activity performed by social workers who were direct service providers, administrators, or supervisors are identified and the knowledge and skill required to perform them described. It is evident from these data that there is a core of activity in social work practice that includes interpersonal helping, workload management, professional development, and gaining expertise regarding the human service delivery system. The competence to perform these activities effectively is at the heart of social work.

The limited activity by social workers in the community change area revealed in the National Task Analysis Study of Social Work Practice represents a deviation from social work's historical mission of working to facilitate change related to both people and the environment. In an effort to provide readers with an illustration of how social workers might prevent social problems from developing or creating opportunities for large groups of people to improve their well-being, Chapter 9 examines prevention as an area of increased emphasis for social work intervention. Prevention intervention models are presented, including ways of preventing gang homicide.

Another challenge is to advance social work as a global profession. Some of the most serious problems throughout the world (e.g., hunger, inadequate housing, assistance to people experiencing mental and physical disabilities, child and spouse abuse, violations of human rights) are all addressed by social workers—either by treating the victims or seeking ways to prevent these problems. As Chapter 10 indicates, social work is relatively new or currently not recognized in many countries, but the social work perspective is nonetheless needed. Although the practice of social work must be modified to respect cultural variations, its potential to positively affect the quality of life throughout the world is important.

CHAPTER 7

Values and Ethics in Social Work

Prefatory Comment At the heart of social work is its values. Values assist the social worker and the social work profession in setting goals related to both clients and society. Of course, like any other population group, every social worker does not have identical values. Yet, there are some common themes in social work that suggest that, by and large, social workers hold some fundamental beliefs in common. As opposed to many other groups of people, for example, social workers tend to believe that society has the responsibility to assist people in meeting their needs, that people should be included in making decisions that affect their lives, that positive change in people's lives can be attained through professional help, and so on. This chapter examines these and other values that are central to social work's belief system.

The most concrete expression of social work's ethical guidelines are embodied in the NASW Code of Ethics. This Code helps social workers to make the inevitable moral choices that arise in their daily practice and is intended to assure clients that the professional monopoly given to social workers will not be abused. If such abuse (i.e., unethical practice) is suspected, the Code also becomes the criteria by which the social worker's ethical behavior is evaluated.

From formulating social programs to helping clients, values affect social work practice. It is evident the social programs created to "promote the general welfare" of the people are influenced by the values held by legislators, board members, or owners of for-profit organizations who created or maintain those programs. Beliefs about who should be responsible for meeting human needs, what role government or private charity should play, and how much of the nation's wealth should be invested in meeting people's social needs are just three examples of factors that have shaped human services programs.

Also, values affect the manner in which human service organizations operate. Values, at least partially, determine the answers to important questions: Should potential clients be encouraged or discouraged from asking for help? Should clients be required to pay for services? Should volunteers, staff with no specific preparation, or professionals provide services? To what extent should an agency attempt to make services readily accessible to clients and assure that the surroundings are comfortable and pleasant? Should a social worker be allowed to terminate services before a client's insurance benefits are exhausted when the agency needs the funds to meet its financial obligations? Should services be terminated just because the client can no longer pay yet continues to need help? In short, the dominant values of an agency can have a direct impact on social work practice.

The values of a social worker's clients, too, affect practice. If a client feels stigmatized, demeaned, or embarrassed to ask for assistance in addressing a social problem, the client's ability to productively use the service is affected. If the client is unnecessarily demanding of a worker's time and attention or resents being required to use social services (i.e., an involuntary client), that, too, affects the way a social worker assists the client. Further, much of practice involves helping clients identify, clarify, and resolve value issues that are almost always present in human interactions.

As members of a profession that has based many of its practice approaches and principles on certain beliefs about people and how they can best be served, social workers must be cognizant of the profession's values. Further, since social work must protect the public from potential abuses of the professional monopoly, it has adopted a code of ethical practice that prescribes certain professional behaviors related to interactions with clients, colleagues, employers, and the community. Each social worker must be prepared to adhere to the NASW Code of Ethics.

Finally, the social worker must be clear about how the profession's values and ethical standards interact with his or her own belief system. Therefore, understanding one's own values becomes critical for the social worker. R. Huws Jones, a British social work educator, is quoted as saying, "A man's values are like his kidneys: he rarely knows he has any until they are upset."[1] Indeed, most of us do not typically contemplate our values unless they somehow are upset or create problems for us as we address the issues we confront in life. This chapter, however, asks the reader to consider the nature of values, their place in promoting people's welfare through shaping social programs, the values and ethics of social workers, and, finally, the fit between social work's values and one's own. Understanding the central place of values and ethics in social work is another important factor in making a career choice or preparing to enter the social work profession.

The Nature of Values

Unlike knowledge, which explains what is, values express what ought to be. Rokeach more precisely defines a *value* as "a type of belief, centrally located in one's total belief system, about how one ought or ought not to behave, or about some end-state of existence worth or not worth attaining."[2] In short, values guide our thinking about how we should behave and what we want to accomplish.

Values are much more than emotional reactions to situations or doing what feels right. Values are the fundamental criteria that lead us to thoughtful decisions. It is important to recognize, however, that people do not always behave in a manner consistent with their values. Values guide decisions but do not dictate choices. People can and do make decisions contrary to their values. Such decisions might be made when other factors are given priority ("I know that I shouldn't have done that, but when will I ever get another chance to make that kind of money?"), the person acts on emotion ("I was just so angry, I hit her without thinking"), or when one fails to adequately think through and understand the value issues in a situation ("It just didn't occur to me that my quitting school would make my parents think that they have failed").

Each person values a variety of things in life. Differences in the strength with which one holds any particular value and the priority a particular value will have among the whole constellation of that person's values, that is, the person's *value system,* is a part of what makes individuals unique. For example, for many people the most important value is feeling secure in their relationships with loved ones. For some, generating income is the driving force in their lives. For others, giving service or maintaining relationships dominates their value system. Still others attempt to maintain some balance among these values.

Dealing with values is particularly difficult for several reasons. First, values are such a central part of our thought processes that we often are not consciously aware of them and therefore are unable to identify their influence on our decisions. The social worker should constantly be alert to values in practice situations as these values may subtly influence the thoughts, feelings, attitudes, and behaviors of both the client and the social worker.

Second, a person may be forced to choose among values that are in conflict with one another. Who can avoid wrestling with a *value conflict* when confronted by a person on the street asking for money to buy something to eat? We may value responding to people in need, but we may equally value encouraging people to use the organized system for receiving financial assistance that does not put the person into the degrading position of panhandling.

Third, addressing values in the abstract may be quite different from applying them in a real-life situation. The social worker must recognize, for example, that clients may not act on the basis of value choices selected in a counseling session when they are confronted with the actual people and conditions where this value must be operationalized.

Finally, values are problematic because they change over time. Various events, experiences, and even new information can lead clients to adapt their system of values to more closely fit their current situation. A person whose job is eliminated, for instance, may be much more supportive of a universal health insurance program than when he or she was employed and receiving health insurance benefits from the employer.

The Place of Values in Social Work

Helping people to be clear about their individual values, that is, *values clarification,* and facilitating their understanding of how the particular set of values they hold influences their goals and decisions is an important aspect of social work practice. At times, clients also must be assisted in recognizing and understanding the values of others. Taking into consideration the values of family members, friends, employers, teachers, or others in that person's environment may be prerequisite to making appropriate and workable decisions. The matter becomes more complicated when social work practice involves more than one person, as it is likely that each will have a somewhat different value system. In that case the social worker may need to help resolve issues that stem from differences in values.

Further, the social worker must be concerned with his or her own values and control for their inappropriate intrusion into practice situations. Value choices that may be viable personally for the social worker may not coincide with the needs, wants, priorities, or realities the client experiences. Ultimately, the client must live with the decisions that are made, and they should be consistent with his or her own value system—not the value system of the social worker. Learning to suspend one's own values (i.e., *value suspension*) to keep the focus of helping on the client or client group is an important, yet difficult task for every social worker.

People are attracted to particular helping professions because they perceive that the work they do will be consistent with their personal values and, therefore, the job will be satisfying. The way a profession views its role in society, its attitudes toward the clients it serves, the knowledge it selects as the basis for its practice, its requirements for ethical practice behavior, and so forth are all influenced by the profession's values.

With social work practice focused at the interface between person and environment, the social worker must simultaneously address several sets of values. It is no wonder that social work has perhaps devoted more attention to values than has any other helping profession. Yet it has not developed a sufficiently clear and adequately tested statement of its core values to offer a definitive description of its central beliefs. At best, there is only rather general agreement that some values are fundamental to social work practice.

Social Values in U.S. Society

Values differ from *needs*. The latter refers to people's basic biological or psychological urges, while values reflect what people hope to get out of life and how this should be accomplished. The choice of which needs a society will attempt to meet depends on what it values. The most predominant feature of Western values is the central place of the individual; that is, the society exists to help individuals lead satisfying and productive lives.[3] Like other parts of Western culture, the values that guide choices in U.S. society focus on the individual. These values have their roots in at least four different sources, all of which are concerned with the responsibilities of the individual toward self and society and/or the society's responsibility to the individual.[4] These sources include:

1. Judaism and Christianity with their doctrine of the integral worth of humans and their responsibilities for their neighbors;
2. The democratic ideals that emphasize the equality of all people and a person's right to "life, liberty, and the pursuit of happiness";

3. The Puritan ethic, which says that character is all, circumstances nothing, that the moral person is the one who works and is independent, and that pleasure is sinful;

4. The tenets of Social Darwinism, which emphasize that the fittest survive and the weak perish in a natural evolutionary process that produces the strong individual and society.

It is evident that much of the disagreement in the United States over the provision of human services results from value conflicts inherent in the U.S. public's value system. Brill points out:

> Even the casual reader will see that a dichotomy exists within this value system. We hold that all men are equal, but he who does not work is less equal. . . . We hold that the individual life has worth, but that only the fit should survive. We believe that we are responsible for each other, but he who is dependent upon another for his living is of lesser worth.[5]

In carrying out the commitments of the social welfare institution to respond to human needs, the social worker becomes an intermediary between people in need and society's value judgments about what needs are to be met. As one cynic phrased it, the social worker stands "between the demanding recipient and the grudging donor." Therefore, the social worker must be particularly knowledgeable about the values that are dominant in U.S. society.

What constellation of values are held by the U.S. population? In this nation of people with widely diverse backgrounds and interests, it is not surprising that there is considerable variation in belief systems. The answer to the question "Am I my brother's (or sister's) keeper?" is not a categorical "yes" or "no." Protecting a woman's "right to choose" in regard to abortion in one person's value system, for example, is viewed as a "license to kill" in another's system of beliefs. Efforts to document preferred values held by the U.S. public are the basis for considerable political debate, but rarely identify a clear consensus on issues.

Kahle's carefully constructed study of the social values held by Americans suggests that value preferences differ substantially for different segments of the population.[6] The study asked respondents to indicate which of eight fundamental social values was the most important for a person to achieve in life.* The data reveal that the more vulnerable groups consistently hold two values, security and being respected, at much higher levels than the general population. Perhaps that is not surprising. If one is poor, has a limited education, is a minority group member, or is old, he or she is likely to worry about having basic health insurance, sufficient income, and safety. It is also likely that he or she is regularly treated with some

---

*The eight social values, in order of numbers of times it was selected as most important, were (1) having *self-respect* (feeling good about oneself and what has been accomplished in life); (2) attaining a *sense of security* (feeling safe and comfortable about the future); (3) having *warm personal relationships* (maintaining satisfying interpersonal relations with friends and family); (4) feeling *successful* in life's undertakings; (5) being *respected by others*; (6) feeling *fulfilled* by the quality of life experiences; (7) experiencing *a sense of belonging* to valued groups of people; and (8) finding *fun, enjoyment, and excitement* in life's activities.

degree of disrespect by other members in the society as many do not have the education and experience to compete well for jobs, are considered "too old" to take on meaningful work, suffer various forms of discrimination, and so forth. Under these conditions, one values highly what he or she does not have—security and respect. From the vantage point of social work, these data reinforce the view that it is important to support the development of social programs that increase people's security and to deliver those programs in a manner that treats the recipients with dignity. With those two basic social values achieved, people are then ready to address other areas of need that can enhance the quality of their lives.

Social workers and other professionals must be particularly alert to what the clients value because those values are not likely to be held with the same strength by the professionals themselves. The data from the Kahle study indicate that attaining such basic values as security and being respected by others were not of high priority to professionals. After all, they really don't need to worry about those basics. Professionals are highly educated, usually have secure jobs with relatively high income, don't typically experience discrimination, and can feel pretty safe about their futures. Their value preferences are related to items that enhance the quality of life such as achieving self-respect, having a sense of accomplishment, and experiencing fulfillment.[7] It takes discipline and commitment to avoid the trap of seeing the world only through one's own eyes and actively seeking to understand and appreciate the value preferences of others.

Values Held by Social Workers

We have seen that the social worker must relate to the values of both the client or client group and the society. In order to avoid imposing personal values on the client or making inappropriate judgments about a client's values, the social worker must have a clear understanding of his or her own personal values. In addition, the social worker must be fully aware of, and guided by, the fundamental values of the social work profession.

What, then, are the values commonly held by social workers? When developing its classification scheme for different levels of practice, the National Association of Social Workers identified ten basic social work values.[8] These statements express the basic values that underpin the profession of social work.

1. *Commitment to the primary importance of the individual in society.* In this value statement social work reaffirms its commitment to the most basic cultural value in Western society—the primacy of the individual. Social work accepts the position that the individual is the center of practice and that every person is of inherent worth because of his or her humanness. The social worker need not approve of what a person does but must treat that person as a valued member of society. Each client should be treated with dignity.

Commitment to the centrality of the individual has also led social workers to recognize that each person is unique and that practice activities must be tailored for that person's or group's uniqueness. Such individualization permits the worker to determine where and how to intervene in each helping situation, while at the same time communicating respect for the people being served.

2. *Commitment to social change to meet socially recognized needs.* Giving primacy to the individual does not minimize the commitment of the social worker to achieve societal change. Rather, it suggests that the social worker recognizes that the outcome of change activities in the larger society must ultimately benefit individuals.

Social work evolved as the primary profession responsible for helping society fulfill its commitment to meet the social needs of people, that is, to operationalize the social welfare institution. The obligation of social work is not only to deliver social provisions and social services to people in need, but also to serve as instruments of social change as a means of allowing each person to realize his or her fullest potential.

Social workers, then, are committed to the belief that the society has a responsibility to provide resources and services to help people avoid such problems as hunger, insufficient education, discrimination, illness without care, and inadequate housing. While social workers accept the primacy of the individual, they also hold the society responsible for meeting social needs. Social workers serve both the person and the environment in responding to social needs.

3. *Commitment to social justice and the economic, physical, and mental well-being of all in society.* The obligation of social workers is to attempt to improve the quality of all people's lives. Social workers believe that social justice must be achieved if each person is to have the opportunity to develop his or her unique potential and, therefore, make his or her maximum contribution to society. Thus, social workers believe that each person should have the right to participate in molding the social institutions and the decision-making processes in U.S. society so that programs, policies, and procedures are responsive to the needs and conditions of all.

Of course, when needs are competing in a diverse society and when resources are limited, choices must be made. Not every person can have all needs met. When they are making choices, the values held by social workers emphasize the importance of responding to the needs of the most vulnerable members of the society. Typically, these vulnerable people are children, the aged, minority group members, the disabled, women, and others who have been victims of institutionalized discrimination. Social workers are committed to ensuring that social justice is achieved for these persons, individually and as a population group.

4. *Respect and appreciation for individual and group differences.* Social workers recognize that there are common needs, goals, aspirations, and wants that are held by all people. In some ways we are all alike. However, social workers also recognize that in other ways each individual's life experience and capacities make him or her different from others. Where some may fear differences or resist working with people who are not like themselves, social workers value and respect uniqueness. They believe that the quality of life is enriched by different cultural patterns, different beliefs, and different forms of activity. As opposed to efforts to assimilate persons who are in some way different from the general population, social workers value a pluralistic society that can accommodate a range of beliefs, behaviors, languages, and customs.

The title of this book, *Social Work: A Profession of Many Faces,* is intended to suggest that social work not only includes people of many backgrounds performing a wide variety of human services but that social workers also provide services to people from virtually all backgrounds and walks of life. The chapters in Part Four,

"Social Work Practice with Special Populations," elaborate on some of these differences and their impact on social work practice.

5. *Commitment to developing clients' ability to help themselves.* If clients are to change their social conditions, their actions that contributed to the conditions must ultimately change. Unlike medicine, where an injection may solve a patient's problem, social change requires that the people affected become personally engaged in the change process and actively work to create the desired change. Underpinning social work practice, then, must be the social worker's belief that each person has an inherent capacity and drive that can result in desirable change.

Social workers do not view people as static or unchanging, nor is anyone assumed to be unable to engage in activities that may produce a more satisfying and rewarding life. Rather, social workers view people as adaptable. Although there are conditions that some people face that cannot be changed, the people themselves or the world around them can be helped to adapt to these conditions. For example, the terminally ill patient cannot be made well, the blind child cannot be made to see, and the severely retarded person cannot be made self-sustaining. Yet in each case the person involved can be helped to adjust to these conditions, and the person's environment can be adapted to more adequately accommodate special needs. Within the individual's or group's capacities, the social worker places high value on helping people take responsibility for their own decisions and actions.

6. *Willingness to transmit knowledge and skills to others.* Perhaps the most important function performed by the social worker in helping clients accomplish the change they desire is to effectively guide the change process. A significant part of this guidance involves helping clients understand the situation they experience from both a personal perspective and the perspectives of others, as well as helping them develop the skills to resolve their problems.

Effective helping avoids making clients dependent on helpers and prepares them to address other issues that arise in their lives. Thus, it is important that social workers assist clients in identifying strengths that can be mobilized for solving the immediate problem and to help them learn how to use these strengths in solving problems that may arise in the future.

A second application of this value concerns the commitment of professionals to share knowledge with colleagues. Knowledge or skills developed by a social worker are not to be kept secret or limited to clients who work only with that social worker. Rather, the social worker is obligated to transmit this information to other social workers so that they might bring the best knowledge and skill possible to their clients.

7. *Willingness to keep personal feelings and needs separate from professional relationships.* It is important for the social worker to recognize that the focus of practice must be maintained on the client—not on the social worker. Because social workers care about the people they work with, it is easy to become overidentified with clients' lives or even to develop personal relationships with them. If that happens, the client loses the benefit of an objective helper, the social worker can be placed in a compromising position, and the quality of the helping process is diminished because the relationship has changed from professional to personal.

As opposed to the many personal relationships that each person has throughout life, professional relationships require that a degree of professional objectivity be maintained. If a social worker becomes too closely identified with a client, the ability to stand back from the situation and view it from a neutral position is minimized. Sheafor, Horejsi, and Horejsi argue the importance of maintaining an appropriate degree of personal distance from clients:

> By the time most clients come into contact with a professional helper, they have attempted to resolve their troublesome situation themselves—by struggling alone or seeking assistance from family, friends, or other natural helpers.
>
> The professional adds a new dimension to the helping process by operating with a degree of emotional neutrality. Maintaining this neutrality without appearing unconcerned or uncaring is a delicate balancing act. The worker who becomes too involved and too identified with the client's concerns can lose perspective and objectivity. At the other extreme, the worker who is emotionally detached fails to energize clients or, even worse, discourages clients from investing the emotional energy necessary to achieve change.[9]

8. *Respect for the confidentiality of relationship with clients.* Although it is rare that the social worker can guarantee "absolute confidentiality" to a client, social workers value achieving the maximum possible protection of information received in working with clients. The very nature of a helping relationship suggests that there is sensitive information that must be shared between the person being helped and the helper. For example, the social worker must learn the reasons a client has been fired from a job, why a person who is chronically mentally ill has failed in a community group home placement, what keeps a homeless person from being able to secure resources to pay rent, why an alcoholic has not been able to stop drinking, or why a couple involved in marriage counseling has not been able to solve problems without fighting, and the like. In each case, some information typically passes between client and worker that could potentially be emotionally or economically damaging if it is inappropriately revealed to other parties. Social workers consider it of critical importance to respect the privacy of this communication.

9. *Willingness to persist in efforts on behalf of clients despite frustration.* Situations that require social work intervention typically do not develop quickly and usually cannot be resolved readily. Recognizing the frustration that they experience when change is slow to occur, social workers have come to value tenacity in addressing both individual problems and the problems that affect groups of people, organizations, communities, and society in general.

When providing direct services, a social worker may become frustrated with a client who, at a given time, is unable or unwilling to engage in activities the social worker believes would improve the situation. Or, when advocating on behalf of a client with another agency to provide needed services, the social worker may also experience frustration when the client is denied service or is placed on a waiting list. Advocacy for classes of clients or in relation to broad social issues can also prove quite frustrating. If delay tactics or the length of the change process is extended, the social worker may understandably become discouraged. Social workers must be persistent.

10. *Commitment to a high standard of personal and professional conduct.* The final value on the NASW list directs the worker to use the highest ethical standards in his or her practice. It suggests that the worker must conduct professional activities in a manner that protects the interests of the public, the agency, the clients, and the social worker.

This value has been operationalized in the form of the NASW Code of Ethics, which is perhaps the single most important unifying element among social workers. Loewenberg and Dolgoff identify the following five functions served by an ethical code:[10]

1. Provide practitioners with guidance when faced by practice dilemmas that include ethical issues.
2. Protect the public from charlatans and incompetent practitioners.
3. Protect the profession from governmental control; self-regulation is preferable to state regulation.
4. Enable professional colleagues to live in harmony with each other by preventing the self-destruction that results from internal bickering.
5. Protect professionals from litigation; practitioners who follow the Code are offered some protection if sued for malpractice.

Shortly after its founding, the NASW began the development of a Code of Ethics that could serve the needs of this profession. The Code was originally approved in 1960 and experienced major reorganization and revisions in 1979 and 1996. During periods between these comprehensive reviews of the Code, incremental revisions are made as complaints of Code violations are reviewed and the need for clarification is recognized or ethical issues not explicitly covered by the Code are identified.

With a clearly explicated Code of Ethics in place, NASW members can be clear about expectations for competent and ethical practice and the profession has a standard against which to assess complaints that the public has been violated. To join NASW, the social worker must sign a statement agreeing to abide by the ethical standards contained in the Code and to participate in the adjudication process if a complaint is made. By renewing one's membership each year, he or she reaffirms the commitment to adhere to NASW's Code of Ethics. NASW has created an elaborate procedure for hearing grievances at the local or chapter level with appeal to the national level possible for all parties to the complaint. A member found to have violated the Code of Ethics can be asked to take corrective actions, may be listed on a published report of Code violators, or may have his or her NASW membership revoked.

A study of a sample of 300 formal complaints filed with NASW between 1982 and 1992 reveals that about one-third of the complaints claiming violation of the Code of Ethics were substantiated (upheld) during the process of review and appeal. In 61 percent of the cases the person making the complaint was another social worker and in another 34 percent it was the client or a member of the client's family.[11] It appears that social workers take seriously the responsibility to file a complaint when they believe a colleague is not abiding by the Code of Ethics. Of those complaints that were substantiated, the most prevalent Code violation related to workers engaging in sexual activity with their clients (29.2%). Other frequently violated provisions in the Code of Ethics were concerned with the social worker having relationships or commitments that were in conflict with the interests of the client (16.9%), withdrawing services without efforts to minimize possible adverse affects for the client (16.7%), and exploiting professional relationships for personal gain (16.4%).

Areas of Practice Addressed by the NASW Code of Ethics

The *NASW Code of Ethics* has evolved from its 1960 format of ten general statements to guide ethical considerations in practice to its 1996 format that consumes twenty-seven pages of ethical prescriptions. Mastering the specifics of the *Code* and interpreting its provisions in actual practice situations is an ongoing challenge for all social workers. This process begins by recognizing the general areas of practice activity that the *Code* addresses.* The following statements summarize the main sections of the 1996 version of NASW's *Code of Ethics*.

1. Standards related to the social worker's ethical responsibilities to clients. This section of the *Code of Ethics* is concerned with such factors and principles as the following: the worker's primary responsibility is to the client; respect for client self-determination; securing client's informed consent; the worker's competence to provide needed services; the worker's cultural competence; avoiding conflict of interest; respecting clients' rights to privacy and confidentiality; the prohibition of sexual involvement, sexual harassment, inappropriate physical contact, and abusive or derogatory language; special considerations when clients lack decision-making capacity; avoiding the interruption of services; and the planful termination of services.

2. The social worker's ethical responsibilities to colleagues. Section 2 is concerned with the social workers' responsibility to treat colleagues with respect; concern for maintaining confidentiality among professionals; appropriate collaboration and teamwork; proper handling of disputes and disagreements; developing appropriate consultation relationships; proper referral of clients to colleagues; the prohibition of sexual harassment and sexual involvement with one's supervisees or students; and the requirement for responsible action in relation to a colleague who is impaired, incompetent, or unethical in his or her practice.

3. The social worker's ethical responsibilities in practice settings. This section of the *Code of Ethics* relates to services performed in relation to social workers and other professionals and only indirectly relates to clients. The items addressed include the competence required for providing supervision, consultation, education, and training; responsible evaluation of the performance of other workers; maintaining proper client records and billing properly; carefully evaluating client needs before accepting transfers; assuring an appropriate working environment and providing ongoing education and training in human services agencies; demonstrating commitment to agency employees; and guidelines for acting responsibly in labor disputes.

4. The social worker's ethical responsibilities as a professional. Section 4 includes items related to the social worker accepting employment and job assignments when

---

*The full text of the *NASW Code of Ethics* can be obtained from the National Association of Social Workers, 750 First Street, NE, Washington, DC 20002-4241, or can be downloaded from NASW's web site (http://www.naswdc.org). The Canadian code of ethics (which contains similar provisions) can be obtained from MYROPEN Publications, 383 Parkdale Ave., Suite 402, Ottawa, ON K1Y 4R4, and additional information on this code can be obtained from the Canadian Association of Social Worker's web site (http://www.ca/~casw-acts/code2-e.htm).

he or she may not be competent to perform that work; prohibition from practicing, condoning, or participating in any form of discrimination; engaging in private conduct that compromises the ability to fulfill professional responsibilities; restriction from engaging in dishonesty, fraud, and deception; the responsibility to address one's own problems if impaired; the requirement to be clear in public statements regarding whether acting as a professional or a private citizen; prohibiting uninvited solicitations for business; and properly acknowledging any contributions to one's written or other work made by others.

5. **The social worker's ethical responsibilities to the social work profession.** The *Code of Ethics* is also concerned with issues related to the social worker promoting high standards for social work and contributing time and energy to the profession's growth and development, as well as addressing items related to social workers continuously monitoring and evaluating social policies, programs, and their own practice interventions.

6. **The social worker's ethical responsibilities to the broader society.** In its final section the *Code of Ethics* charges social workers with promoting the general welfare of the society and seeking to assure social justice for all people; participating in public debate to shape social policies and institutions; providing services in public emergencies; and actively engaging in social and political action.

The maintenance of a code of ethics helps to satisfy social work's obligation to be responsible in performing its duties as a recognized profession. It provides guidance to social workers as they make ethical decisions in their day-to-day practice, spells out expected behaviors in areas where ethical compromises may arise, and provides clarity to the general public, employers, and other professionals who may feel that a social worker has violated the principles of ethical practice and wish to have NASW and/or the courts determine if a social worker has violated the public trust granted to professions.

An Illustration of Values and Ethics Operating in Social Work Practice

For most social workers, theoretical or abstract discussion of values and ethical dilemmas is not a daily event. It is usually when these issues are experienced when working with clients that they take on full significance. Hokenstad notes that "half of professional decision making requires ethical rather than scientific judgment. . . . Such judgment requires the capability to make moral precepts operational in specific situations and calls for tolerance or ambiguity in some cases and the ability to resolve conflicts between principles in others."[12] It is through consideration of a case example describing a social worker in action that the reader may be able to extend his or her more applied understanding of how values and ethical decisions affect social work practice.

In her book *Never Too Old*, Twente presented a case illustration of a social worker providing service to an aged widower who was unsuccessfully attempting to establish a new life with his son and his son's family.[13] In the following excerpt from this case, some value and ethical issues become evident:

> When Miss Jones visits Mr. Brandon, Sr., he at first seems determined not to enter into any kind of a discussion. He answers with a curt "no" or "yes" or "hmmm." Some reference to an old chair in which he sits brings forth the comment that it belonged to "mom and me." It was bought secondhand when they "set up housekeeping."
>
> "How long ago was that?" asks Miss Jones.
>
> "Fifty-one years last February," Mr. Brandon is struggling with tears.
>
> "It must be hard to go on without her," comments Miss Jones quietly. Mr. Brandon nods. There is a sob. Miss Jones rises, walks to the bedtable and looks closely at a photograph. "Is this she?"
>
> "Yes." Miss Jones sits down again. There is a silence. "There never was a better wife or mother than she." Miss Jones nods sympathetically.
>
> "Is the other picture on the table of your granddaughter?" she asks. "There seems to be a resemblance."
>
> "There is," responds Mr. Brandon, and for the first time his face lights up. "She is like my wife, Peggy is. Sometimes she comes into my room and asks me questions. All kinds of fool questions. She'll say, 'Grandpa, how did you meet grandma?' or 'What did you do when you took her out?' or 'Did you and grandma dance at parties?' And when I'll say, 'Yes, but not the kind of dances you kids dance,' she'll get up and do some funny turns and say, 'Was it like this, Grandpa?' I tell her, 'No. We waltzed and sometimes I jigged.' 'Show me, Grandpa,' she says. And I get up, but these stiff hips of mine won't move like they ought to." Then he becomes silent again.

The gentle probing of Miss Jones in this part of the case allows her to understand some of the things that Mr. Brandon values, such as the satisfaction from the warm relationship he had with his wife and the joy he gets from his granddaughter. The social worker reflects her value of the worth of Mr. Brandon and treats him with dignity by listening carefully and showing interest in his experiences and feelings. She also allowed him the privilege of only minimally participating in the discussion until he was ready to become involved. Mr. Brandon is important not because of his charm or good looks but because of his humanness. The case continues:

> "You aren't very happy here, are you?"
>
> The next comments come like the rush of water through a broken dam. "No, I'm not happy. How can I be? I am just an old man in everybody's way. Oh, perhaps that is not quite true of Peggy. She likes to visit me, I think. But she has many friends. You know how popular young girls are. Tom is a good son. He works hard, and sometimes he comes in to talk to me. But I can tell he would rather read about sports or look at TV."
>
> "How about Tom Junior?" prods Miss Jones.
>
> "Oh, young Tom is like all young fellers. He is so busy going off on hikes and playing ball and the likes, he doesn't know I exist. I have his room. That should not be. The boy needs his own room to keep things like rocks and frogs and snakes." Again, there is that impish expression. Now there can be no mistaking it. "Margaret doesn't like them things in the house, and she's put her foot down about bringing them alive into the basement.

She says she has to do the washing down there and she doesn't want the critters around her feet."

"You don't get along too well with Margaret," said Miss Jones.

"Oh, Margaret's all right. She is just too persnickity. When I first came I said, 'Now, Margaret, you let me do the dishes.' She said it would be hard for me to get them clean because I don't see so well. Well, I washed them, and then I saw her wash them over again. I don't see so bad, but I could see what she did." Then, after a short pause, "I am just in the way. I am an old farmer, and I am what I am. Margaret doesn't like the way I eat. When they had fancy company, she said to me, 'Grandpa, would you prefer to eat in your own room? I can fix your dinner on the card table.' I knew the score. She just didn't want me."

In this passage Mr. Brandon reflects his loss of a sense of self-respect. He views himself as an unimportant old man who doesn't suit the tastes of his daughter-in-law and is a burden for the rest of the family. Like many older people, he feels that he is of little use in a society that values work and productivity. While his life may have been fulfilling before and there was a real sense of achievement when he was managing the farm, life was hollow for Mr. Brandon now. Miss Jones communicates genuine concern about his well-being and seeks to understand the roots of the problem. The story goes on:

After a while Miss Jones asks him if he knows anyone in town besides Tom and his family. "No, all of my friends are out in the country, what is left of them. I can't go out there and they can't come in. Too far."

"And how about church?" asks Miss Jones.

"Mom and I always went to the Methodist Church. Tom and Margaret go to the Christian. Disciples of Christ, they call it. That was Margaret's church. Tom had to be 'ducked' before he could belong." Mr. Brandon does not want to be baptized again. "Once is enough." And he doesn't know anybody. So he stays at home and listens to the radio. Anyhow, his stiff hips can't do those steps very well.

"Did you ever like fishing or hunting?" asks Miss Jones.

"No, you know, where we lived there was no water for miles around. And as to hunting, there are jackrabbits and prairie dogs, but I was never one to shoot except to protect the crops."

"When you and your wife had company on Sunday afternoons, what did you men do?" Miss Jones continues her questions.

"Oh, we talked politics and things like that, and looked at crops; and sometimes we played horseshoe," replies Mr. Brandon. "Horseshoe was fun, then, but with these hips, it's out of the question."

"How about Sunday afternoons in the winter?" Miss Jones is not giving up.

"Well, we played checkers and dominoes and sometimes Flinch."

"Did you enjoy that?" asks Miss Jones.

"Yes." His face brightens. "Hank Brown and I used to play checkers. We played to win. Maggie, that was my wife, and Elizabeth, Hank's wife, had to remind us that the stock had to be fed and we had to go home."

"Would you care to play checkers now, that is, if there were someone to play with you?"

"No. Anyhow, there's nobody to play with."

"There is a Center on Elm Street and retired men get together for checkers and cards. They seem to have fun."

Here Miss Jones moves the conversation to understand better the uniqueness of Mr. Brandon. Although he faces problems experienced by other old people, Mr. Brandon is a unique individual with his own interests and abilities. Miss Jones responds to his need to belong and searches for interests that match community resources that would provide him with an opportunity to make new friends. She knows that men in Mr. Brandon's age group especially need to have warm relationships with a group of friends. Miss Jones reflects the belief that people can change in a new environment and that Mr. Brandon could once again enter the mainstream of life, yet she is ethically bound to present options and let Mr. Brandon determine what, if any, changes he will make in his life. She is persistent and does not let his despair frustrate her efforts to help find a solution:

Mr. Brandon shakes his head. "I've heard about the Center but it does not appeal to me. Anyhow, I won't be in town very long. I overheard Tom and Margaret discuss me. They want me to go into a home." He seems resigned.

"And do you want to go?" Miss Jones keeps on digging.

"Hell, no. But what can an old man like me do? I don't want to stay where I am not wanted. Not me."

"I am not sure that you are not wanted," says Miss Jones. "Why don't you talk it over with Tom and Margaret and tell them how you feel?"

"I couldn't do that," says Mr. Brandon. "Anyhow, what's the use? I shouldn't have blabbered so much to you. I wasn't going to, and then I went and did it anyhow."

"Do you want me to talk to Tom and Margaret and perhaps with Peggy and young Tom present, too?" asks Miss Jones.

"What would Peggy and young Tom have to do with it?" He is almost shouting. "They are not responsible for me. Not them young kids."

"No, they aren't, but they are a part of the family and they know whether they want you to stay or to leave. I think Peggy, especially, would hate to see you go to a home."

"Well, I'm going and that is that." Mr. Brandon is trembling. "Like I told you, I am not going to be in anybody's way."

Miss Jones asks for at least a minimum level of informed consent. Mr. Brandon, now that he knows there may be some options, is in a position to judge if he wants to continue with this service from the social worker.

"Do you want me to tell you about the homes nearby?" asks Miss Jones.

The answer sounds something like assent. Miss Jones lists the four different kinds of institutions in the county and briefly describes each one. Mr. Brandon is silent. After a while he says, "You sure know about all these things, don't you?"

"It's my business to know," says Miss Jones.

There is another pause. This time it is a long one. "Does Tom know about all of this, I mean all of these homes?"

"Yes," replies Miss Jones. "I told them when they came in to see me."

"And they want me to go?"

"Only Tom and Margaret and Peggy and Tom Junior can answer that," says Miss Jones. "I do think they would like to see you happier than you have been here."

"Well, I would be! A damn sight happier!" Then, in quite another voice, "Can family visit you in those places? I mean, can young kids come too?"

"Yes, they can, especially during visiting hours."

"What do you have to do with all of this?" he then asks.

"Really very little, Mr. Brandon. We do give information when it is wanted and needed, and sometimes we help with the finances. Most of all we are interested in trying to help families find the best solutions in situations like yours. Tom and Margaret told us they were concerned about you. They know you are lonely and unhappy. They thought a home might be a solution and they asked for information."

"Did they also ask you to come and talk with me?" Mr. Brandon is shouting again.

"Yes, but they understood that I would not try to persuade you to go to a home or do anything else you don't want to do. I think this is up to you and your family."

"And that includes Peggy and Tom Junior?"

"To me it would seem so."

Soon after that, Mr. Brandon comments, "Well, I've got something to think about."

We find Miss Jones reflecting the social work value of helping the clients help themselves. She recognizes that people must be permitted to determine what is best for them and take responsibility for these decisions. Miss Jones is also aware that Mr. Brandon said some things he would not want her to report back to Tom and Margaret. She is ethically obligated to protect the confidentiality of their conversation by asking if he wants her to talk with the family about his views. Yet she refuses to be drawn into the role of an interpreter for the family and, instead, helps them come together to talk about the problems and possible solutions. The final decision, however, is left to them. Although frustrated at times, she continues to pursue working with the family until a satisfactory solution is achieved.

Examples of Ethical Issues in Social Work Practice

What are the ethical dilemmas one faces in social work practice? The Code violations substantiated by NASW described previously center around social workers making judgments in practice situations in which they placed their own wants and needs above their obligation to serve their clients. Within the expectations of a profession, those decisions were clearly wrong. Most ethical decisions, unfortunately, are not so clear. They require the social worker to make choices when, sometimes, none of the alternatives are desirable. The worker must weigh one choice against others and make a decision about which option is best or, too often, which is least harmful.

Consider the following examples of a range of decisions a social worker must make that have ethical elements to them:

- What should a social worker do if a client announces the decision to return to an abusive spouse when the worker fears for the client's safety?

- Is it ethical for a social worker to attempt to provide specialized therapeutic services for which he or she is not trained if the worker doubts the competence of the only credentialed person with that expertise in the area where the client lives?

- Should a social worker accept a personal gift from a client beyond the fee the client pays for the professional service? In lieu of a fee for professional service?

- Should a social worker report a colleague to NASW or the state licensing board if that colleague reveals that he or she has developed a sexual relationship with one of his or her clients?

- What should a social worker do if a grand jury requests a client's file that contains case notes that may be damaging to the client?

- What should a social work intern do if a field instructor is touching him or her inappropriately in the course of field instruction activities?

- Is a social worker obligated to do anything if he or she believes a colleague has developed a substance abuse problem?

- If requested by the agency's executive director, is it okay for a social worker to provide supervision to another staff member in a practice area in which the worker has limited knowledge and competence?

- What should be done if a client asks a social worker in a probation setting to overlook (and not mention in the case record) a violation of a condition of parole—promising not to repeat the activity?

- Is it okay for a social worker not to record information given by a client in confidence in the case file when the agency's administrative procedures require recording all pertinent information to the case? If state law requires reporting that information to a central registry or a protective services agency?

- What should a social worker in private practice do if a local company considering a substantial service contract with the worker requests the names and addresses of current clients to contact in order to assess their satisfaction with the worker's performance?

- If the administrator in a nursing home directs the social work staff to transfer out of the agency all patients who do not have insurance or other benefits because the nursing home is experiencing financial difficulty, should the social workers abide by this directive?

- Is it ethical for a social worker who develops a successful helping technique to obtain a patent and market the technique for a profit to other social workers?

- Is a social worker obligated to engage in social and political action when his or her job description does not specify such activity?

The NASW Code of Ethics offers some guidance on each, but at times more than one Code provision applies, and, even more frustrating, sometimes if the worker follows one Code guideline another may be violated.

Concluding Comment

One cannot understand social work without being sensitive to values. Values represent a highly individual and personal view that must be constantly examined during practice.

The social worker must be aware of the value system of the client or client group and the values held by society that impinge upon the client. Research reported in the chapter identifies the dominant values in U.S. society that form the context in which social programs are formulated and in which social workers and their clients engage in the helping process. These values, however, are not held equally by all people, and client groups can be expected to vary in the intensity with which they hold particular values.

The social worker must be especially cognizant of his or her personal values, lest they intrude into the helping process. Certainly it would be unrealistic to expect, or even desire, that the helping process occur in a value-free environment. Yet the social worker must attempt to avoid imposing personal values inappropriately on the client or client groups. In order to practice social work, one must be prepared to accept and understand people who hold values that are different from their own.

The social worker also must be guided by the values and ethics of the social work profession. These beliefs are not held exclusively by social workers. Some overlap with the values of other professions, and there is indication that professionals hold distinctly different values from the general population.[14] Social work's constellation of core values, however, is unique. Roberts, for example, has identified five areas where the values of physicians and those of social workers are quite different, including attitudes about such factors as saving life versus quality of life, the professional's control versus patient autonomy in establishing treatment plans, and so on.[15] Further, Abbott's research identified areas of significant difference in the values held by social workers, physicians, nurses, teachers, psychologists, and business people. Of these groups, psychologists were most like social workers in their beliefs.[16]

In many ways, values or beliefs about how things ought to be or how people ought to behave are the cornerstone of social work. Even when the knowledge available to guide practice is limited, the social worker who falls back on the values of the profession cannot go far wrong in guiding the helping process. When the worker is value-sensitive and effectively supplies the competencies of social work practice, clients receive the quality of services they should expect from a professional.

KEY WORDS AND CONCEPTS

Values	Value suspension
Ethics	Western society's values
Knowledge versus values	U.S. society's values
Value conflict	Social workers' values
Value system	Social workers' ethics
Values clarification	NASW Code of Ethics

SUGGESTED READINGS

Bullis, Ronald K. *Clinical Social Worker Misconduct: Laws, Ethics, and Personal Dynamics.* Chicago: Nelson-Hall, 1995.

Gambrill, Eileen, and Pruger, Robert. *Controversial Issues in Social Work Ethics, Values, and Obligations.* Boston: Allyn and Bacon, 1997.

Levy, Charles S. *Social Work Ethics on the Line.* New York: Haworth, 1993.

Reamer, Frederic G. *Social Work Values and Ethics,* 2nd Edition. New York: Columbia University Press, 1999.

Wells, Carolyn Cressy, with Masch, M. Kathleen. *Social Work Ethics Day to Day: Guidelines for Professional Practice,* 2nd Edition. Prospect Hills, IL: Waveland Press, 1991.

ENDNOTES

1. R. Huws Jones, "Social Values and Social Work Education," in Katherine A. Kendall, ed., *Social Work Values in an Age of Discontent* (New York: Council on Social Work Education, 1970).

2. Milton Rokeach, *Beliefs, Values, and Attitudes: A Theory of Organization and Change* (San Francisco: Jossey-Bass, 1968), p. 124.

3. Shepard B. Clough, *Basic Values of Western Civilization* (New York: Columbia University Press, 1960), p. 5.

4. Naomi I. Brill, *Working with People: The Helping Process,* 4th Edition (New York: Longman, 1990), p. 29.

5. Ibid., p. 12.

6. Lynn R. Kahle and Susan Groff Timmer, "A Theory and a Method for Studying Values," in Lynn R. Kahle, ed., *Social Values and Social Change: Adaptation to Life in America* (New York: Praeger Publishers, 1983), pp. 47–108.

7. Ibid., p. 110

8. National Association of Social Workers, *NASW Standards for the Classification of Social Work Practice, Policy Statement 4* (Silver Spring, MD: The Association, September 1981), p. 18.

9. Bradford W. Sheafor, Charles R. Horejsi, and Gloria A. Horejsi, *Techniques and Guidelines for Social Work Practice,* 5th Edition (Boston: Allyn and Bacon, 2000), p. 70.

10. Frank Loewenberg and Ralph Dolgoff, *Ethical Decisions for Social Work Practice,* 5th Edition (Itasca, IL: F. E. Peacock, 1996), p. 35.

11. National Association of Social Workers, "Overview of a Decade of Adjudication," mimeo (Washington, D.C.: The Association, 1995).

12. M.C. Hokenstad, "Teaching Practitioners Ethical Judgment," *NASW News* 32 (October 1987): 4.

13. Esther E. Twente, *Never Too Old: The Aged in Community Life* (San Francisco: Jossey-Bass, 1970), pp. 151–158.

14. William C. Horner and Les B. Whitebeck, "Personal versus Professional Values in Social Work: A Methodological Note," *Journal of Social Service Research* 14 (Issue 1/2 1991): 21–43.

15. Cleora S. Roberts, "Conflicting Professional Values in Social Work and Medicine," *Health and Social Work* 13 (August 1989): 211–218.

16. Ann A. Abbott, *Professional Choices: Values at Work* (Silver Spring, MD: National Association of Social Workers, 1988), pp. 74–75.

CHAPTER 8

Competencies Required for Social Work Practice Today

Prefatory Comment Equipped with adequate social programs to meet client needs, sanction to perform professional services, a suitable agency or private practice environment, and the requisite professional values and ethical guidelines, the social worker is prepared to deliver helping services. Little of this background for practice is usually recognized or even of interest to clients, although the absence of any one of these factors would minimize the social worker's ability to be helpful. Instead, the clients' primary concern is with the social worker and the social worker's competence to be of maximum assistance in addressing their needs and enhancing their general well-being.

To understand social work, then, it is important to be familiar with the competencies needed to perform this professional activity. In this chapter, a major national study of social work practice serves as the basis for describing the competencies typically required of a social worker.

The term *competence* is a particularly useful descriptor for professional practice, because it not only includes the expertise to perform a function but also suggests the capability to translate that expertise into useful actions. Synonyms for competence include skill and knowledge, art and science, as well as talent and proficiency. Competence, then, requires the worker to not only have the requisite information, but he or she must be able to use that knowledge to effectively assist clients in changing their social functioning or bringing about change in the functioning of some part of their environment.

What must a social worker be competent to do? As a profession with a mission to facilitate change in both people and the environment, a wide range of competencies are required. The requisite knowledge and abilities appear quite different depending on which part of social work one is exploring. One might wonder if there is sufficient similarity in the activity performed by social workers in the various fields of practice (e.g., criminal justice, family services, community planning), social work practice settings (e.g., schools, nursing homes, private practice), and professional education levels (i.e., BSW, MSW, DSW) to fit under the umbrella of a single profession. Indeed, throughout most of social work's evolution from volunteerism to a recognized profession it has sought to identify the characteristics that all social workers have in common. As Chapter 2 indicated, social work found such a common theme at the rather lofty conceptual level of its mission, that is, to help people simultaneously address both person and environment. But are there competencies that most social workers use on a day-to-day basis that indicate the presence of a single profession at a more concrete level?

The Competencies Required for Social Work Practice

In the most comprehensive study of social work practice to date, a representative sample of 7,000 social workers from throughout the United States indicated how often they performed 131 different tasks as part of their jobs and how important each task was for successfully doing their jobs.* The sample was made up of approximately 21 percent basic social workers, 75 percent who had the MSW as their highest degree, and the remainder were doctoral-level social workers. Through a statistical procedure commonly referred to as cluster analysis, the tasks were statistically grouped into eighteen distinct clusters of work activity. The mean (or average) score for each cluster could range from a low score of 1.00 (the cluster is not a part of the social worker's job activity) to a high of 5.00 (the activities in the cluster are almost always performed).

To identify the competencies required for various career paths in social work, the task analysis data provide a useful structure. First, the mean scores for each of the eighteen clusters can be compared to determine which are tasks most likely to be performed by social workers and which are the least common activities. In the remainder of this chapter the clusters are presented in that order with the mean score for the composite sample ($n = 7,000$) indicating the frequency with which the typical social worker performs those tasks.

---

*All data reported in this chapter, as well as the eighteen cluster descriptions, are from Robert J. Teare and Bradford W. Sheafor, "National Task Analysis Study of Social Work Practice." (Unpublished materials. School of Social Work, University of Alabama, Tuscaloosa.) The most complete description of the methodology used in collecting and analyzing the data and the most comprehensive published report of the full study can be found in Robert J. Teare and Bradford W. Sheafor, *Practice-Sensitive Social Work Education: An Empirical Analysis of Social Work Practice and Practitioners* (Alexandria, VA: Council on Social Work Education, 1995).

Second, the data indicate that the most significant factor that affects the task a social worker performs is his or her *primary job function.* With some variation, the profile of activities is similar for *direct service* practitioners (i.e., social workers who work primarily in face-to-face contact with clients) regardless of field of practice or employment setting. Social workers who are agency *administrators* also do similar things wherever they are employed. As will become evident when examining the data in this chapter, with the exception of a few clusters administrators have a very different set of activities to perform when they carry out the job of managing human services agencies than do social workers in direct practice jobs. The third job function analyzed, *supervision,* reflects the need for a blend of direct service and administrative competencies. Each job function offers a challenging career track for a social worker.

Third, a significant factor in one's career decision relates to whether he or she will prepare for practice by obtaining the BSW degree or secure the MSW to practice at the specialized or independent levels. Thus, it is useful to compare the activities of BSWs with those of MSWs. Because relatively few BSW-level social workers are engaged in supervision and administrative jobs, only the mean scores for direct service practitioners from the task analysis study are presented for each cluster of activity. Examination of the data will indicate that the profiles for practice levels are similar with the exception of MSW-level practitioners being more treatment oriented (e.g., individual and family treatment, group work) and the BSWs more likely to engage in more concrete and tangible activities such as case planning and ongoing case maintenance, dispute resolution, and connecting clients into the service delivery system.*

Finally, knowing what social workers do leads to the identification of the competencies one needs to carry out those job activities. These competencies, although not empirically derived as part of the task analysis study, help the prospective social worker recognize the knowledge and skills one must master to become a social worker. They also assist social work education programs to identify content they should include in their curricula.

THE UNIVERSAL SOCIAL WORK COMPETENCIES

Two clusters of tasks, interpersonal helping and professional competence development, were consistently performed by most social workers at all levels of practice, in all job functions, and in all practice areas and settings. They represent the most clear indication of a common set of work activities that help to bind social workers into a single profession.

---

*Preliminary results from a 1997 update of the task analysis data from all MSW-level social workers ($n = 4,266$) indicate little change in the cluster scores. In general, there was a slight increase in direct service activities and a decrease in indirect services over the intervening twelve years.

INTERPERSONAL HELPING. The cluster of tasks most frequently performed by all social workers requires the worker to engage in interpersonal helping. To perform this set of activities the social worker must be prepared to use basic helping skills (e.g., interviewing, questioning, counseling) to assist individuals and/or families in understanding the problems they experience in social functioning and in helping them to examine possible options for resolving those problems. In carrying out these activities, the worker actively involves individuals and families in discussions designed to explore options for solving problems. The worker encourages people to express their points of view and share their feelings. Throughout this process the worker attempts to communicate an understanding of other people's points of view and establish a relationship of trust with clients.

The high frequency with which social workers use interpersonal helping, especially in direct practice jobs, is indicated by the mean scores achieved in the task analysis study. Box 8-1 reveals the universal application of these skills.

What competencies are needed to carry out these interpersonal helping tasks? Different social workers would, no doubt, approach practice situations in a manner that reflects their individual ways of working with clients. However, most social workers would probably include at least the following items in a list of interpersonal helping competencies:

1. *Self-awareness and the ability to use self in facilitating change.* The primary tool for helping by a social worker is the social worker himself or herself. The social worker cannot give a client an injection that will cure a social problem or surgically remove some impediment to healthy social functioning. To use oneself effectively, a social worker must be sensitive to his or her own strengths and limitations, be aware of areas of knowledge and ignorance, and recognize the potential to be both helpful and harmful when serving clients.

2. *Knowledge of the psychology of giving and receiving help.* Often a part of the motivation for entering a helping profession is the desire to give of oneself to improve the lives of others. It is rewarding to help others, but social workers must take care to focus the helping process on what is needed by the client. Also, social workers must remember that clients are often uncomfortable when receiving help—both because our society suggests that one has somehow failed if he or she needs assistance and because we sometimes offer social programs in a manner that is demeaning to clients.

BOX 8-1 **Mean Scores for Interpersonal Helping Tasks**

All Social Workers: 3.98	
BSW Direct Practitioners: 4.27	MSW Direct Practitioners: 4.40
	MSW Supervisors: 3.77
	MSW Administrators: 3.35

3. *Ability to establish professional helping relationships.* Prerequisite to all successful helping is the establishment of a positive helping relationship. Whether working directly with clients, coworkers, or others in the community, the social worker must establish a relationship characterized by mutual respect and trust. Personal characteristics of the worker that have been found to be critical for creating such a helping relationship include empathy, positive regard, warmth, and genuineness. Research has further indicated that the social worker whose interaction with clients is characterized by concreteness, objectivity, and the ability to introduce and maintain structure in the helping process further improves the worker's success rate.

4. *Understanding differing ethnic and cultural patterns, as well as the capacity to engage in ethnic-, gender-, and age-sensitive practice.* One's social functioning, and even perceptions of what is positive social functioning, is affected by a person's appreciation of variations in cultural background experienced by various subgroups of the population. The various ethnic and racial minority groups in the United States have had a very different experience, both in cultural background and in their experience with the dominant white culture, than have members of the majority. Similarly, women have had more limited opportunities than men, and older people often have a quite different place in society than when they were younger. To engage in effective interpersonal helping the social worker must not only be aware of these different life experiences but must also be aware of how they affect the social functioning of individual clients. In short, the effective social worker engages in ethnic-, gender-, and age-sensitive practice. That same sensitivity should be applied to other population groups such as the physically and mentally disabled, gay and lesbian persons, persons of varied religious backgrounds, and so on.

5. *Knowledge and application of the Code of Ethics as a guide to ethical practice.* Inherent in the practice of any profession is the expectation that the public trust evident in granting professional sanction is rewarded by the professional mandate to engage in ethical practice. Each social worker is expected to conduct his or her practice in a manner that attempts to bring the best services possible to clients and, at a minimum, does no damage. The NASW Code of Ethics represents social work's effort to spell out the minimum requirements for ethical social work practice. Adhering to the Code of Ethics must be part of carrying out every practice task from interpersonal helping to research and policy analysis.

6. *General understanding of individual and family behavior patterns.* Interpersonal helping must be underpinned by knowledge of people, both individually and as part of families or other households. Effective interpersonal helping requires doing more than just what feels right. The social worker needs a thorough grounding in expected human growth and development patterns throughout the life cycle, understanding of different family structures and their influence on family members, and sufficient knowledge of human physiology and anatomy to recognize biological factors that may affect one's social functioning. It requires synthesizing knowledge from the disciplines of biology, psychology, and sociology to understand the bio-psycho-social functioning of clients.

7. *Skill in client information gathering.* Interpersonal helping requires a set of specific skills for gathering information that will help determine the social worker's course of action in regard to the client's situation. Perhaps the most fundamental skill a social worker must have is the ability to conduct an interview that not only reveals important information but also facilitates a continuing professional relationship. A substantial and rich literature on interviewing is available to the social worker.[1] Skills such as focusing an interview, listening, questioning, reflecting feeling and content, interpreting meaning, confronting, and many other techniques are necessary for the social worker to master. Information-gathering skills are used by social workers in virtually every setting, practice area, and job function and apply to work with individuals, couples, families, and even professional teams and committees.

8. *Ability to analyze client information and identify both the strengths and problems evident in a practice situation.* Once information is collected about a client situation, the social worker must interpret its meaning and arrive at an assessment about its effects on the client's situation. This assessment often will be based on a combination of the social worker's experience or practice wisdom, as well as on various assessment tools that have been developed for social work practice.[2] Arriving at an accurate understanding of the problems in a case situation is central to most interpersonal helping. Yet the identification of problems does not provide a sufficient basis to resolve or overcome them. Social workers must also seek to identify client strengths as essential resources for problem resolution.

9. *Capacity to counsel, problem solve, and/or engage in conflict resolution with clients.* Interpersonal helping also includes basic skills in assisting clients to understand, accept, and come to grips with the issues in their lives that brought them to the social worker. Skills in counseling, values clarification, problem solving, and conflict resolution, for example, must be a part of the social worker's equipment. When working with clients, social workers should avoid, where possible, actions that take over aspects of clients' lives. Instead, they should attempt to maximize a client's participation in the change process and leave final decisions in the client's hands. After all, it is the client who must live with the results of those decisions.

10. *Possession of expertise in guiding the change process.* When engaged in interpersonal helping, social workers attempt to help their clients to bring about some kind of change in their lives. The social worker has a particularly important role in guiding that change process through its various phases. Typically, a helping situation is initiated by a client requesting service or being referred either to a human services agency or private practitioner. The worker must first *engage* the client in addressing and clarifying the situation and determine if the agency is the proper source of help. The latter is known as making an *intake* decision. Second, the worker and client cooperate in *data collection* and *assessment* of the information obtained so that both fully understand the nature of the problem or situation, as well as the various factors that may have contributed to it. Here, especially, the social worker must direct the process carefully, as the tendency is to move too quickly to action.

Third, the worker and client must develop a *plan* for accomplishing the agreed-upon change and reach agreement (i.e., a formal or informal *contract*) about how to address the issues and choose the activities each will carry out. Fourth, the actual *intervention(s)* will occur, and the social worker will *monitor* the change activities to determine if they indeed are helping. Finally, when the helping activity has run its course, the process will be *terminated* with the expectation that the client's social functioning has been stabilized at an appropriate level. Ultimately, the social worker should *evaluate* the overall process and apply what is learned from this evaluation to future practice activities. It is evident that the competence required for assisting clients in changing their social functioning is substantial and requires a social worker who is both knowledgeable about that process and skilled at moving through its several phases.

PROFESSIONAL COMPETENCE DEVELOPMENT. To their credit, all social workers devote a considerable amount of energy to improving the quality of their practice. To maintain high-quality practice the social worker in every position must carefully monitor his or her own work and continually engage in activities that will improve their job performance. To accomplish these goals, the social worker must regularly engage in activities that strengthen one's own practice effectiveness and expand one's professional competence. Some of the tasks involve self-assessment, that is, periodically taking stock of one's performance by evaluating actions and decisions made within the context of practice. Other tasks involve attendance at workshops, seminars, or professional meetings, as well as reading professional journals, magazines, and newspapers in order to keep abreast of new developments. The focus of the cluster is the perception of professional development as an ongoing process.

In their task analysis study, Teare and Sheafor found little variation among social workers in their commitment to the careful examination of their practice and the pursuit of increased knowledge and skill (see Box 8-2).

Professional development is a lifelong process. It includes both learning about practice and making contributions back to the profession through sharing one's own learning. Among the competencies required for professional development are the following:

1. *Ability to be introspective and critically evaluate one's own practice.* At the heart of professional development is self-assessment. One must be willing to critically

BOX 8-2 **Mean Scores for Professional Competence Development**

All Social Workers: 3.64	
BSW Direct Practitioners: 3.72	MSW Direct Practitioners: 3.61
	MSW Supervisors: 3.63
	MSW Administrators: 3.68

examine his or her own work and engage regularly in reflective thinking about practice events. When limitations are evident, there must be an effort to correct them. It is important in a profession to focus on both ethical aspects of practice and the quality of services provided. A thorough understanding of the *NASW Code of Ethics* is an important prerequisite to addressing ethical issues, while the availability of professional supervision and/or consultation provides a valuable perspective for recognizing and resolving professional issues. The social worker should also develop the capability to engage in ongoing practice evaluation wherein one's practice activities can be tracked and compared to service results.

2. *Ability to make use of consultation.* Effective professional practice requires that the worker obtain regular consultation regarding his or her service provision activities. While a professional is expected to practice with considerable autonomy and has final responsibility for his or her practice decisions, the social worker is not expected to conduct these activities alone. The use of consultation from peers is a hallmark of professions. Sometimes this consultation is provided by a supervisor, while at other times consultation from persons outside the administrative structure of the agency is obtained. In either case, the purpose is to offer guidance in making practice decisions or to provide a second opinion regarding decisions that have already been made.

3. *Ability to consume and extend professional knowledge.* The social worker must be committed to participating in a range of external activities that build his or her base of practice knowledge and skills. This might include attending staff training sessions and professional workshops and conferences, and regular reading of the professional literature. In addition, as social workers gain experience and insights from their practice, they are expected to share their understanding with others in the social work profession. The NASW Code of Ethics, for example, indicates that "the social worker should contribute to the knowledge base of social work and share with colleagues knowledge related to practice, research, and ethics."[3] That means contributing to social work's knowledge base and involves being competent to make conference presentations and prepare articles for publication in professional journals.

FREQUENTLY UTILIZED SOCIAL WORK COMPETENCIES

Six additional clusters of activity were regularly performed by most social workers, but were especially emphasized in work in one or more of the job functions. The competencies to perform these tasks, however, are sufficiently important for all social workers to master.

CASE PLANNING AND MAINTENANCE. The tasks included in the case planning and maintenance cluster require the worker to be competent to perform ongoing case planning, coordinate any additional services the client requires, monitor and evaluate case progress, obtain case consultation when appropriate, and complete required paperwork for case records. Tasks include preparing and reviewing case materials to assess progress, coordinating service planning with agency staff and providers from other agencies, and carrying out appropriate procedures (e.g., obtaining consent, explaining rights, and maintaining security in order to ensure that client's rights are protected).

As Box 8-3 indicates, this cluster of activities is most prominent among the direct service worker and supervisors—and is especially important for the basic social workers.

In addition to using the basic interpersonal helping skills required to perform these tasks, the particular competencies required for case planning and monitoring include the following:

1. *Expertise in service planning and monitoring.* Social work practice often involves oversight of a battery of services being offered to an individual or family. With the client, the social worker identifies the services already being provided and those still needed, and helps to develop plans for clients to gain access to resources that might prove helpful. Once the service plan is in operation, the social worker may then shift emphasis to monitoring the progress of the case to ensure that the plan, in fact, is working. This may include reviewing case records, consulting with other service providers both within the employing agency and elsewhere, and maintaining a professional relationship with the client to assess his or her ongoing perception of the helpfulness of the services being provided.

2. *Ability to carry out the employing agency's programs and operating procedures.* Agency-based social workers are agents of the organizations that employ them. Whether the programs are social provisions, social services, or social action, they are important tools for helping, and the social worker must know how to access those resources to benefit their clients. Often agencies require a frustrating amount of paperwork, but it is, nevertheless, essential to complete the required forms and recording. Human services agencies typically have a variety of procedures in place that must be followed by the worker so that information is recorded that will, for example, ensure that funds continue to be generated by the agency, continuity can be achieved should the social worker assigned to a case change positions, and appropriate monitoring by supervisors can take place.

3. *Knowledge of client background factors.* In conjunction with the case assessment that is part of one's interpersonal helping competence, the social worker involved in case planning must gather specific background information that can be

BOX 8-3 **Mean Scores for Case Planning and Maintenance**

All Social Workers: 3.46	
BSW Direct Practitioners: 4.02	MSW Direct Practitioners: 3.79
	MSW Supervisors: 3.45
	MSW Administrators: 2.89

used in creating a comprehensive approach to helping. Included among this information is the identification of such resources as friends, family, neighbors, coworkers, teachers, clergy, and other personal contacts that may offer assistance. The social worker must also obtain information from the client about current or past experiences with the human services delivery system in order to make judgments about the merits of connecting clients to particular resources as part of a package of helping services. Finally, the social worker serving as a case manager is responsible for ensuring that clients are informed of their rights and that confidentiality regarding their situation is properly protected even though services are being provided by several agencies.

4. *Skill in interagency coordination.* The social worker, as orchestrator of a battery of services and service professionals, must be knowledgeable about the availability of various resources and the requirements for gaining access to them and be capable of making sound professional judgments about their potential helpfulness. Further, the social worker must be skilled in communicating with persons with various professional backgrounds and creating networks among agencies and professionals to facilitate a coordinated approach to client services. This may mean exchanging information among agencies, planning and leading case conferences, securing case consultation when needed, and negotiating decisions about who will provide which services to an individual or family—and, importantly, who will pay for them.

5. *Ability to engage in case advocacy.* Ideally, services will be given to clients when they are needed. In reality, that is not always possible. At times, clients in crisis are placed on an agency's waiting list, an agency's eligibility requirements are rigidly interpreted in a way that does not fit the uniqueness of a particular client's situation, or many other factors may interfere with clients receiving needed services. In those cases, the social worker may become an advocate for the client and make appeals to his or her own or another human services agency to help clients obtain needed services. This may involve activities such as informing clients about an agency's appeal process, making a personal appeal to a social worker in another agency, or even representing a client before an agency's appeal board.

INDIVIDUAL AND FAMILY TREATMENT. Another set of tasks frequently performed by social workers in direct service positions involves providing treatment to individuals and families. Individual and family treatment requires that the social workers select and use clearly defined formal treatment modes or models to help individuals and/or families improve their social functioning or resolve social problems. Activities include the use of any of a wide array of interventive techniques and strategies ranging from nondirective to confrontational approaches.

This set of activities, as would be expected, is used mostly by direct service practitioners and especially by the specialized and independent-level practitioners as indicated in Box 8-4.

Box 8-4 **Mean Scores for Individual and/or Family Treatment**

All Social Workers: 3.24	
BSW Direct Practitioners: 3.35	MSW Direct Practitioners: 3.61
	MSW Supervisors: 3.14
	MSW Administrators: 2.89

Certainly the social worker engaged in treatment activities mixes the specific treatment approach selected with the basic interpersonal helping skills. However, the worker must also possess the following:

1. *Sufficient knowledge of human development to make in-depth psychosocial assessments.* The social worker engaged in clinical or treatment activities with individuals and families is required to have considerable knowledge about human functioning. He or she must be prepared with sufficient information about expected functioning for persons at different developmental levels to make a valid psychosocial assessment on which treatment plans can be developed. In addition to knowledge of normal development, the social worker must have sufficient knowledge to diagnose pathology, recognize deviance, and help clients recognize their own or others' dysfunctional behaviors.

In some settings the social worker is required to identify client issues according to the categories of the *Diagnostic and Statistical Manual for Mental Disorders* (DSM–IV).[4] This manual, developed by the American Psychiatric Association, describes symptoms, suggests criteria for making a diagnoses, and so on, for more than 200 mental disorders. Although it is not specifically intended for the diagnosis of problems in social functioning, many agencies utilize the DSM–IV, making it necessary for social workers employed in those agencies or in private practice to be knowledgeable about these diagnostic categories.

2. *In-depth knowledge of family functioning.* Just as the social worker must be skilled at assessing normal and problematic individual social functioning, one must also be prepared to diagnose factors affecting the functioning of families and other households. A rather substantial literature exists that identifies various types of family structures including the two-parent, single-parent, postdivorce, remarried or blended, and gay/lesbian households. Each has particular issues it must address if it is to attain stability and offer a positive environment to its members. Clinical social workers, especially, need to recognize that interactional patterns of families can have a profound and lasting impact on family members and that, with professional help, harmful patterns can often be corrected.

3. *Skill in the selection and application of individual and/or family treatment modalities.* To engage in individual and family treatment, the social worker must have mastered one or more specific treatment approaches. The range of specific approaches that a social worker might draw from is quite broad. Sheafor, Horejsi, and Horejsi, for example, identify the following as some of the practice frameworks social workers typically use:[5]

Psychosocial therapy	Task-centered model
Behavior modification therapy	Addictions model
Cognitive–behavioral therapy	Clubhouse model
Person-centered therapy	Self-help approach
Reality therapy	Family systems approach
Interactional model	Family therapy approach
Structural model	Family problem-solving approach
Crisis intervention	Family preservation model

This list would be extended considerably if one were to compile a list of all of the specialized individual and family treatment models and approaches that might be a part of a clinical social worker's repertoire. A social worker will typically begin by developing the necessary skill to carry out one or two approaches and later add to his or her repertoire as subsequent practice experience indicates the need for additional approaches.

DELIVERY SYSTEM KNOWLEDGE DEVELOPMENT. Among the helping professions it is social workers who are most likely to help clients manage the complex web of human services that exists in most communities. The tasks included in the delivery system knowledge development cluster suggest that the social worker must learn about the community's service delivery system and develop an understanding of various regulations, policies, and procedures that affect social programs. The focus of this cluster is on the gathering of information about the network of services and service resources within the social worker's geographic area. Activities include visiting agencies, attending meetings, and making contacts in order to become acquainted with or keep up-to-date with changes in the services provided, developing cooperative service arrangements among agencies, and keeping current on regulations, organizational policies, and agency guidelines.

Developing knowledge about the human services delivery system is an *indirect service*. It is work that develops important background information when serving clients, but it is usually conducted outside the presence of clients and is done without reference to a single client or group of clients. Engaging in interagency contact that yields this valuable information is a function performed by all social workers. However, as indicated in Box 8-5, the work of creating service agreements and participation in interagency coordination meetings is primarily the responsibility of supervisors and administrators. To carry out these activities the social worker must have the following competencies:

BOX 8-5   **Mean Scores for Delivery System Knowledge Development**

All Social Workers: 3.09	
BSW Direct Practitioners: 2.97	MSW Direct Practitioners: 2.89
	MSW Supervisors: 3.32
	MSW Administrators: 3.48

1. *Ability to maintain up-to-date knowledge of a variety of human services programs.* The effective social worker cannot be agency-bound. He or she must know the community—or at least the human services delivery system in the community. The worker must read about local, state, and national programs, visit human services agencies to gain in-depth knowledge of their programs and procedures for gaining access to those services, and regularly attend interagency meetings where one can be updated about changing programs.

2. *Skills in building interagency coordination and linkage.* Rarely is merely acquiring information sufficient for social work practice. Social workers must be prepared to act on that knowledge. In the case of knowledge about human services, social workers often develop linkage arrangements to facilitate information-sharing processes among agencies that regularly interact when serving clients. Sometimes that takes the form of interagency teams, such as a domestic violence team, where social workers must be skilled at interagency and interprofessional team building.

STAFF INFORMATION EXCHANGE.   As an agency-based profession, social workers must also be thoroughly versed about the programs and operating procedures in their own agencies. In addition, a worker must be prepared to contribute to the effective operation of that organization by working to resolve problems in agency functioning and contributing to decisions that strengthen the agency. This exchange of information among staff members is another indirect service activity of social workers. To be effective in information exchange, the social worker must be prepared to organize and/or participate in meetings or use other means of communication to exchange information with staff members, resolve job-related problems, and/or make decisions that affect agency functioning. The essence of the tasks in this cluster is the presentation and receiving of information, with individuals and in group meetings, in order to accomplish task-centered objectives.

Box 8-6 indicates that almost all social workers participate in this intra-agency exchange of information and decision making to some degree, although MSW-level private practitioners are an exception. However, the primary responsibility for facilitating this exchange falls to the supervisors and agency administrators.

To achieve effective intra-agency communication, all members of the staff must regularly participate in the giving and receiving of information. The following competencies are required of the social worker when performing these tasks:

1. *Ability to prepare and consume written and oral presentations regarding agency programs.* Much of the information about agency operation is transmitted

Box 8-6 **Mean Scores for Staff Information Exchange**

All Social Workers: 2.94	
BSW Direct Practitioners: 2.72	MSW Direct Practitioners: 2.56
	MSW Supervisors: 3.40
	MSW Administrators: 3.48

through written communication or formal staff meetings. This activity can consume considerable time, and, if it is not to detract from client services, the social worker must learn to read and write such materials quickly and accurately. Oral communication skills, too, are important. Knowing how to make formal presentations that are interesting and lively, yet emphasize the important content, facilitates effective communication of in-house materials. The bottom line, however, is that all staff members must have thorough knowledge of the employing agency's policies, programs, and operating procedures.

2. *Capacity to facilitate staff members' ability to make decisions and resolve problems.* In addition to sharing information, the members of an agency staff must regularly engage in activities that help the agency resolve problems and find ways to function more effectively. Typically this activity occurs through staff meetings, committee assignments, or team meetings. Knowledge of group dynamics, parliamentary procedure, and skill in moving group processes ahead all help to facilitate this activity. At times, the social worker may be required to use skills in consensus building, mediation, or negotiation in order to complete the work in this cluster of tasks.

3. *Ability to facilitate interdisciplinary collaboration.* In agencies that use the talents of several professions or disciplines in delivering their social programs, problems in interdisciplinary collaboration inevitably occur. Although the professions have carved out their boundaries or unique missions in general terms, in practice there are overlapping areas. Further, individual practitioners often drift in their practice activities toward the orientation of their colleagues, blurring even further the boundaries between the disciplines. When professional drift becomes excessive, clients lose the advantage of the perspective that each discipline offers and, sometimes, services are given by persons without sufficient preparation. Professionals, including all social workers, must be vigilant regarding interdisciplinary collaboration—facilitating appropriate collaboration and guarding against inappropriate professional drift.

RISK ASSESSMENT AND TRANSITION SERVICES. All direct service providers must carefully assess a variety of case situations. They regularly have to make judgments about the urgency for services or the consequences of not providing services. Based on that assessment they determine the type of services needed, facilitate the transition of clients from one service to another, and/or decide on the appropriateness of terminating the helping process. To perform these tasks, the worker must have the competence to assess a case situation to determine its difficulty (i.e., risk, urgency, or need) and engage clients either in making use of services or preparing them for transition or termination of services. Tasks include the observation of individuals and the gathering of information in order to decide if specialized services are required. In certain circumstances the worker will be expected to deal with hostile or unco-operative clients.

Sound assessment is prerequisite to all change efforts. However, as Box 8-7 sug-gests, the assessment of changing client conditions is more associated with the activ-ities of basic social workers. Their work often places them in the role of making intake decisions and planning for clients' transition from agency services to other agencies or, hopefully, providing them with the ability to maintain themselves with-out the support of social workers or human services programs.

It takes considerable knowledge to accurately assess a practice situation. The social worker must learn the client's perception of the reasons services are required, the viewpoints of significant people in the client's immediate environment, and, if working as part of an interdisciplinary team, obtain information others have col-lected. To engage in these assessment activities, the social worker should have the fol-lowing competencies:

1. *Ability to apply general systems and/or ecosystems theory when assessing fac-tors affecting a practice situation.* It is evident that the perspective one brings to the assessment process will affect the conclusions that are eventually reached. Due to the need for social workers to assess both personal and environmental factors, social workers have increasingly found various system-based theories particularly valuable because they allow the social worker to address interactions between systems (e.g., individual, family, neighborhood). The focus of the ecosystems perspective, for exam-ple, is on interaction among five elements in a practice situation: (1) individual(s) characteristics; (2) family life-style and dynamics; (3) cultural values and beliefs; (4) environmental-structural factors such as racism, sexism, or ageism; and (5) his-torical experiences that have contributed to the client's situation. Meyer notes that the ecosystems perspective allows "social workers to look at psychological phenom-ena, account for complex variables, assess the dynamic interplay of these variables, draw conceptual boundaries around the unit of attention of the case, and then gen-erate ideas for interventions."[6]

BOX 8-7 **Mean Scores for Risk Assessment and Transition Services**

All Social Workers: 2.79	
BSW Direct Practitioners: 3.20	MSW Direct Practitioners: 2.99
	MSW Supervisors: 2.85
	MSW Administrators: 2.43

2. *Skill in engaging clients in examining problems in social functioning.* An important part of social work practice involves helping clients explore the severity and intensity of the situation being addressed and determining if routine or emergency service is required. The most critical source of information for making such judgments is the client. The worker must be skilled in engaging clients in problem analysis. In some cases clients are involuntarily receiving services and sometimes are hostile or resistant to providing such information. In such cases, it is especially important that the social worker is skilled in recognizing client resistance and engaging clients in problem assessment.

3. *Skill in utilizing social work assessment techniques.* The ability to use specific assessment tools effectively is critical if a social worker is to make valid judgments about the severity of a particular case situation or is to make a decision about terminating service and/or helping clients with transition to other services. Examples of competencies a social worker might possess to accurately assess a client situation include mastery of assessment techniques such as ecomaps, genograms, or life history grids; the competence to help clients accurately identify and specify the problems to be addressed; and the ability to prepare clear and concise social functioning assessment reports for agency records and communication with other professionals.

4. *Skill in the use of crisis intervention.* If a risk assessment determines that a client (i.e., individual or family) is in crisis, the social worker must be prepared to act immediately. Meaningful change frequently occurs when the client is experiencing a crisis and the opportunity to be helpful is missed if the worker is not prepared to act. Crisis intervention requires rapid response over a limited time that is focused on a specific client emergency. The worker's focus is on helping the client make decisions that will resolve the crisis, and, if necessary, crisis intervention may require taking action that will protect the client as well as others.

5. *Ability to facilitate client transitions between services and/or to terminate service.* Helping clients make transitions from one service to another also requires considerable care and planning. Transitions might involve, for example, moving from one's own home to a foster home, from a hospital to a nursing home, from one agency to another, or simply from one social worker to another. Workers must be sensitive to the difficulty of such transitions for clients and carefully prepare them for these changes. When the service activity is completed, or if for some reason a different social worker is assigned to a case, clients must be prepared for the termination of the professional relationship. At times clients can feel that a meaningful person in their lives is lost, making termination a painful event.

STAFF SUPERVISION. Agency-based human services practice requires an additional indirect service competence—supervision of a variety of personnel with differing qualifications and job assignments. Some may be volunteers who provide various helping services, others may be staff members such as custodians and clerical staff, and still others are other social workers or human services providers. To provide staff supervision, one must be prepared to guide the day-to-day work of staff members (e.g., professional and clerical employees, volunteers, and/or students) by orienting them to the organization and its requirements, by assigning work and teaching them to perform their jobs, as well as by monitoring and assessing their performance. The tasks in this cluster encompass the array of tasks typically associated with supervision including the provision of job orientation and training by means of regular case review and critique, clarification of job duties and work expectations with individuals and groups, and the evaluation, interpretation, and feedback of job performance evaluations.

As Box 8-8 reveals, the oversight and direction of the work of agency personnel is not a significant responsibility of direct service practitioners, although it is not uncommon for either a BSW- or MSW-level social worker to direct the work of volunteers. Supervision is, however, a substantial part of the job of social workers who perform management roles in human services agencies—either as supervisors or agency administrators.

Many of the skills required for interpersonal helping are also important for supervising employees and volunteers. One must be skilled at collecting pertinent information, developing productive working relationships, assessing situations, and so on. In addition, the social worker engaged in staff supervision must have the following competencies:

1. *Knowledge of the literature regarding the supervisory process.* A rather abundant literature has emerged that can be of assistance to social workers who assume supervisory responsibilities.[7] This literature, for example, helps supervisors recognize that there is an administrative or monitoring component to supervision, a role in providing professional support to the worker, and an educational component through which the worker is helped to grow and develop in practice competence. This literature also suggests ways to structure supervisory learning processes so that it is of maximum value to the worker and yet is efficient in terms of the time invested by both the worker and supervisor.

2. *Capacity to facilitate the work of supervisees.* The ultimate payoff from good supervision is having supervisees who can perform their work efficiently and effectively. The supervisor must be clear about the job assignments of the workers and able to assess their strengths and limitations related to performing various assignments. Of critical importance is the ability to provide a sound orientation to the agency and job requirements when the worker (or student) begins the supervisory process. When necessary, supervisors also teach the workers practice skills and/or

BOX 8-8   **Mean Scores for Staff Supervision**

All Social Workers: 2.62	
BSW Direct Practitioners: 1.97	MSW Direct Practitioners: 2.28
	MSW Supervisors: 3.98
	MSW Administrators: 3.14

facilitate their attendance at training sessions or professional seminars in which their competence can be enhanced.

3. *Ability to conduct worker evaluation and professional development.* For the protection of both clients and the agency, the work of supervisees must be constantly monitored to ensure that high-quality service is provided and agency policies and procedures are appropriately carried out. In addition, the supervisor must be prepared to formally evaluate worker performance on a periodic basis, discuss that overall evaluation with the worker in a manner that will enhance professional growth, and supply the results of the evaluation for the agency's personnel records. Since these evaluations often become the basis for job promotion and salary increments, or possibly even job termination, they require accurate, fair, and sensitive interpretation and feedback from the supervisor.

COMPETENCIES OCCASIONALLY NEEDED BY SOCIAL WORKERS

The following seven task clusters of social work practice activity are occasionally performed by most social workers and more regularly required in one or more specialized job functions or practice areas. The competencies required to perform these activities should be a part of each social worker's repertoire of knowledge and skill, but one would not expect to use them on a daily basis in most social work jobs.

GROUP WORK. A cluster of tasks that have been a part of social work from the initial days of the Settlement House Movement are those associated with working with groups of clients. Although a powerful and efficient tool in both treatment and teaching activities, the use of group-centered techniques has diminished in recent years. Group work requires the social worker to use small groups as an environment for teaching clients skills for effective performance of daily living tasks, communicating information to enhance social functioning, or for facilitating problem resolution or therapeutic change. In these tasks, the worker consciously uses the group process in order to teach individuals how groups work and how to act as a member of the group. These tasks involve the worker in therapeutic groups as well as task-oriented work groups in organizations and communities.

The mean scores for the groups of social workers reported in Box 8-9 indicate that work with groups is at least a small part of all social workers' practice. However, it is the direct service practitioners at the specialized or independent levels that are most likely to apply group techniques as a part of their practice approach.

Like the individual and family treatment cluster, group work activities require the conscious selection of group processes as a means to address a practice situation. Group skills appear to be used most as a method of treatment by MSW-level social workers, but they also have application when teaching skills to clients or staff and in team meetings or other agency-related activities. Competencies required to perform these tasks include the following:

1. *Knowledge of group structure and function.* A sizable body of theory exists about the nature of groups and the dynamic nature of their functioning. Groups may

Box 8-9 **Mean Scores for Group Work**

All Social Workers: 2.43	
BSW Direct Practitioners: 2.36	MSW Direct Practitioners: 2.85
	MSW Supervisors: 2.37
	MSW Administrators: 2.16

be formed in social work practice for such varied purposes as therapy, training, mutual support, or social action. Some will be structured to maximize members' input into deliberations, while others will be focused on accomplishing specific tasks or making decisions. All, however, will be concerned with interaction among members as they engage in their work. The social worker needs knowledge of the phases of group development and skills in handling the power issues that characteristically arise in groups.

2. *Capacity to perform the staff role within a group.* Social workers are often responsible for constructing groups. They must be able to identify the criteria for selecting clients or others to participate in the group, recruit and screen potential members, and conduct the initial planning activities (e.g., arrange time and place to meet, invite members) that allow the group to come together. Depending on its purpose, when the group does meet, the social worker is most likely to perform such functions as helping the group determine its goals, providing information, teaching particular skills to the members, building consensus, discouraging those who tend to dominate and encouraging those who are reluctant to become involved, supporting group leaders, and so on.

3. *Ability to engage in group therapy.* In therapeutic groups, a social worker is likely to be particularly active in guiding the group's process. The worker should have considerable knowledge about each member and guide the process to ensure that his or her goals for being in the group are met while, at the same time, the group's goals are being attained. In this capacity the social worker is typically viewed as the group leader and an expert in facilitating group interaction. Yet the process belongs to the members, and the worker helps them to clarify their own issues by discussing them with each other and by using the group as a sounding board for decision making.

DISPUTE RESOLUTION. Like every form of organization, disputes inevitably arise in human services agencies. At times those disputes are between clients and the agency. A client may have been judged ineligible for service or may have expected resources that were not provided in a timely manner. Or a staff member may have been viewed as discourteous or unhelpful. It is within a client's rights to dispute these matters or even to file a formal grievance. Disputes may also exist between staff members or between a staff member and the administrator or board of an organization. Such disputes must be resolved if the agency is to devote maximum attention to client services. To be prepared to help resolve disputes, the social worker should be prepared to use advocacy, negotiation, and mediation to resolve interpersonal problems among staff members or between client/staff and the organization. These tasks involve interpersonal interactions in a "charged" organizational climate. The worker is expected to then listen to dissatisfied parties and mediate disputes at various levels in the organization.

As the person in the chain of command to whom a client would complain about a worker's actions and as the link between workers and agency administration, it is not surprising that supervisors are more likely to engage in dispute resolution than social workers in other jobs (see Box 8-10). It is also not surprising that the MSW direct practitioners are less involved in dispute resolution because those in private practice are not a part of an agency and therefore would not be expected to assist in such disputes.

In addition to using basic interpersonal helping skills to assist in dispute resolution, a social worker must also have the following two additional competencies:

1. *Understanding of agency procedures and its decision-making structure.* To address disputes, the social worker must not only be thoroughly familiar with the client's concerns but must be prepared to accurately relate those concerns to the agency's functioning. If a client's rights have been violated, the worker must understand how that relates to agency policies and procedures in order either to correct the problem or explain why it occurred. The worker also needs to understand the agency's structure so that the correct person or persons can be approached to address the problem or a strategy can be developed to correct agency procedures and prevent similar problems from occurring in the future.

2. *Skill in advocacy, negotiation, and mediation.* The social worker involved in dispute resolution is often in a position to help resolve the issue by advocating for the client's or another worker's interests, mediating the problem between the affected parties, or helping to negotiate a resolution of the matter. These skills should be a part of the repertoire of all social workers, but most specifically those who hold administrative or supervisory positions.

SERVICE CONNECTION. The maze of human services that has evolved is often confusing and difficult for clients to utilize. Social workers engaged in direct practice, in particular, must be able to help clients obtain the services they want or need. As brokers for the human services who link clients with community resources, social

---

Box 8-10 **Mean Scores for Dispute Resolution**

All Social Workers: 2.30	
BSW Direct Practitioners: 2.41	MSW Direct Practitioners: 2.07
	MSW Supervisors: 2.71
	MSW Administrators: 2.50

workers must be prepared to employ techniques that help clients to connect with established services and take action to eliminate barriers that prevent them from receiving those services. Activities in this cluster center on the linkage function, although some advocacy on the part of the worker may be required. Tasks include arranging transportation, following up by phone, and carrying out intake procedures.

It is the front-line workers who are most likely to spend time linking clients with services. Therefore, as Box 8-11 indicates, it is the BSW direct practice positions that make the heaviest demand on the service connection competency.

Service connection tasks overlap with some of those used in case planning and maintenance, but they differ to the extent that the worker engaging in service connection helps the client make the desired connection with a community service and then drops out of the picture. Service connection also overlaps somewhat with interpersonal helping, because those basic helping skills must be used to assist clients in determining the services needed. Additional competencies that are particularly important in this cluster of activity are the following:

1. *Maintaining an ongoing critical assessment of the battery of social programs in the community and region.* Social programs change rapidly. Printed and computerized directories are available in most communities, but they still do not provide the quality of information that a social worker needs to communicate to clients. When making service connections, social workers must be careful to provide accurate information because clients can become frustrated and discouraged if a referral is inappropriate and may not follow through and thus not receive needed assistance.

2. *Ability to make an accurate intake assessment of a client's needs and to skillfully refer clients to appropriate resources.* When clients enter the human services delivery system they often are not clear about just what services they need or where to get them. A familiar agency is sometimes the starting point, and the social worker must be prepared to help clients gain clarity about the issues that concern them and the services they require. Sometimes the social worker or others in the agency can provide the needed services, but at other times referrals must be made elsewhere. A social worker must make judgments regarding how directive to be when making a referral and might use techniques ranging from giving the client the name and telephone number of an agency, to making an appointment for the client, to arranging for transportation, or even to taking the client to the appointment. Research into the referral process indicates that fewer than one-half of all referrals actually result

Box 8-11 **Mean Scores for Service Connection**

All Social Workers: 2.30	
BSW Direct Practitioners: 3.08	MSW Direct Practitioners: 2.20
	MSW Supervisors: 2.16
	MSW Administrators: 1.95

in the client receiving service.[8] Human service brokering requires considerable care if a social worker is to successfully connect clients with other human services.

3. *Expertise in advocating for clients with human service programs.* Efforts to connect clients with services often fail because clients are placed on lengthy waiting lists or agencies are unwilling to make flexible interpretations of eligibility requirements that might permit serving the client that has been referred. It is important that social workers follow-up with clients who have been referred elsewhere to be sure that the connection was made. If the client has not received service, the worker may elect to actively advocate for that client with that agency. At times agencies will respond more favorably to the request of another helping professional than to the application of the client.

PROGRAM DEVELOPMENT.   Social workers who hold administrative or management positions often carry responsibility for either modifying existing programs or creating new ones. They must have the competence to document and interpret the need for additional human services programs, develop working relationships with relevant resources for program support (e.g., boards, funding sources, legislative bodies, referral sources), oversee implementation of new programs, and evaluate program success. The tasks in this cluster focus on the development of *new* programs or the *alteration* of existing ones. Workers convert program goals and concepts into specific plans, develop budgets and staffing plans, "sell" the program(s) to funding sources and other decision makers, and compile data for evaluation purposes. In this cluster, workers meet with resource people, explain needs, and encourage resource contributions.

As evidenced in Box 8-12, direct practice workers are usually only minimally involved in program development. A social worker in a supervisory position could expect some involvement, but it is the administrators who must possess the ability to assess community needs, design programs, garner support from funding agencies, install the new program in the agency, and evaluate its success.

The competencies required to successfully carry out this indirect service activity include:

1. *Skill in community and organizational data collection and analysis.* Program change or the creation of new social programs can be quite time consuming and expensive. Social workers engaged in program development must do their homework carefully to ensure that client services are not jeopardized by the enthusiasm for innovation. The skills required for program development include collecting and analyzing data about the adequacy of programs offered in their own agencies, as well as the ability to conduct community needs assessments that will help to place their programs in the context of the battery of human services in the community.

2. *Skill in the design and implementation of social programs.* Once a careful analysis of information regarding existing programs is completed, the social worker engaged in program development must develop a plan for new or revised programs that will more adequately respond to the community's needs. The program must be carefully designed and issues addressed as to who will be eligible, where services will

Box 8-12   **Mean Scores for Program Development**

All Social Workers: 2.27	
BSW Direct Practitioners: 1.87	MSW Direct Practitioners: 1.82
	MSW Supervisors: 2.44
	MSW Administrators: 3.19

be provided, what it will cost, who will deliver the service or social provision, what practice approach will be used, and how its effectiveness will be evaluated. The social worker must then develop a budget identifying the anticipated income and expenditures required to start the operation of the program and describe specific plans for its implementation.

3. *The capacity to obtain agency and/or community support for new or revised programs.* Gaining support for change requires considerable effort. The social worker promoting either program modification or the creation of a new program must have the support of the staff and board (or responsible legislative body) where it will be located. Securing such support requires knowledge of organizational change processes and skill in presenting and interpreting the merits of the proposed programs. Typically, this does not happen without a long period of planning and involvement of board and staff members in the process of developing the proposal for change.

Obtaining support for new programs from the community requires additional skills. It often requires coalition building among human services agencies and other interested parties. The coalition can then select a strategy and create an action plan to develop support for the program. Program development, at times, involves the social worker in the preparation of grant applications for initial support of the program, and in public education activities such as speaking before community groups, preparing news articles, conducting radio and TV interviews, and lobbying individuals for support.

INSTRUCTION.   Most social workers engage in a certain amount of teaching. Much of their teaching is in informal work with clients to help them learn skills for addressing the issues they face in life. However, many social workers also engage in instructional activities in which a planned curriculum is delivered to groups of clients, agency staff members or volunteers, students, or community groups. To provide instruction effectively, the social worker must be prepared to plan, arrange, conduct, and evaluate programs that enhance the knowledge or increase the skills of staff members, students, agency volunteers, or participants in community groups. This cluster deals with formal instruction rather than the kind of informal teaching associated with orientation or on-the-job training. Activities involve course planning, syllabus design, test construction, and course evaluation.

Formal instructional activities are typically a relatively minor part of the direct practitioner's workload (see Box 8-13) but are a more substantial part of the work

Box 8-13   **Mean Scores for Instruction**

All Social Workers: 2.20	
BSW Direct Practitioners: 1.80	MSW Direct Practitioners: 1.81
	MSW Supervisors: 2.32
	MSW Administrators: 2.50

of supervisors and administrators. These experienced agency staff members are the persons usually designated to perform the more advanced teaching roles in both the agency and the community.

Several special competencies are required to fulfill the formal teaching roles of social workers and include the following:

1. *Capacity to develop curriculum for instruction or training programs.* Sound instruction requires a carefully developed curriculum. Whether helping parents learn more effective ways to deal with the inevitable problems their children experience or teaching foster parents about expected phases of child development, the curriculum must be based in the best available literature and delivered in a carefully sequenced and organized manner. Unfortunately, it is rare that a social work education program, even at the doctoral level, teaches how to develop curriculum. On some topics prepackaged curricula are available, but more typically social workers are on their own to develop a curriculum.

2. *Skill in planning workshops, seminars, or classroom sessions.* Once a curriculum is developed, it must be delivered. The logistics of announcing the meetings, recruiting the participants, ensuring that there is a quiet and comfortable meeting space with plenty of parking, arranging for refreshments, having the necessary instructional materials available, and so on, all call for careful planning. Failure to attend to these planning matters can negate even the best content.

3. *Ability to engage students, trainees, or groups of clients in learning activities.* Social workers are usually skilled in engaging their audience in learning. Their skills in group work, adapting to client interests, and basic communication skills serve them well when teaching. Because the content is typically aimed at helping the audience learn how to do something, the teaching style is likely to be more interactional than the styles used in standard classroom instruction where the goal is more oriented to transmitting information to students.

4. *Capacity to assess and evaluate instructional activities.* Instructional programs tend to be repeated and, while good instruction requires adapting to each audience, critique of instructional activities provides an important base for the next round of instruction. The competent instructor, therefore, must develop or adopt instruments that accurately assess the students' learning experience and invite suggestions for ways to improve the value of the experience for participants.

STAFF DEPLOYMENT. Human services agencies are labor intensive, that is, they work with relatively few tangible products and most of their resources are invested in people. Therefore, an important indirect service activity for some social workers is the deployment of staff in a way that makes efficient use of staff time (the most valuable commodity for an agency) and ensures that the appropriate personnel are available to serve clients. To perform this set of tasks effectively, a social worker must recruit and select staff (e.g., professional and clerical employees, volunteers, and students), arrange staffing patterns and workload assignments, monitor staff productivity, and oversee compliance with organizational policies. Tasks in this cluster concentrate on the ensurance of staff coverage and equitable workload distribution, along with scheduling and coordinating working hours, leave, and vacation, and monitoring service demands.

The data in Box 8-14 make it clear that direct service practitioners rarely engage in staff deployment activities. This work, however, is a substantial part of the activity of supervisors and administrators who are charged with the responsibility to implement the programs of the agency in a way that is both efficient and effective.

As opposed to most other supervisory tasks that are focused on the development of the staff members, staff deployment tasks are primarily concerned with the functioning of the agency. These tasks require the following competencies:

1. *Capacity to match personnel with job assignments.* To accurately select and assign staff and volunteers to the various tasks that must be performed, it is necessary for the supervisor or administrator to have considerable knowledge of the work to be done and the capacities of available staff members. If needed skills are not present, it is important to then seek that competence through additional personnel and, at times, the replacement of existing personnel. Thus, the social worker in this capacity must be skilled at personnel selection and recruitment, as well as in appropriately matching the resources to the needs of the agency.

2. *Ability to create a clear organizational structure for conducting the work of the agency and a fair means of assigning the workload.* Human services workers are known for their dedication and willingness to extend well beyond the typical expectations for a job. They are equally known for their intolerance of time wasted due to organizational inefficiencies. It is, therefore, important that those social workers involved in personnel deployment are skilled at maintaining an equitable plan for

Box 8-14 **Mean Scores for Staff Deployment**

All Social Workers: 2.08	
BSW Direct Practitioners: 1.48	MSW Direct Practitioners: 1.57
	MSW Supervisors: 3.18
	MSW Administrators: 3.14

assigning workload, a clear and fair set of personnel rules and regulations that provides for both professional autonomy and agency responsibility, and a reasonable plan for monitoring the performance of the staff members. Specific activities that might be performed to accomplish these goals include assigning tasks, coordinating working hours, planning vacation time, making arrangements when personnel are on sick leave, and so on.

3. *Skill in the development of instruments for the evaluation of worker performance.* Supervisors are responsible for the evaluation of those staff members they supervise. The staff deployment personnel, additionally, are responsible for assessing the broader picture of how well all of the personnel mesh their talents to meet the agency's goals. To make those judgments, it is important to monitor changing service demands and worker competencies in order to determine staffing requirements. Worker performance evaluation requires carefully constructed performance measures that can be applied to workers throughout the organization and will yield valid information for assessing the agency's effectiveness.

PROTECTIVE SERVICES. The very young and the very old are among the most vulnerable members of U.S. society, and social workers are often in a position to protect both children and older people from potential physical, mental, or economic abuses. Some social workers are employed for the primary function of serving as agents of the society to offer protective services when there is suspected abuse. To provide those services, the social worker is required to collect and analyze data to be used in assessing at-risk clients and presenting information to appropriate authorities if clients are judged to be in danger of physical and emotional maltreatment or of having their basic rights violated. This includes the observation and assessment of children and/or adults to determine whether they have been abused or neglected. As part of this process, the worker may be expected to start legal proceedings and testify or participate in court hearings involving custody, competence, outplacement, or institutionalization.

Box 8-15 provides evidence that the provision of protective services is not a universal activity of social workers, despite the amount of television time devoted to social workers removing children from abusive situations. It is primarily basic social workers working on the front lines of public human services agencies that deal with the complex family situations that require protective services.

The following are examples of special competencies required to provide effective protective services. These specific competencies need to be used in addition to the competencies already described, especially those associated with interpersonal helping, individual and family therapy, case planning and maintenance, and risk assessment:

1. *Capacity to identify at-risk factors such as physical and emotional maltreatment.* Abusive situations are difficult to identify because abuse often occurs within a family or other living situation and is not readily evident to outsiders. The abusers attempt to conceal the maltreatment, and the persons being abused are often intimidated to the point they are fearful of reporting or even admitting they

Box 8-15 **Mean Scores for Protective Services**

All Social Workers: 2.03	
BSW Direct Practitioners: 2.39	MSW Direct Practitioners: 1.98
	MSW Supervisors: 2.15
	MSW Administrators: 1.71

have been abused. A variety of literature and workshops are available to help social workers providing protective services develop the needed competencies to work in these situations.

2. *Knowledge of the law and legal processes concerning protective services.* In most states it is mandatory that any helping professional report suspected abuse or maltreatment. When abuse is suspected, the legal and human services systems join together to investigate and, when appropriate, take action to prevent further abuse and resolve issues that contribute to the abuse. To perform this service the social worker not only needs good clinical skills but must also be thoroughly familiar with the relevant laws and legal processes that apply.

3. *Knowledge of local resources to be contacted if clients are in danger.* In some abusive situations the client is in immediate danger and the social worker must be prepared to seek police protection, make arrangements for temporary placement outside the home, or take other needed actions to protect the client. The worker engaged in child protection work must be thoroughly informed about the available resources and how to gain access to them.

4. *Ability to deal with conflictual situations.* People are typically frightened and angry when a social worker enters an abusive situation. The worker must be able to diffuse situations where high levels of conflict are present and assist clients to attempt resolution of issues in a calm and peaceful manner.

ORGANIZATIONAL MAINTENANCE. A certain amount of effort in every organization is devoted to carrying out its programs as efficiently as possible. Organizational maintenance activities require a social worker with the necessary knowledge and skills to manage the ongoing operation of a program or administrative unit to ensure its efficient and effective functioning by securing, allocating, and overseeing the utilization of its resources (e.g., staff, funds, supplies, space) and marketing its services. This cluster includes a wide array of tasks concerned with the operation of an existing program or unit. Some of the tasks center on financial operations, for example, estimating budgets, documenting and reviewing expenditures, and compiling billings, cost reimbursement, and cost control documents. Other tasks deal with the maintenance of a physical plant, control of inventory, and working with staff and vendors in order to ensure smooth program operations.

This day-to-day detail work is not usually the responsibility of a social worker unless he or she serves in an administrative role in the agency. For administrators (see Box 8-16), however, organizational maintenance tasks are a key part of the work to be done.

The following competencies are necessary to conduct the activities associated with organizational maintenance:

1. *Understand the operation of basic business systems and the requirements for oversight of agency resources.* The administrator must see that the scarce resources available to most human services organizations are used prudently. Public scrutiny of these agencies is typically high, requiring that administrators create and implement carefully developed measures of accountability. Systems must be developed for such activities as estimating budgets, documenting and reviewing expenditures, compiling billings, managing funds, maintaining the physical plant, securing necessary supplies, and so on. These administrative activities are essential for the efficient operation of the agency.

2. *Skill in creating and managing agency paperflow.* At times the excessive demand for accountability in human services agencies creates an enormous amount of paperwork, and administrators must attempt to protect workers from devoting excessive time to this administrative detail. To plan programs that maximize staff efficiency, social work administrators should possess knowledge of computer word processing and data analysis, should be able to create systems for the collection and storage of agency records, and should be skilled in implementing cost control programs.

3. *Skill in marketing and fund-raising for human services organizations.* Organizational maintenance also requires that the social worker be prepared for the continuing activity of making the services of the agency known in the community. Potential clients need to be made aware of the services that might be secured from the agency, and the general public needs to be informed on a regular basis about the important role the agency plays in enhancing the quality of life in the community. This public relations activity is a prerequisite for another important activity, that is, securing funds to operate the agency's programs. In addition to documenting, justifying, and monitoring the regular flow of funds from client fees, tax sources, and/or United Way allocations, effort must also be made to generate supplemental funds through such sources as foundation grants, agency benefit events, and personal bequests.

Box 8-16 **Mean Scores for Organizational Maintenance**

All Social Workers: 1.82	
BSW Direct Practitioners: 1.56	MSW Direct Practitioners: 1.42
	MSW Supervisors: 2.00
	MSW Administrators: 2.64

LOW UTILIZATION COMPETENCIES
FOR MOST SOCIAL WORKERS

The final two task clusters, research and policy development and tangible service provision, were not a central part of the activity of any group of social workers. Both sets of activity were central to social work in its historical development but appear to be at best a secondary activity for social workers today. The low scores for research and policy development, when combined with somewhat low scores for program development and public education (i.e., instruction), generates an important question for social work. Has this profession abandoned its mission to address the societal, as well as the individual, causes of social dysfunctioning? The even lower scores for tangible service provision also raises a question. Has social work abandoned its commitment to the most vulnerable members of the society, that is, those who are in need of the most basic resources of food, clothing, and housing?

RESEARCH AND POLICY DEVELOPMENT. From its early development in the state boards of charity, settlement houses, and charity organization societies, research and social policy development has been an integral part of social work practice. If social workers are to assist communities to improve social conditions or contribute to improved social conditions through influencing laws or regulations at the state or federal levels, they must be skilled at collecting data about those social conditions and assist policy makers as they apply that knowledge to various social policies and programs. In short, the worker must be prepared to collect, analyze, and publish data; present technical information to the general public, legislators, or other decision makers responsible for changes in human services programs or community conditions; and/or interact with community groups. While the tasks in this cluster involve a wide assortment of research, public relations, and community outreach activities, most of them are concerned with influencing public opinion, public policy, or legislation. The worker may collect and compile information, conduct surveys, present or publish findings from studies, testify as an expert witness, or organize and take part in campaigns or demonstrations.

The data presented in Box 8-17 indicate that for the typical social worker it is very rare to engage in this activity. Even the MSW-level administrators (Mean = 1.99) who are in roles where they are most likely to interface with community decision makers are not regularly involved in research and social policy development activities. The data may, however, underrepresent the full involvement of social workers

---

Box 8-17 **Mean Scores for Research and Policy Development**

All Social Workers: 1.72	
BSW Direct Practitioners: 1.48	MSW Direct Practitioners: 1.51
	MSW Supervisors: 1.66
	MSW Administrators: 1.99

in this area. The job function data do not report the social work educators (5.6% of the sample) who conduct the major part of social work research. These university-based social workers had a 2.63 score on this cluster of tasks.

What competencies does a social worker need to perform the research and policy development tasks? The following are necessary:

1. *Ability to develop and implement program and needs assessment research.* Sound policy development begins with valid information. Much discussion of social policy is highly tinged with emotion and political rhetoric. An important mechanism for minimizing the effect of political manipulation in policy and program decisions is fact. If social workers simply bring more or different emotion to the bargaining table, helpful social policy is unlikely to emerge. Thus, social workers must be prepared to collect accurate data to serve as the foundation for social policy analysis.

2. *Skill in social policy analysis and influencing decisions of policy makers.* With a sound data base, social workers are then prepared to assess existing and proposed social policies to determine a proposed policy's potential for resolving social problems and/or enhancing the overall quality of life for members of the society. For most social policy changes, some people will gain and some will lose. Social workers must be prepared to use one or more of the available policy analysis techniques to arrive at their conclusions and develop defensible positions on the proposals. Armed with a solid analysis, the social worker then calls on an additional set of competencies as he or she carries out a strategy to influence the outcome through actions intended to influence the decisions of those who finally establish the policy or program.

3. *Capacity to inform the public regarding social problems and potential solutions.* A part of influencing social policy is public education. An uninformed public is unlikely to support any significant change. Social workers are often in a position to see the effects of existing social policies as they affect their clients in positive or negative ways and, therefore, it is important for them to share that knowledge through speaking to public groups, working with the media, and so forth.

TANGIBLE SERVICE PROVISION.   At the heart of social work's self-image is its concern that the poor and most at-risk members of the society have their basic needs met through the provision of adequate food, housing, clothing, and fundamental social supports. To provide these basic human services, social workers must be prepared to deliver a variety of "hard" tangible services designed to assist people coping with problems or activities associated with daily living. These activities focus on meeting the basic needs of clients as they cope with everyday life. Tasks include teaching budgeting, money management, food preparation and homemaking skills; helping clients find jobs and housing; and putting clients in touch with people of similar backgrounds and experience. Workers may visit clients to assess the suitability of living arrangements and take part in leisure activities to help them reduce loneliness.

The scores from the task analysis study contained in Box 8-18 suggest that most social workers are not meaningfully involved in delivering tangible services. Only

Box 8-18 Mean Scores for Tangible Service Provision

All Social Workers: 1.60

BSW Direct Practitioners: 1.98   MSW Direct Practitioners: 1.56
                                          MSW Supervisors: 1.51
                                          MSW Administrators: 1.49

the BSW direct practitioners report even a limited amount of practice activity that involves assisting clients to receive basic social provisions.

Those social workers who are involved in tangible service provision need to be competent in the following areas:

1. *Knowledge of local resources that provide clients with social provisions such as shelter, food, clothing, money, and employment.* In virtually all communities and in most legislation creating social programs, the responsibility for implementing programs is assigned to several different human services agencies. For example, financial assistance, housing, job counseling and placement, and a food bank would usually be located in different agencies in different locations. "One-stop shopping" is rare in the human services. The social worker, then, must be familiar with the social provisions that are available and know how clients can gain access to them.

2. *Ability to develop positive helping relationships with clients requiring basic social provisions.* Social stigma is often attached to needing these basic services. To help clients make use of these provisions and, where possible, become self-supporting, social workers need to establish good working relationships characterized by empathy and trust. Such a relationship can become both supportive and a motivating factor in bringing about lasting change.

3. *Competence in teaching clients to use resources effectively.* It is said that the successful social worker works himself or herself out of a job. Indeed, the competent social worker can teach clients to do many things for themselves—including how to gain access to resources when needed and how to use those resources in a way that helps them achieve independence from the human services.

Concluding Comment

For a profession with the broad mission of helping people interact more effectively with their environments, it is not surprising that the identification of common features that bind social work practitioners into one profession has proven difficult. It is only at the somewhat general level of defining its mission that social workers have gradually moved toward consensus. Agreement at this broad conceptual level, however, does not necessarily indicate that at the more concrete level of day-to-day practice there is sufficient similarity in the work performed to consider this a single profession.

Drawing on data from a national task analysis study of social work and examining the clusters of work activity regularly performed by social workers, it has been possible to obtain a reasonably clear picture of social work practice. It is evident from these data that there is a core of helping tasks that most social workers regularly perform, as well as some that only a relatively few perform. One can reasonably conclude that in practice, as well as in theory, social work can stand as a single profession. Many tasks are regularly performed by most social workers, supporting the view that a common core of activities exists in the many expressions of practice.

In the preceding pages a set of competencies social workers are expected to possess are identified. These expressions of the tasks associated with each cluster provide a relatively clear overview of social work practice and represent one of the first data-based descriptions of what social workers need to be able to do to carry out their professional obligations.

KEY WORDS AND CONCEPTS

Competence	Primary job function
Mean	Direct practice
Task analysis	Supervision
Cluster of practice activity	Administration
Universal practice competencies	Indirect service activities

SUGGESTED READINGS

Raymond, Ginny Terry, Teare, Robert J., and Atherton, Charles R. "Is 'Field of Practice' a Relevant Organizing Principle for the MSW Curriculum?" *Journal of Education for Social Work* 32 (Winter 1996): 19–30.

Sheafor, Bradford W., Horejsi, Charles R., and Horejsi, Gloria A. *Techniques and Guidelines for Social Work Practice,* 5th Edition. Boston: Allyn and Bacon, 2000.

Teare, Robert J., and Sheafor, Bradford W. *Practice-Sensitive Social Work Education: An Empirical Analysis of Social Work Practice and Practitioners.* Alexandria, VA: Council on Social Work Education, 1995.

ENDNOTES

1. For example, see Laura Epstein, *Talking and Listening: A Guide to the Helping Interview,* 3rd Edition (New York: Macmillan, 1991); Alfred Kadushin, *The Social Work Interview,* 3rd Edition (New York: Columbia University Press, 1990); Bradford W. Sheafor, Charles R. Horejsi, and Gloria A. Horejsi, *Techniques and Guidelines for Social Work Practice,* 5th Edition (Boston: Allyn and Bacon, 2000), pp. 134–170; and Lawrence Shulman, *The Skills of Helping: Individuals, Families, and Groups,* 3rd Edition (Itasca, IL: F. E. Peacock, 1992).

2. Sheafor, Horejsi, and Horejsi, pp. 301–396.

3. National Association of Social Workers, *Code of Ethics* (Washington, D.C.: National Association of Social Workers, 1996).

4. American Psychiatric Association, *Diagnostic and Statistical Manual of Mental Disorders,* 4th Edition (Washington, D.C.: American Psychiatric Association, 1994).

5. Sheafor, Horejsi, and Horejsi, pp. 97–113.

6. Carol H. Meyer, "What Directions for Direct Practice?" *Social Work* 24 (July 1979): 271.

7. See, for example, Douglas R. Bunker and Marion J. Wijnberg, *Supervision and Performance: Managing Professional Work in Human Service Organizations* (San Francisco: Jossey-Bass, 1988); Alfred Kadushin, *Supervision in Social Work,* 3rd Edition (New York: Columbia University Press, 1992); Bradford W. Sheafor and Lowell E. Jenkins, eds., *Quality Field Instruction in Social Work* (New York: Longman, 1982); and Carlton Munson, *An Introduction to Clinical Social Work Supervision,* 2nd Edition (New York: Haworth, 1993).

8. Laura Epstein, *Brief Treatment and a New Look at the Task-Centered Approach,* 3rd Edition (New York: Macmillan, 1992), p. 137.

CHAPTER 9

Prevention as a New Direction: The Future of Social Work

Prefatory Comment

The nature of social work practice has been able to demonstrate flexibility based on public needs within the context of political and economic opportunities and constraints. The latter appears to be the case in the late 1990s and as we enter into the twenty-first century. Assisting social work practice in this regard are intervention concepts such as *prevention,* originally developed by the medical and public health professions. The social work profession is challenged to develop its own prevention theories grounded on psychosocial concepts as demonstrated in this chapter. Following an in-depth discussion of *prevention,* the remainder of the chapter will examine the topic areas of: (1) the role of social workers ensuring a person's right to treatment, or nontreatment, and even preventing treatment abuse with involuntary clients; (2) the potential role of social work intervention in the prevention of violence and homicide in gangs; (3) the application of advocacy and empowerment concepts in working with clients as a foundation to develop primary prevention strategies for nonclient populations; and (4) the continued development and testing in the courts or *class action social work* as a primary mental health prevention tool.

Prevention: An Evolving Concept Going into the Twenty-First Century

As human services budgets were drastically reduced during the 1980s and into the 1990s, an increasing number of people continued to need services. Substance abuse, child abuse, crime and delinquency, homelessness, AIDS, and the breakdown of the family are social problems that also continue to increase. Even in the most favorable economic periods for the human services, the mental health needs of the U.S. population have far surpassed the nation's financial and manpower resources to meet these needs. For example, it is estimated that there are anywhere from 1 to 2 million children in the United States each year who suffer physical or sexual abuse or neglect. Considering that each case could cost society $7,000 to treat, the total treatment expenditure might amount to $14 billion. The Department of Health and Human Services, however, spends less than $30 million per year for the treatment of child abuse and neglect. Federal and state agencies spend approximately $500 million per year for alcohol treatment services and yet treat less than 10 percent of all addicted alcohol abusers.[1] To live with increasingly limited financial and professional personnel resources while not losing sight of the potential of progressive health and welfare policies, were they to be someday passed by Congress, could result in less costly interventive approaches impacting larger numbers of people. Theories of *prevention*, therefore, have to be developed and applied to practice.

PREVENTION

Contemporary mental health conceptual formulations of prevention have as their foundation public health prevention theories and practice. In public health terms, prevention, as previously noted, has three stages. *Primary prevention* indicates actions taken prior to the onset of a problem to intercept its cause or to modify its course *before* a person is involved. It is the elimination of the noxious agent at its source. Through systematic spraying of affected ponds, for example, malaria-carrying mosquitoes, their eggs, and larva are destroyed before they have the opportunity to infect humans. *Secondary prevention* involves prompt efforts to curtail and stop the disease in the affected persons and the spreading of the disease to others. *Tertiary prevention* involves rehabilitative efforts to reduce the residual effects of the illness, that is, reducing the duration and disabling severity of the disease. In its most succinct form, therefore, prevention has three stages: prevention, treatment, and rehabilitation.

In 1977, the National Institute of Mental Health established an Office of Prevention to stimulate and sponsor large-scale programs of research on prevention. This office has also assisted the Council on Social Work Education to prepare curriculum materials about prevention.[2] The director of the Office of Prevention developed the following definition of primary prevention within a mental health context:

> Primary prevention encompasses activities directed towards specifically identified vulnerable high risk groups within the community who have not been labeled psychiatrically ill and for whom measures can be undertaken to avoid the onset of emotional disturbance and/or to enhance their level of positive mental health.[3]

Primary preventive programs were for the promotion of mental health, as educational rather than *clinical* in conception and practice, with their ultimate goal being to help persons increase their ability for dealing with crises and for taking steps to improve their own lives.[4] Goldston identifies two goals in primary prevention: (1) to prevent needless psychopathology and symptoms, maladjustment, maladaptation, and "misery" regardless of whether the end point might be mental illness; and (2) to promote mental health by increasing levels of wellness among various defined populations.[5] This places an emphasis on strength and positive qualities, in contrast to the problem-centered focus found in the medical model.

In applying primary prevention to child abuse, for example, intervention program efforts can be developed at three different levels. On a macro, social-reform level, prevention interventions may include legislation to protect children's rights, abolishment of corporal punishment, advocacy for abortion, and a more equitable economic distribution of resources. A second level of primary prevention intervention, also macro in impact, may utilize educational approaches aimed at a variety of audiences. This may include, for example, educating and sensitizing society to basic issues in child abuse and its deterrents, the use of newsletters and "crash courses" to provide helpful information to young families, and teaching adolescents in public schools essential skills needed in their future parental roles. A more focused primary prevention practice strategy, which is directly concerned with the operation of intrafamilial variables, involves utilizing homemaker and home visitor services to provide support and crisis assistance to at-risk families with young children. The visitors could be hospital-based personnel, day care, child support workers, or community volunteers.[6]

Preventing Treatment Abuse with At-Risk Populations

An at-risk population group with whom social workers should be concerned is juveniles who in fact have *not* committed crimes, yet are involuntarily coming to the attention of private psychiatric hospitals and the public juvenile justice system. Congress enacted the Juvenile Justice and Delinquency Prevention Act of 1974 as a decriminalization and deinstitutionalization effort designed to prevent young people from entering a "failing juvenile justice system," and to assist communities in developing more sensible and economical alternatives for youths already in the juvenile justice system.[7] The Act was successful; arrests for status offenses or "crimes" which, had they been committed by adults, would not have been considered crimes (such as truancy, running away, or incorrigibility), declined 15.8 percent (569,481 arrests to 466,885 arrests) between 1974 and 1979.[8] The 1980s presented a mixed picture, as juvenile crime nationally was decreasing yet more juveniles were institutionalized. In Minnesota, for example, even though there was a decrease in institutionalization in public juvenile training institutions, there was a tremendous growth in the numbers of youths admitted "voluntarily" to inpatient psychiatric settings in private hospitals.[9]

Many allege that poor adolescents who are genuinely mentally ill but whose parents do not have the economic resources or insurance coverage are not receiving the specialized treatment that affluent youths with less severe problems receive, and the poor are tracked instead into the public juvenile justice system.[10] Setting aside the potential economic conflict-of-interest issue for private hospitals and the double standard of treatment for the affluent and the poor, are the rights of hospitalized, affluent adolescents being abused?

Saul Brown, head of psychiatry at Cedars-Sinai Medical Center in Los Angeles, believes the issue of patients' rights is a misguided one and that giving adolescents the right to decide whether they need treatment abrogates a certain kind of parental reason. The United States Supreme Court ruled in 1979 that parents had the right to commit their children to a psychiatric facility if qualified medical professionals did the admitting. However, the ruling applied *only* to state hospitals. This situation has been referred to as a *legal twilight zone*. The California Supreme Court has asked the legislature to conduct an inquiry into psychiatric facilities being used by parents as "private prison hospitals for their incorrigible children."[11]

On the one hand, while some affluent white adolescents expressing behavioral disorder symptoms are being involuntarily committed by their parents to private psychiatric hospitals, risking the long-term psychosocio-political consequences of a psychiatric label, some poor adolescents—mostly minorities—who have not committed any crimes and are expressing behavioral disorder symptoms are being labeled criminal by law enforcement officials and tracked prematurely into the public juvenile justice system. They will have to suffer the long-term consequences of a criminal label. The U.S. Department of Justice has developed and funded the SHODI (Serious Habitual Offenders—Drug Involved) program in five cities: Oxnard and San José, California; Portsmouth, Virginia; Jacksonville, Florida; and Colorado Springs, Colorado. The purpose of the SHODI program, according to Oxnard Police Chief Robert Owens, is to (1) identify the most serious offenders, ages thirteen to seventeen; (2) ensure they receive stiff sentences; and (3) keep the youths off the streets for the longest period of time. The criteria to be labeled a SHODI is three arrests in the past year and two previous arrests (three of the five arrests must be for felonies); or three arrests in the past year and seven previous arrests (eight of the ten arrests must be for petty theft, misdemeanor assault, narcotics, or weapons violations).[12] The most controversial aspect of the program is that a juvenile who has never been convicted of a crime (or allegations found to be true and sustained in a juvenile court proceeding) could be classified by police as a habitual offender because criteria are based on arrests, *not convictions!*

With reference to the affluent white and poor minority adolescents being prematurely labeled and tracked into the private psychiatric hospitals and public juvenile justice systems, the values social workers place on self-determination, right to nontreatment, opposing discrimination, and treatment abuse may require them to assume a position and take action. Those adolescents who are definitely a danger to themselves or others, who are severely psychiatrically disabled, or who chronically damage property or commit acts of violence, based on *convictions*, may indeed have to be institutionalized for their and/or society's protection. Social workers must support these detentions and make sure the youths receive proper treatment rather than punishment. This role would be consistent with *tertiary prevention*. However, for those youngsters whose acting out is not harmful or who have numerous arrests that are related more to police deployment practices rather than predelinquent behavior of poor minority adolescents, social workers should assume a *secondary prevention* role as advocates encouraging intervention at the family and community level rather than harsher measures such as institutionalization. *Primary prevention* intervention involving educational and employment alternatives for at-risk families and youths might consist of evening workshops or seminars for affluent families concerning the stresses and pressures some affluent adolescents suffer; for example, the fear that they will not be able to achieve as well as their parents in a tight economy that places the cost of a home out of reach for many. For poor communities, primary prevention community education programs could focus on helping families learn to cope with the stresses of migration, urbanization, gangs, and drugs. Youths would be provided assistance in school or helped to obtain employment if they chose not to remain in school.

Gang Violence and Homicide Prevention

Numerous polls show that the nation's number one problem is youth violence. In addition to pending crime bills, President Clinton is advocating proposals that limit the availability of guns and is attempting to influence the media to show less violence on the screen. U.S. Attorney General Janet Reno has threatened a "crackdown" on Hollywood over television violence.[13] Reno goes even further when she states that the United States has passed white South Africa as having the highest number of people in jail per capita. She is described as being "remarkably" interested in *preventing* crime rather than just punishing it, reflecting a shift in priority that, if she succeeds, could leave a lasting mark on law enforcement nationally.[14]

Youth violence is increasing dramatically. According to the Department of Justice between 1987 and 1991 the number of adolescents arrested for homicide in the nation increased by 85 percent. In 1991 youths from ten to seventeen accounted for 17 percent of *all* violent crime arrests. Youths are not only the perpetrators, they are also the victims. Violent youth gangs, which are now present in 126 cities across the nation, are responsible for many of these homicides.[15] Like the nation, the president, and the U.S. attorney general, the profession of social work has to be concerned and challenged and has to address this national problem of gang violence and homicide with its own psychosocial-based theories of prevention. What follows is one approach in addressing this problem, first anticipated and reported in social work in this text in the late 1980s.

A seventeen-year Chicago study involving 12,872 homicides reported that more than half of Hispanic youth victims were killed in gang-related altercations.[16] In 1985, 10.5 percent of 2,781 homicide victims in California were killed by gangs, and in Los Angeles 24 percent of 1,037 homicides were gang-related.[17] Other large urban areas with gangs also have significant numbers of persons being assaulted and/or killed by gangs. This violence exacts an extremely high toll in injuries, death, and emotional pain and adversely impacts the quality of life for thousands of poor residing in the inner cities.

The public health profession, with its focus on epidemiologic analysis and prevention, believes it can make a substantial contribution to solving problems of interpersonal violence. Former Surgeon General C. Everett Koop stated that "violence is every bit a public health issue for me and my successors in this century as smallpox, tuberculosis, and syphilis were for my predecessors in the last two centuries."[18] The health professions are making their initial bold entry into this major problem area, following in the footsteps of criminology, sociology, and the criminal justice system. Psychiatry and psychology have been investigating the issue primarily from a biological (brain chemistry) and behavioral (modifying the behavior of *individuals*) perspective. The social work profession, with its micro- to macrolevel knowledge and skills base, is ideally suited to apply its techniques with individual gang members, gang groups, and the community to reduce urban gang violence and homicide. In addition to employing social work's traditional approaches in dealing with the problem, the present task is to devise ways in which prevention theory, with corresponding intervention models, can be applied.

It was stated earlier that *primary prevention* in a public health context involves averting the initial occurrence of a disease, defect, or injury. Primary prevention in homicide requires national efforts directed at the social, cultural, educational, technological, and legal aspects of the macro environment which facilitate the perpetuation of the country's extremely high homicide rate—indeed a tall order. A national strategy would involve public education on the seriousness and ramifications of violence, contributing factors, high-risk groups, and need for social policy as a physical health and mental health priority in the United States. The topic must become a higher priority in medical schools and schools of nursing, social work, and psychology. At the community level community self-help groups, social planning councils, and other civic groups need to work toward educating U.S. citizens about the causal relationship of alcohol, illegal drugs, firearms, and television violence to homicide and violence.[19] In theory these strategies, when directed at high-risk populations, are supposed to reduce those conditions that are seen as contributing to violence and homicide.

Secondary prevention in a public health context concerns the cessation or slowing down of the progression of a health problem. It involves the early detection and case finding by which more serious morbidity may be decreased. Applying this concept to homicide, such case finding requires the identification of persons showing early signs of behavioral and social problems that are related to increased risk for subsequent homicide victimization. Variables such as family violence, childhood and adolescent aggression, school violence, truancy or dropping out of school, and substance abuse are early indicators of many persons who later become perpetrators of violence and homicide. Secondary prevention intervention strategies with individuals already exhibiting these early symptoms interrupts a pattern that may later result in serious violence or homicide.[20]

Tertiary prevention pertains to those situations in which a health problem is already well-established, but efforts can still be made to prevent further progress toward disability and death. In the case of homicide, the problems of greatest concern are those of interpersonal conflict and nonfatal violence, which appear to have a high risk for homicide. Aggravated assault is one early significant predictor related to homicide.[21] In a study in Kansas, in 25 percent of the homicides either the victim or the perpetrator had previously been arrested for an assault or disturbance.[22] Victims of aggravated assault, such as spouses or gang members, are at especially high risk for becoming homicide cases.

Attempts have been made to develop program models aimed at preventing youth violence and homicide, although some of these programs are not specifically aimed at *gang* homicide prevention. These educational-, court-, and community-based programs seem to be functioning mainly at the primary (reducing conditions contributing to homicide) and secondary (identifying persons showing early signs of sociobehavioral problems) prevention levels. A few of these programs, as examples of prevention models, will be discussed.

EDUCATIONAL PREVENTION MODELS

The *Boston Youth Program* instituted in four Boston high schools had a curriculum on anger and violence. The ten-session curriculum provided (1) information on adolescent violence and homicide; (2) the discussion of anger as a normal, potentially constructive emotion; (3) knowledge in developing alternatives to fighting; (4) role-playing and videotapes; and (5) the fostering of nonviolent values. Following the completion of the program, an evaluation of a control group (no curriculum) and an experimental group (curriculum) revealed that there was a significant, positive change of attitude in the experimental group. The researchers cautioned, however, that further study had to delineate the actual impact the curriculum would have on actual *behavior,* and the longevity of the impact.[23] The Boston Youth Program was directed at minority students, but it was not indicated whether any of these students were gang members.

Peer Dynamics is another school-based program, sponsored by the Nebraska Commission on Drugs, which was designed to reduce the incidence of destructive risk-taking behaviors associated with juvenile delinquency and substance abuse among high school adolescents in fifty-six public schools. With the goal of developing improved self-esteem and better communication skills, the program trained and supervised students who participated in group interaction activities with other students. A follow-up evaluation found that in relationship to other students, program participants showed a noticeable drop in discipline referrals. The final evaluation noted that Peer Dynamics affected both sexes equally and that the greatest changes were noted in eighth-, tenth-, and eleventh-grade students. No significant change in attitude toward themselves or others was reported in the control group.[24] Again, this was not a program designed specifically for gang youths, although some gang members may have been participants. The question remains, however, whether improved *attitudes* result in less violence and homicide.

A third school-based prevention program functioning in the city of Paramount in Los Angeles County is called the *Paramount Plan.* This was designed to be a "gang-prevention" model and, unlike the Boston Youth Program and Peer Dynamics that target high school youths, it is an educational model directed at *all* fifth and sixth graders in the school district. The program consists of neighborhood parent meetings and an antigang curriculum taught to students in school for fifteen weeks. Prior to the program, 50 percent of students were "undecided" about joining gangs. After the fifteen weeks, 90 percent said they would not join gangs.[25] No mention was made of the 10 percent of students who did not change their minds about joining gangs. In poor urban areas where there are gangs, only 3 to 5 percent of youths become delinquents and/or join gangs. In other words, at least 95 percent of youths do not join gangs even without a gang-prevention program such as the Paramount Plan. Further research is needed to determine if those in the 10 percent who did *not* change their minds about joining gangs actually do, and second, whether they later become either perpetrators or victims of gang homicide. Perhaps one of the major research challenges is to be able to measure what was prevented.

COURT- AND COMMUNITY-BASED PROGRAMS

In Baltimore, Maryland, *Strike II* was developed as a court-based program linking juvenile justice with health care. Its "clients" were court adjudicated first-time offenders (secondary prevention) for violent crimes, assault, robbery, arson, and breaking and entering. Noninstitutionalized probationers were eligible for the program, which was a probation requirement. This multidisciplinary program employed paralegal staff, counselors, social workers, and psychiatrists. The juvenile probationers were involved in five programs: recreation, education, job readiness, and ongoing counseling and medical care as needed. These services were in *addition* to traditional probation supervision.

The recidivism rate for Strike II clients was only 7 percent, compared to 35 percent statewide and 65 percent for those leaving corrections institutions. The basic cost (excluding medical and job readiness services) was $100 per client.[26] With impressive results, the Strike II program dealt largely with violent juveniles in a physical health/mental health, educational, employment, juvenile justice program. Although gang members were not mentioned specifically, it would appear that with a reduction in recidivism these perpetrators would also have been at reduced risk for becoming violence/homicide victims.

Another community-based program, aimed specifically at gangs, was called *House of Umoja*. It was developed in Philadelphia by two inner-city black parents whose son had joined a gang. His fellow gang members were invited to live with the family, following the model of an extended African family. In response to increased gang-related homicides in 1974 and 1975, the House of Umoja spearheaded a successful campaign to reduce gang violence by obtaining peace pledges from eighty youth gangs. From this experience evolved a community agency called Crisis Intervention Network that worked toward reducing gang violence through communication with concerned parties and organizational efforts.[27] This approach later was called the *Philadelphia Plan*.

In 1978 the state of California Youth Authority reported its findings concerning its *Gang Violence Reduction Project* in East Los Angeles. The project's basic strategy was to (1) promote peace among gangs through negotiation; and (2) provide positive activities for gang members. Directors maintain they reduced gang homicides in East Los Angeles 55 percent, from eleven homicides in seven months of one year down to five homicides during a similar seven-month period the following year. The project researchers admitted that "any judgment that a relationship exists between the changes in gang-related homicide and violent-incident statistics and the activities of the Gang Violence Reduction Project must be based on inference."[28]

Another community-based peace-treaty program targeting high-risk gang youth, patterned after the Philadelphia Plan, is the *Community Youth Gang Services Corporation* in Los Angeles. CYGS counselors in fourteen street teams were able to convince forty-four of 200 gangs they worked with to come to the table to develop a "peace treaty." During the period the peace agreement was in effect, from Thanksgiving of 1986 through the New Year's holidays of 1987, there was only *one* act of violence among the forty-four gangs. The peace-treaties model can "buy time" for all concerned, but if society does not respond with the needed resources (employment, job training, physical health/mental health services, education), peace treaties are very difficult to maintain. Obviously, *all* the above approaches are needed.

GANG HOMICIDE PSYCHOSOCIAL PREVENTION MODELS

Continuing efforts have to be made in further refining homicide prevention models in order for them to correspond more closely with the specific type of homicide one wishes to prevent. There are different types of homicide that vary according to circumstances. Robbery, spousal, and gang homicide are all different and require different prevention strategies. If, for example, Asian Americans are at extremely high risk for being robbed and murdered at 2 AM in Uptown, U.S.A., through a community education effort Asian Americans would be informed about the high homicide risk in visiting Uptown at 2 AM. Adhering to the warning could immediately reduce the number of Asian American homicide victims.

In addition to attempting to get a "close fit" between the prevention model and the specific type of homicide, it is equally important that the high-risk person be clearly identified in order to maximize the impact of the prevention model. In the educational- and community-based violence prevention models previously discussed, the focus of intervention appeared to be more on the perpetrator or the "pre-perpetrator" (the person showing early behavioral signs indicating he or she *might* become a perpetrator) who was at high risk for committing a violent act. In theory all potential victims in an *unspecified* population are spared victimization when the perpetrator ceases to be violent. Furthermore, there did not seem to be specific prevention programmatic strategies focusing on the violence *victim* or the person most likely to become a victim. What seems to be needed is a guideline or framework that assists in the identification of high-risk gang members.

Using California as an example, Table 9-1 represents a "general to specific" profile framework for identifying and "zeroing in" on the high-risk gang members who will be the target population for homicide prevention.

For our purposes, we will attempt to develop a hospital-based and community-based youth gang psychosocial homicide prevention model in which social workers play a key intervention role. The focus of these prevention models will be on the gang member who actually becomes a violence or homicide victim of a gang and goes or is taken to the hospital. In Table 9-1 these victims would be the gang members found in items 2b and 2c. In this respect the prevention models are largely tertiary in nature. However, they become primary prevention models when intervention strategies are aimed at younger children and latency-age siblings of the victim who are not yet gang members. By preventing children in high-risk families from becoming future gang members, the likelihood of the children being killed may be significantly reduced, because gang members are nearly sixty times more likely to be killed than persons in the general population (519/100,000 versus 10/100,000).

TABLE 9-1	**Area and Demographic Characteristics Related to Homicide Risk**
I. United States	One of the most violent countries in the world, ranked no. 5 out of 41 countries
II. California	Along with Southern states, ranks among the most violent states
III. Los Angeles	Among the more violent cities in the U.S.
IV. Inner City (L.A.)	The poorest areas, often the scene of most violent crime
A. Minority Groups	Overrepresented among the disadvantaged, poor, and those residing in the inner city
1. Profile of Perpetrators and Victims	
a. Males	4 to 5 times more likely than females to be killed
b. Age	15–25 age category at highest risk
c. Substance Abuse	Found in 50 to 66 percent of cases
d. Low Education	50 percent school drop-out rate not uncommon
e. Low Income	High unemployment, many living in poverty
2. Gangs	Quite prevalent in inner city and a product of social disorganization
a. Minor Assaults	Gang members are at high risk for being assaulted
b. Aggravated Assaults	Gang members are at high risk for being victims of aggravated assault; occurs 20 to 35 times more often than homicide
c. Homicide	Gang members are at high risk for becoming homicide victims, rate being 519 per 100,000 in the 150,000 gang-member population

Sources: M. L. Rosenberg and J. A. Mercy, "Homicide: Epidemiologic Analysis at the National Level," *Bulletin of the New York Academy of Medicine* 62 (June 1986): 382; H. M. Rose, "Can We Substantially Lower Homicide Risk in the Nation's Larger Black Communities?" *Report of the Secretary's Task Force on Black and Minority Health,* Vol. 5 (Washington, D.C.: U.S. Department of Health and Human Services, January 1986); I. A. Spergel, "Violent Gangs in Chicago: In Search of Social Policy," *Social Service Review* 58 (June 1984): 201–202; A. Morales, "Hispanic Gang Violence and Homicide," Paper presented to the Research Conference on Violence and Homicide in Hispanic Communities, Los Angeles, September 14–15, 1987, p. 13; *Los Angeles Times,* Wednesday, October 5, 1995, p. B-9; A. Morales, "Homicide," in Richard L. Edwards, ed., *Encyclopedia of Social Work,* 19th Edition (Washington, D.C.: NASW Press, 1995).

HOSPITAL-BASED MODEL. Health professionals in community clinics and hospitals are actually in the "trenches," dealing with thousands of violence and homicide casualties related to gang violence. These professionals are usually the first to touch these bodies, and in medical settings they function in a tertiary prevention role, literally trying to control bleeding and save lives. Wounded gang victims of gang violence are in reality a "captive audience," which creates an excellent intervention opportunity for secondary prevention.

Through the physician, social worker, nurse, or other health practitioners on the hospital emergency room team inquiring *how* the victim was injured (which may be confirmed by police, family members, or interested parties), professionals could ascertain if the incident was gang-related. Through in-service staff training concerning gangs and their culture, health staff would be able to determine whether the victim was a gang member. Specifically, dress codes, mannerisms, graffiti, language, tattoos, and other gang symbols could help establish or rule out the gang identity of the victim. Police, family members, peers, and/or witnesses could also be good sources for gang identity confirmation.

If the injuries were caused by gang members and the victim is a gang member, a designated health team member (the social worker) would be responsible for referring the matter to the hospital's SCAN Team. "SCAN Team" refers to Suspected

Child Abuse and Neglect, or in some hospitals, Supporting Child Adult Network.[29] SCAN Teams, which are found in many hospitals, are composed of multidisciplinary health staff in which at least one member is a social worker. SCAN Teams were originally developed to investigate suspected child sexual or physical abuse or neglect cases coming to their attention in medical settings. In cases of suspected child abuse, for the protection of the child SCAN Teams are required to take immediate action by involving law enforcement and the child-welfare department.

Our gang-homicide prevention model would require that gang violence victims also become a SCAN Team intervention priority. However, one additional social worker on the SCAN Team would be a gang "specialist" and have primary treatment-coordinating responsibility with the gang victim, his or her family, and the community.

Although not intentional, the emergency room provides access to a high-risk population (victims and families) that is often too embarrassed, frightened, or reluctant to seek assistance from traditional social work agencies. The anonymity of a large, busy, impersonal hospital can be less threatening.[30] Additionally, medical crises may make some persons psychologically vulnerable, hence more amenable to change during the crisis period.

In working with gang members who have been seriously injured as the result of gang assault, the author has found that often this is when their psychological defenses are down because they are suffering adjustment disorder or posttraumatic stress disorder symptoms (PTSD). In the acute stage of PTSD symptoms, victims may have recurrent, intrusive, distressing recollections of the event, including nightmares, flashbacks, intense stress at exposure to events resembling the traumatic event, persistent avoidance of stimuli associated with the event, sleeping problems, hypervigilance, anxiety, and fear. They are sometimes reluctant to leave the home and even become fearful of their own friends in gang "uniform."

During this acute stage, which may last about six months, they are quite motivated to abandon "gang banging" (gang fighting). If the social worker is not the primary therapist, arrangements should be made for the youth to receive prompt treatment for PTSD while hospitalized, as untreated PTSD may become chronic and last for years. It is at this point that the social worker can also obtain needed employment, educational, recreational, or training resources for the vulnerable gang member. The parents may also be emotionally vulnerable, having just gone through an experience in which they almost lost their son or daughter. They may be more willing to accept services for themselves, if needed, and/or for younger siblings who might be showing some early behavioral signs of problems (deteriorating school performance, truancy, aggressiveness). Helping the family and young siblings is a *primary prevention* role, as these efforts may prevent future gang members (perpetrators or victims) from developing in this at-risk family.

There also may be situations in which the gang member arrives deceased at the hospital or dies during or after surgery. These cases would still be referred to the SCAN Team social worker for service. The focus of help would be—with the family's permission—helping the parents and other children deal with grief and providing any additional assistance they may need in burying their loved one. If there are adolescent gang members in the family, they may be quite angry and want to get even for their brother or sister's death. If not already involved, the social worker would call on community gang group agencies to assist in reducing further conflict. If there are younger siblings in the family, an assessment would be made of their needs, and efforts would be made to mobilize resources to meet these needs. These intervention strategies would have the objective of preventing future homicides in a high-risk family.

The preceding gang homicide prevention model operating from a medical-based agency is presented to illustrate how social work may be able to have intervention impact on a very serious problem shortening the life of many poor, inner-city youths. Figure 9-1 illustrates the various intervention strategies of the hospital-based gang homicide intervention model. Other models can be developed, such as the community agency-based model described in the following paragraphs.

COMMUNITY AGENCY-BASED MODEL. An example of an inner-city community agency-based model that the author is currently developing and implementing with the help of a full-time social worker and a second-year clinical social work intern, is a clinical program funded by the Kellogg Foundation. The agency, Challengers Boys and Girls Club, founded in 1968 by Lou Dantzler, is located in South Central Los Angeles, a poor, predominantly African American area. This community was the hardest hit in all of Los Angeles as a result of the April 29, 1992, riot, which was this nation's most destructive and deadliest riot, resulting in sixty deaths and nearly a billion dollars of damage.

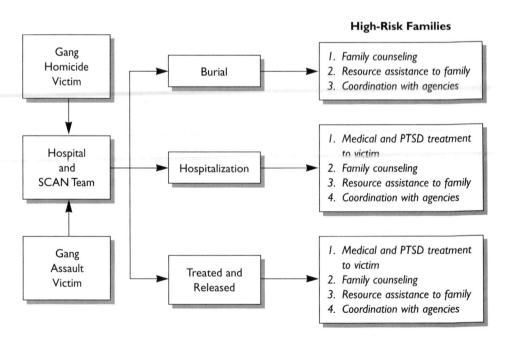

FIGURE 9-1 Gang Homicide Psychosocial Prevention Model

Within a three-mile radius of the agency are approximately 22,000 youths in a population of 379,000 persons, with 43 percent of the households headed by 15,000 single mothers over sixteen years of age with children up to eighteen years of age. This community has exceptionally high rates of school dropouts (56% of seventeen-year-old African American youths are functionally illiterate), AIDS, diseases of the heart, sexually communicated diseases, and homicide. Neighborhood homicide rates at 95 per 100,000 are almost twelve times the national rate, four times the Los Angeles rate, and at 600 per 100,000 in the neighborhood's gang population.

The agency, with 2,100 enrolled families, has an average daily attendance of 400 boys and girls (ages six to seventeen) during the summer months; 200 during the rest of the year. Program services, in addition to athletic and recreational services, include tutoring, classes in basic math, reading comprehension and computers, photography, woodshop, job application training, a new basic dental and health examination program, and mental health crisis intervention.[31]

In establishing a gang-homicide psychosocial prevention model, an assessment has to be made regarding the severity of the gang-related violence and homicide problem. Local law enforcement statistics are mandatory in this regard. Table 9-2 demonstrates the extent of the problem in the above targeted area.[32]

The target area is a very active, violent community, clearly contributing to making many young ethnic/racial youths an endangered species as they approach adolescence and young adulthood, being killed at the rate of 600 to 1,000 per 100,000 in the gang population, depending on the gang-related homicides for a given year.

The mental health crisis intervention program, staffed by the author as a mental health consultant, a full-time social worker, and a clinical social work trainee is available to those member families who experience a sudden, severe crisis such as the premature death of a family member brought on by an accident, suicide, or

TABLE 9-2 **Prevalence of Gangs and Gang-related Violent Crimes**

Total No. of Gang Members	24,200
Latino Gangs	204
African American *Crips*	109
African American *Bloods*	45
Types of Gangs: *Criminal* (making $); and *Conflict* (turf-oriented)	

No. of Gang-related Crimes (5/1992 to 5/1993)	
Homicide	133
Attempted Homicide	247
Felony Assault	1259
Robbery	1034
Discharging Firearm into Inhabited Dwelling	61
Battery on Police Officer	19

Source: South Bureau, Los Angeles Police Department, 1993.

homicide. These tragic events are known to leave a spouse or parent emotionally immobilized for months and, at times, even for years. The death of a child results in a more severe grief reaction for a parent than that of any other family member.[33] The surviving siblings' loss may be more than that of the surviving parent because they have lost not only an immediate family member but also the grieving parent(s) who is temporarily emotionally unavailable to them. During this time, depending on their prior adjustment, age, and emotional strength, these children are at high risk for emotional, educational, and behavioral problems. Prompt intervention (assessment, counseling, and possible referral in acute cases) may lessen and *prevent* a child from having more serious difficulties and problems of adjustment. In specific cases where the sibling was a gang member and the victim of a gang homicide, younger adolescent or pre-adolescent siblings are at especially high risk for becoming either future victims or perpetrators of gang violence and homicide.

In this inner-city, agency-based, gang-homicide psychosocial prevention model, nearly 100 high-risk African American and Hispanic elementary school children (mostly males) were referred for treatment for assaultive, fighting behavior directed at peers either at school, at home, in the neighborhood, or at Challengers. Of these, ten cases were more directly impacted by violence. For the purposes of brevity, only two of these cases will be commented on.

In one case, a fourteen-year-old Challengers member was the victim of a "drive-by" shooting outside his home by a gang group. The youth was not a gang member, yet met the general, stereotypic profile of a gang member held by many police and gang members; that is, he was a minority male adolescent residing in the poor, inner-city neighborhood. A bullet to his brain resulted in four months' hospitalization and permanent neurological impairments, including dependence on a wheelchair. Ongoing supportive visits were made with the youngster at the hospital, along with conversations with medical and social service staff and his guardian aunt. (His mother had passed away three years previously due to illness, and his father was in a correctional facility.)

On release, efforts were made to reintegrate the youngster into the Challengers program components, with supportive counseling as needed and assistance in applying for victim's assistance and Social Security benefits. The victim did not have younger or adolescent siblings, hence other family members were not at risk for gang homicide as future victims or perpetrators.

The second case concerned a ten-year-old suicidal boy, whose father had been killed by a robber twelve months previously, and his paternal uncle three months before. The boy was experiencing school behavioral problems, sleep disturbance, and some somatic complaints, including vomiting. The mother had already taken the boy to a child guidance-counseling program and was now enrolling the youngster in the Challengers recreational program. The agency made available to the mother an adult supportive counseling group, led by the mental health consultant and social worker, for family members who have lost a loved one due to a sudden, premature death. The mother herself was seen individually, with plans to later involve her in a group with similarly affected families. Such groups are also needed for children and adolescents. Additionally, outreach efforts are made with law enforcement and other community agencies, hospitals, and churches to identify high-risk families who had a child who was a gang member and was killed as the result of gang violence. These families, in their psychological state of vulnerability, were extended an invitation to become part of the Challengers program. As they began to participate in the program, they received a host of social, recreational, educational, dental, health, and mental health services. It was anticipated that the cycle of gang violence and trauma, with its accompanying sequelae of psychosocial problems, was lessened.

Advocacy, Empowerment, and Prevention

Briar defines the social worker advocate as one who is:

> . . . his client's supporter, his advisor, his champion, and if need be, his representative in his dealings with the court, the police, the social agency, and other organizations that affect his well-being.[34]

On the other hand, Brager sees the social worker advocate as one who:

> . . . identifies with the plight of the disadvantaged. He sees as his primary responsibility the tough-minded and partisan representation of their interests, and this supersedes his fealty to others. This role inevitably requires that the practitioner function as a political tactician.[35]

Briar's concept represents advocacy on behalf of an *individual*, whereas Brager's concept represents advocacy on behalf of a group or *class* of people. The latter concept is similar to the role social workers would perform in *class action social work*, discussed later in this chapter.

Gilbert and Specht report that advocacy as a social work role (social change versus psychological change) has presented a dilemma for generations of social workers. Each generation redefines this issue in its own terms. For example, in 1909 Richmond defined the issue in terms of the "wholesale" versus the "retail" method of social reform. Lee approached it in 1929 as "cause" versus "function," and in 1949 Pray perceived it as "workmanship" versus "statesmanship." In 1962 Chambers conceptualized the matter in terms of "prophets" versus "priests," and in 1963 Schwartz analyzed this conflict in terms of providing a service as opposed to participating in a movement.[36] In 1977, in a special issue of the journal *Social Work* on conceptual frameworks for practice, Morales perceived the issue differently. He saw social workers as persons armed with appropriate knowledge and skills that enabled them to do clinical work in poor communities as well as to intervene via social action and advocacy in larger community systems.[37]

Social workers can help clients help themselves through the application of concepts such as *empowerment*. Solomon defines *empowerment* as:

> . . . a process whereby persons who belong to a stigmatized social category throughout their lives can be assisted to develop and increase skills in the exercise of interpersonal influence and the performance of valued roles. Power is an interpersonal phenomenon;

if it is not interpersonal it probably should be defined as "strength." However, the two concepts—power and strength—are so tightly interrelated that they are often used interchangeably.[38]

According to Solomon, empowerment, as a social work practice goal in working with African American clients or other persons living in oppressed communities, implies the client's perception of his or her intrinsic and extrinsic value and the client's motivation to use every personal resource and skill, as well as those of any other person that can be commanded, in the effort to achieve self-determined goals. Solomon attempts to develop a conviction in the client that there are many pathways to goal attainment and that failure is always possible, but the more effort one makes the more probable success must be.[39]

Solomon suggests three practitioner roles that hold promise for reducing a client's sense of powerlessness and leading to empowerment: the resource consultant role, the sensitizer role, and the teacher/trainer role. The resource consultant role finds the practitioner linking clients with resources in a manner that enhances the clients' self-esteem and problem-solving capacities. Minahan and Pincus identify five specific practitioner tasks for accomplishing this.[40] In the sensitizer role, the practitioner incorporates all the role behaviors that are designed to assist the client to gain the self-knowledge necessary for him or her to solve the presenting problem or problems. The teacher/trainer role, according to Solomon's conceptualization, finds the practitioner as manager of a learning process in which the principal aim is the completion of certain tasks or the resolution of problems related to social living.[41]

A *voluntary* relationship seems to be implied in Solomon's conceptualization when she speaks of the practitioner assisting the client to gain self-knowledge to solve problems. The practitioner does not appear to be working from a social control perspective in which the presenting problem is defined by someone other than the client. Such "helping" transactions might make *involuntary* clients feel powerless.

In prevention theory a social worker helping *clients* through advocacy and empowerment concepts would seem to be using a secondary prevention strategy, because the target population is already identified as persons with problems. The social worker has a significant role and performs specific key tasks in advocacy and empowerment efforts with the client. In applying advocacy and empowerment concepts toward primary prevention goals, however, the social worker's role is not central as it is in working with client populations. Rather, the role is multiple since the at-risk target population is comprised largely of nonclients or "unaffected" persons. The focus must be on strengths foremost in the target population, as opposed to problems, weaknesses, and inadequacies.[42]

One of the essential tasks of the social worker in working with an at-risk population toward primary prevention will be to network. Network may be defined as the process of developing multiple interconnections and chain reactions among support systems.[43] There are four levels of networking approaches: (1) personal networking; (2) networking for mutual aid and self-help; (3) human services organization networking; and (4) networking within communities for community empowerment.[44] The last approach will be highlighted as it has *primary* prevention goals.

The community empowerment model and process has several goals. The first is to create community awareness of neighborhood strengths and needs, with emphasis on strengths as perceived by the target population. The second goal is to strengthen neighborhood helping networks by developing linkages among natural helpers in the community, among helpers and neighborhood leaders, and among neighborhood residents themselves. A third goal is to strengthen the professional helping networks by organizing a professional advisory committee in the target population area to advise this community empowerment-directed process. Fourth, linkages are formed between the lay and professional helping networks. The fifth goal is to form linkages between the lay and professional helping networks and the macro system. In a mental health primary prevention context, mental health professionals would help the target population put together a database of information regarding federal, state, county, and local mental health and human services plans, or the macro system. The sixth and final goal would be to institutionalize the networking process, thereby creating a new mental health constituency, integrated into but not assimilated or taken over by the larger, bureaucratic human services system. Through such a networking process leading to community empowerment and an improvement in the quality of life, those problem areas that the professional system traditionally ends by treating (secondary and tertiary prevention) rather than preventing, the at-risk population may be spared unnecessary pain, stress, and anguish.[45]

Class Action Social Work and Prevention

The enormous mission of social work is to enhance the quality of life for all persons. Some of the injustices and obstacles that damage the quality of life are poverty, racism, sexism, and drug abuse; there are many more.[46] Social work's impact on these problems is sometimes limited by the clinical model, by inappropriate interventive strategies, and by the fact that it becomes too time-consuming and inefficient to try to help people on a case-by-case basis. On other occasions a referred client with a "problem" may not really have a problem. The problem may be in the referral system.

For example, a school may refer a problem student to a social worker to help him or her adjust to the requirements of the school system. The school system, however, may have serious defects that are the primary cause of the student's problem. The goal of the social worker should then be to help tailor the school system to meet the educational needs of the student. The student in this situation may represent a *class* of people, that is, a number of students in a similar predicament. Rather than the social worker working individually with each student to document the deficiencies in the school system, one student can represent all students in a *class action* suit to improve conditions in the school. Class action is a legal concept that has promising implications for social work. Closer working relationships will have to be cultivated with the legal profession to enable lawyers to conceptualize broad social work concerns and to translate these into legal class action suits. Such an approach can be called *class action social work*. Victories in the courts could provide relief for thousands of poor people.

There is precedent for having an organized body of social workers and lawyers, providing the potential for broader collaborative impact through class action suits on behalf of the poor. Recognition of matters of natural interconnection and mutual interest between lawyers and social workers led in 1962 to the creation of the National Conference of Lawyers and Social Workers, a joint committee composed of sixteen members, eight appointed from each parent organization. The Conference met twice a year.[47] In 1967 the Conference developed cooperative goals for the two professions to work toward in serving the needy. Some of these goals included:[48]

1. Identification of needs requiring their individual or joint professional competencies
2. Resolution of situations that involve both social and legal problems—including recognizing and reconciling respective professional orientations, especially with regard to the adversary role
3. The development of machinery and procedures for effective referral relationships

The nine papers in *Law and Social Work,* one of the Conference's publications, envisioned a rather narrow role for social workers working with lawyers, following the traditional clinical, case-by-case model. For example, social workers defined their function as providing "expertise in psychosocial diagnosis including evaluation of the *individual's* potential for social functioning."[49] The collaborative potential of class action suits to help the poor on a broad scale is not mentioned in this 1973 document. Let it again be emphasized that the central theme of the Conference—"lawyers and social workers, as close collaborators in situations involving both social and legal problems, should seek to utilize to the full the resources of each profession to help the poor"—provides the foundation for social work to have a greater impact on social reform.

In some states social workers have already made pioneering efforts to enter the legal arena. In California, for example, the Greater California Chapter of the NASW presented an award to John Serrano, a social worker, for his actions as a concerned citizen in the widely publicized *Serrano* v. *Priest* case, which argued that the quality of a child's education should not be dependent on the wealth of a school district.[50] The California Supreme Court, in this class action suit filed by the Western Center on Law and Poverty, Inc., ruled 6 to 1 that the California public educational finance scheme, which relies heavily on local property taxes, violated the equal protection clause of the Fourteenth Amendment to the U.S. Constitution. The court held that the financing system invidiously discriminated against the poor. The court also asserted that the right to a public education was a fundamental interest that could not be dependent on wealth, and it therefore applied the strict equal-protection standard. Finding no compelling state interest advanced by the discriminatory system, the court held it unconstitutional.[51]

The significance of the *Serrano* v. *Priest* decision transcends California boundaries because all states except Hawaii use similar educational finance systems. Wealthier districts are favored to the detriment of poorer school districts. A direct relationship exists between the number of dollars spent per child and the quality of education available to that child. In *Serrano* v. *Priest* it was discovered that poor communities were paying two to three times as much school tax per $100 of assessed valuation as were wealthy communities, yet wealthy communities received two to three times as many educational dollars per child from the state as did the poorer communities.[52]

In *Serrano* v. *Priest* the court's policy considerations focused on the pervasive influence of education on individual development and capacity within modern society and on education's essential role in the maintenance of free enterprise democracy. It was considered that the combination of these factors sufficiently distinguished education from other governmental services for it to merit recognition as a fundamental interest.[53] No court had previously placed education within the framework of interests meriting strict equal-protection scrutiny, and this decision represented the first time any type of governmental service had been held to involve fundamental interests.[54]

Considering the *Serrano* precedent, might not the areas of welfare, health, and mental health services also represent a set of circumstances as unique and compelling as education? A right to public education may not be maximally enjoyed if a child is poorly housed, impoverished, malnourished, or in need of physical or mental health care. *Serrano* v. *Priest,* as a social work class action concept, has the potential to be the cutting edge of social reform in a wide range of governmental services, including several in which social workers already have knowledge and experience. In view of the regressive social and economic policies of Reagan, Bush, and now Clinton with his harmful new welfare reform, the opportunity for class action collaboration between law and social work as a significant tool of intervention is possible. The class action social work concept and its application was tested by one of the authors in the courts as a mental health primary prevention activity.

Class action is a legal procedural device for resolving issues in court affecting many people. Those persons actually before the court represent the unnamed members of the class in a single proceeding in equity, thereby avoiding multiple case-by-case actions. *Class action social work,* developed by the authors, is a forensic social work/legal profession collaborative litigation activity involving social work concerns, with the goal of obtaining a favorable court ruling that will benefit the social welfare of a group of socioeconomically disadvantaged persons. Class action social work in a mental health primary prevention context finds social workers and attorneys pursuing a court ruling that will have a positive psychosocial impact on a disadvantaged class of people who, prior to the ruling, were at risk in developing psychological or psychiatric disorders or symptoms. Among the requirements needed to accomplish the primary prevention goals are—to borrow from public health terminology—a small sample of "infected" organisms, an identification of the suspected toxic agent, and a laboratory procedural test to show whether the toxic agent caused the infection in the organism. Translating this into class action mental health primary prevention terms using an actual case (*Nicacio* v. *United States INS*), the "infected organisms" were thirteen Hispanic plaintiffs (the injured, complaining parties) who were exhibiting psychiatric symptoms, allegedly caused by stressful interrogations conducted by patrol officers of the United States Immigration and Naturalization Service (INS). The courtroom became the laboratory in which the suspected toxic evidence (behavior of the INS officers) was analyzed as to potential harm. If found to be harmful, the court could issue an order terminating the toxic behavior of the INS, which thus prevented psychosocial harm (psychiatric symptoms) in a specific at-risk population (millions of Hispanics residing in the Southwestern states or the State of Washington area, depending on court boundary definitions).

In *Nicacio* v. *United States INS*, Hispanic plaintiffs brought suit contending that (1) the border patrol agents of the INS were conducting roving motor vehicle stops in search of "illegal aliens" on the roadways of the state of Washington that were in violation of Fourth Amendment rights to be free from unreasonable searches and seizures; (2) that the actions of INS officials were unlawful; and (3) that the plaintiffs were entitled to monetary damages for humiliation, embarrassment, and mental anguish suffered as a result of a violation of their Fourth Amendment rights.[55] The facts of the case were that (1) all plaintiffs were of Mexican descent and were either born in the United States, U.S. citizens, or permanent resident aliens who resided in the Yakima Valley area of the state of Washington; (2) the plaintiff class was defined by the court as "all persons of Mexican, Latin, or Hispanic appearance who have been, are, or will be traveling by motor vehicle on the highways of the state of Washington"; (3) at the time litigation was initiated, INS agents were regularly conducting roving patrol motor vehicle stops, detentions, and interrogations in the Yakima Valley area; (4) many of the stops were based solely on Hispanic appearance, the agents' subjective feelings or intuition, or the suspected "illegal aliens'" innocuous behavior, appearance, or traits; and (5) persons stopped were required, in most cases, to provide identification or documentation of legal presence in the United States.[56]

In attempting to document the amount of humiliation, embarrassment, and mental anguish suffered by the plaintiffs as a result of their contact with INS officers, plaintiffs' attorneys contacted one of the authors as an expert witness to conduct a mental health evaluation of all the plaintiffs. Having been sworn in by the court and qualified and accepted as an expert witness, the author rendered a DSM-III-R diagnosis of each plaintiff. The findings were that (1) not one of the thirteen plaintiffs had ever been hospitalized or treated on an outpatient basis for a mental health problem; (2) eleven of the plaintiffs suffered adjustment disorder symptoms, either with depressed mood, anxious mood, or mixed emotional features; (3) one plaintiff suffered acute posttraumatic stress disorder symptoms; and (4) one plaintiff was symptom-free.

The findings of the court were that (1) the INS border patrol practices were unlawful; (2) plaintiffs and class action members were entitled to a declaratory judgment covering future conduct of INS officers in stopping vehicles on public highways; and (3) plaintiffs were *not* entitled to recover monetary damages for their suffering, since plaintiffs were unable to specifically identify the officers.[57] The favorable court ruling affected *all* persons of Mexican, Latin, or Hispanic appearance residing only in the state of Washington, rather than in the Southwestern states, as had originally been requested by plaintiffs' attorneys. Even so, the court order stopped the noxious activities of the INS directed at Hispanics in the state of Washington. *All* Hispanics in the state of Washington, therefore, were spared INS-provoked psychiatric symptoms in future contacts with the INS. This case shows the growing potential of class action social work with a mental health primary prevention goal and outcome using social work psychosocial practice concepts.

Class action social work, as a macrolevel practice intervention prevention tool, can also be used to ensure that children at risk receive the welfare benefits and services to which they are entitled. Clinton's new welfare reform law could be a test case. As more children are growing up poor and without stable families, Harris impresses on social workers and the social work profession that they must renew their commitment to child welfare and continue to play an important role in the development and formulation of public policy and child welfare services to strengthen the ability of vulnerable families to raise healthy children.[58]

In many instances, it is not necessary to develop and formulate new public policy concerning child welfare; simply creating new laws will not solve the problems. There may be many national and local situations in which child welfare laws and policies already exist to benefit children, but are not—for any number of reasons—being implemented. It is in these cases that class action social work intervention can be applied to prevent children from experiencing harm when they are not receiving the services to which they have a right.

Stein suggests that child welfare agencies are vulnerable to class action suits, alleging that clients are being deprived of constitutional guarantees or entitlements specified in federal or state policy. In this recession era of reduced spending at the continued expense of domestic programs, reductions in personnel and social services increase welfare agency vulnerability to class action suits, as the lack of funds *is not* a defense for failing to provide federal and state legally mandated services.[59]

Class action suits on behalf of children have charged that state agencies have failed to develop case plans; made inappropriate placements of children, ignoring racial/ethnic factors; failed to pursue adoptive placements; and failed to provide preventive services. Currently, two class action suits are pending that allege state failure to provide preventive services, and one suit alleging maltreatment of children in foster care and failure to develop and implement permanent plans.[60] The specific role of social workers in these class action suits is not clear, that is, whether they are defendants, expert witnesses, or initiators and/or collaborators with the attorneys in the suits. It is when social workers are in the initiating, collaborating role with attorneys that it conforms to the earlier definition of class action social work.

Social workers need to pay careful attention to existing national and state benefits and welfare policies and to laws and regulations affecting vulnerable client groups, such as children, the homeless, welfare families, and institutionalized psychiatric and corrections populations, to ensure that they are receiving the services and benefits to which they are entitled. Continued denial of resources to clients by agencies, even after notification of mandated requirements, may have merits for attorney–social worker collaboration that eventually could result in a class action social work type of intervention. A favorable court remedy would prevent continued harm to the immediately affected client population (secondary prevention) and to future client populations (primary prevention).

Concluding Comment

Escalating costs, coupled with increasing need for human services and the fact that there will never be sufficient mental health practitioners to meet these needs, require the development and application of helping concepts, such as primary prevention, designed to benefit large numbers of persons *before* they are symptomatic. Because social work is one of the helping professions most involved in interacting with and helping communities, it is anticipated that the profession will play an increasingly vital role in applying primary prevention concepts in the twenty-first century.

Urban gang violence and homicide was highlighted in this chapter to indicate to the social work profession that, from a historical practice experience standpoint, it is best suited for the health and mental health professions to assume a leadership role in developing micro- to macro-intervention strategies to deal with a problem that is killing thousands of inner-city youths. Primary, secondary, and tertiary violence and homicide prevention programs were discussed and analyzed as to their impact on violence and gang homicide. A framework for identifying high-risk gang victims was developed to correspond to a suggested hospital-based prevention program. A bold, new approach based on prevention in dealing with violence is the "handwriting on the wall," with U.S. Attorney General Janet Reno being the writer and the nation's leading advocate. She is firmly supported by President Clinton. The social work profession and its schools need to "tool up" and meet this new challenge if they wish to become more relevant to the needs of society, especially those of the inner city.

More and more social workers are leaving the public welfare arena, going into private practice, and shifting their target population to the middle class. Lacking public agency bureaucratic constraints, they are potentially free to help the poor through social action activities such as writing proposals, conducting needs surveys, or building coalitions to apply pressure on government. Related strategies of advocacy and client empowerment may result in a transfer of power so that client groups in need of services gain and exercise their own economic and political might. A community empowerment model built with networking methods can, in the final result, produce a mental health primary prevention outcome.

Class action social work, which was first introduced into the literature in this text in 1977, continues to show promise as a macrolevel intervention strategy. *Serrano* v. *Priest,* a class action victory, established the precedent of the right to an equal education; it paved the road for the poor to fight for the right to health and welfare in order to maximize their new educational opportunity. Increasing an individual's opportunities through such assistance is in the best interests of the individual and society. The effectiveness of class action social work with a mental health primary prevention goal was demonstrated in *Nicacio* v. *United States INS,* in which a positive court ruling will have the effect of preventing literally thousands of at-risk Hispanics from developing psychiatric symptoms caused by discriminatory law enforcement practices. A rare opportunity for social work to help the poor on a broad scale seems very possible in light of *Serrano* and *Nicacio.* Examples were also provided to show how class action social work intervention can be applied on behalf of vulnerable client populations who are being denied legally mandated services. Collaboration with the legal profession should be vigorously pursued by social workers.

KEY WORDS AND CONCEPTS

Prevention

Primary prevention

Secondary prevention

At-risk population

Tertiary prevention

Class action social work

Gang homicide psychosocial prevention model

SUGGESTED READINGS

Johnson, Yvonne M. "Indirect Work: Social Work's Uncelebrated Strength," *Social Work* 44 (July 1999), No. 4.

Middleman, Ruth R., and Goldberg, Gale. "Social Work Practice with Groups," *Encyclopedia of Social Work,* 18th Edition, Vol. II. Silver Spring, MD: National Association of Social Workers, 1987, pp. 714–729.

Morales, Armando. "The Mexican American Gang Member: Evaluation and Treatment," in Rosina M. Becerra, Marvin Karno, and Javier Escobar, eds., *Mental Health and Hispanic Americans: Clinical Perspectives.* New York: Grune & Stratton, 1982.

Report of the Secretary's Task Force on Black and Minority Health, Vol. 5. U.S. Department of Health and Human Services, January 1986.

Roberts, Albert R., and Brownell, Patricia. "A Century of Forensic Social Work: Bridging the Past to the Present," *Social Work,* Vol. 44, No. 4, July 1999.

Solomon, Barbara Bryant. *Black Empowerment: Social Work in Oppressed Communities.* New York: Columbia University Press, 1976.

Soricelli, Barbara A., and Utech, Carolyn Lorenz. "Mourning the Death of a Child: The Family and Group Process," *Social Work* 30 (September–October 1985): 429–434.

Spergel, Irving A. "Violent Gangs in Chicago: In Search of Social Policy," *Social Service Review* 58 (June 1984): 199–226.

Stein, Theodore J. "The Vulnerability of Child Welfare Agencies to Class Action Suits," *Social Service Review* 61 (December 1987): 636–654.

ENDNOTES

1. H. John Staulcup, "Primary Prevention," in Aaron Rosenblatt and Diana Waldfogel, eds., *Handbook of Clinical Social Work* (San Francisco: Jossey-Bass, 1983), p. 1059.
2. Feldman et al., p. 6.
3. Stephen E. Goldston, "Defining Primary Prevention," in George W. Albee and Justice M. Joffe, eds., *Primary Prevention of Psychopathology* Vol. I: The Issues (Hanover, NH: University Press of New England, 1977), p. 20.
4. Ibid.
5. Ibid., p. 21.
6. Steven L. McMurtry, "Secondary Prevention of Child Maltreatment: A Review," *Social Work* 30 (January–February 1985): 43.
7. United States Senate Committee on the Judiciary, *Ford Administration Stifles Juvenile Justice Policy* (Washington, D.C.: U.S. Government Printing Office, 1975), p. 2.
8. Barry Krisberg and Ira Schwartz, "Rethinking Juvenile Justice," *Crime and Delinquency* (July 1983): 340.
9. Ibid., pp. 360–361.
10. Ron Schultz, "A New Prescription for Troubled Teens," *Los Angeles* 30 (January 1985): 159.
11. Ibid., p. 205.
12. *Los Angeles Times,* Part II, March 24, 1985, p. 2.
13. *Los Angeles Times,* Part I, Friday, October 22, 1993, p. 24.
14. "Truth, Justice, and the Reno Way," *Time,* Vol. 142, No. 2, p. 26.

15. "Teen Violence—Wild in the Streets," *Newsweek,* August 2, 1993, pp. 40–49.

16. Carolyn Rebecca Block, "Lethal Violence in Chicago over Seventeen Years: Homicides Known to the Police, 1965–1981," Illinois Criminal Justice Information Authority, p. 69.

17. Department of Justice, "Homicide in California, 1985" (Bureau of Criminal Statistics and Special State of California, 1985), p. 17; "Fiscal Year 1985–86 Statistical Summary," Los Angeles County Sheriffs Department; "Statistical Digest, 1986," Automated Information Division, Los Angeles Police Department.

18. Cited in N. Meredith, "The Murder Epidemic," *Science* 84 (December 1984): 42.

19. *Report of the Secretary's Task Force on Black and Minority Health,* Vol. 5, U.S. Department of Health and Human Services, January 1986, pp. 43–44.

20. Ibid., pp. 46–50.

21. Ibid., p. 50.

22. Police Foundation, *Domestic Violence and the Police: Studies in Detroit and Kansas City* (Washington, D.C.: The Foundation, 1976).

23. The Boston Youth Program, Boston City Hospital, 818 Harrison Ave., Boston, MA, cited in *Report of the Secretary's Task Force,* pp. 235–236.

24. C. Cooper, "Peer Dynamics, Final Evaluation Report, 1979–1980," Nebraska State Commission on Drugs (Lincoln: Nebraska State Department of Health).

25. "Early Gang Intervention," Transfer of Knowledge Workshop, Department of the California Youth Authority, Office of Criminal Justice Planning, 1985, pp. 11–12; also see Tony Ostos, "Alternatives to Gang Membership." (Unpublished paper, Paramount School District, Los Angeles County, California, October 1987.)

26. "Strike II," Hopkins Adolescent Program, Johns Hopkins Hospital, Park Building, Baltimore, MD, 1986.

27. Fattah Falaka, "Call and Catalytic Response: The House of Umoja," in R. A. Mathias, P. De Muro, and R. S. Allinson, eds., *Violent Juvenile Offenders: An Anthology* (San Francisco: National Council on Crime and Delinquency, 1984), pp. 231–237.

28. "Gang Violence Reduction Project, Second Evaluation Report: October 1977–May 1978," Department of the California Youth Authority, November 1978, pp. i, iii.

29. T. Tatara, H. Morgan, and H. Portner, "SCAN: Providing Preventive Services in an Urban Setting," *Children Today* (November–December 1986): 17–22.

30. Karil S. Klingbeil, "Interpersonal Violence: A Comprehensive Model in a Hospital Setting from Policy to Program," in *Report of the Secretary's Task Force,* p. 246.

31. Lou Dantzler, "Executive Summary, Challengers Boys and Girls Club" (Los Angeles, CA, 1990), brochure.

32. As reported to the author by the Los Angeles Police Department South Bureau, June 1993.

33. Barbara A. Soricelli and Carolyn Lorenz Utech, "Mourning the Death of a Child: The Family and Group Process," *Social Work* 30 (September–October 1985): 429–434.

34. Scott Briar, "The Current Crisis in Social Casework," *Social Work Practice, 1967* (New York: Columbia University Press, 1967), p. 28.

35. George A. Brager, "Advocacy and Political Behavior," *Social Work* 13 (April 1968): 6.

36. Neil Gilbert and Harry Specht, "Advocacy and Professional Ethics," *Social Work* 21 (July 1976): 288.

37. Armando Morales, "Beyond Traditional Conceptual Frameworks," *Social Work* 22 (September 1977): 393.

38. Barbara Bryant Solomon, *Black Empowerment: Social Work in Oppressed Communities* (New York: Columbia University Press, 1976), p. 6.

39. Ibid., p. 342.

40. Anne Minahan and Allen Pincus, "Conceptual Framework for Social Work Practice," *Social Work* 22 (September 1977): 348.

41. Solomon, p. 354.

42. Felix G. Rivera and John Erlich, "An Assessment Framework for Organizing in Emerging Minority Communities," F. M. Cox et al., eds., *Tactics and Techniques of Community Practice*, 2nd Edition (Itasca, IL: Peacock, 1984).

43. Lambert Maguire, "Networking for Self-Help: An Empirically Based Guideline," in *Tactics and Techniques of Community Practice*, p. 198.

44. Ibid., p. 199.

45. Ibid., pp. 206–207.

46. Scott Briar, "The Future of Social Work: An Introduction," *Social Work* 19 (September 1974): 518.

47. National Association of Social Workers, *Law and Social Work* (Washington, D.C.: The Association, 1973), p. vii.

48. Ibid., p. 15.

49. National Association of Social Workers, *Law and Social Work*, p. 25. [Emphasis ours.]

50. *NASW Newsletter*, Greater California Chapter, April 1975, p. 1.

51. Robert B. Keiter, "California Educational Financing System Violates Equal Protection," *Clearinghouse Review* 5 (October 1971): 287.

52. Ibid., p. 297.

53. Ibid., p. 298.

54. Ibid., p. 299.

55. *Nicacio* v. *United States INS*, 595 F. Supp. 19 (1984), p. 19.

56. Ibid., p. 21.

57. Ibid., pp. 19, 25.

58 Dorothy V. Harris, "Renewing Our Commitment to Child Welfare," *Social Work* 33 (November–December 1988): 483–484.

59. Theodore J. Stein, "The Vulnerability of Child Welfare Agencies to Class Action Suits," *Social Service Review* 61 (December 1987): 636–654.

60. Ibid., p. 640.

CHAPTER 10

Social Work Throughout the World

Prefatory Comment Throughout the world, people need assistance in addressing social issues that affect their lives and help in resolving or reducing the social issues that they confront. As the profession dedicated to both serving people and improving social conditions, the need for social work is global.

The prior sections of this book have focused on the ways in which social work has evolved in the United States. Lest the reader assume that the functioning of social workers in the United States is the only model for this profession, this chapter is concerned with similarities and differences in the expressions of social work throughout the world. In addition, it reflects the growing globalization of social work and the evolving efforts to address international social issues with a single voice.

World Population Changes: Creating a Global Demand for Social Work

In August 1999, the world population reached 6 billion people. This number had doubled in less than forty years and, prior to that, it had taken all of human history until 1804 for the world population to reach 1 billion persons. Given this rapid rate of growth in recent years, experts predict that the world population will increase another 3 billion by 2025, creating a severe drinking water shortage and limited food supply.

The world population continues to expand in spite of a reproductive revolution that has resulted in half of the world's married women using family planning interventions, compared to only 10 percent of fertile women thirty years ago. Even though up to 71 percent of women in the United States use some form of birth control, it has the highest fertility rate among wealthy industrialized countries. Projections are that the United States will double its current population of 270 million by the year 2060. In addition, it is projected that as early as 2025 there will be an explosion of retirees sixty and older in the United States, which will draw on savings and pension funds, causing a shortage for capital investment. Long-term population growth in the United States and other industrialized countries poses problems for the future. Yet these problems are relatively insignificant compared to the rest of the world. For example, 95 percent of the world's fertile young people live in developing countries, which are already characterized by lack of resources in education, housing, employment, and health care. Such global population stresses call for world communication, collaboration, and planning to address such impending problems.[1] Social work has an important role to perform in helping the world address these and related issues, but action is sometimes hampered by the difficulty of speaking with a single professional voice. There are several reasons for social work's slowness to develop into a global profession.

SOCIAL WELFARE: THE CONTEXT

Social work has developed differently in various countries because unique social, political, cultural, economic, and historical forces shape the manner in which human services are provided. Due to the fact that social work is highly interactive with a country's human services delivery system, this profession's evolution in any country is affected by the philosophy that underpins that country's social programs.

In Chapters 1 through 4 of this book, the manner in which social work evolved in the United States was described in tandem with the ebbs and flows of changing philosophies and support for the social welfare institution. Unlike medicine, nursing, and occupational therapy, which are tied mainly to the physical aspects of human functioning and display relatively little variation from one country to another, social work is based on the social structures that each society creates, making it inevitable that there will be substantial differences among countries. Indeed, no two countries have evolved identical human services (although they have borrowed ideas from each other), and thus the configuration of activities for social workers varies considerably.*

Several social welfare philosophies are helpful for characterizing the different approaches to human services throughout the world. For example, in preindustrial or agriculture-based societies, social needs are met primarily by families, churches,

---

*A particularly informative source when examining social work in several different countries is M. C. Hokenstad, S. K. Khinduka, and James Midgley, eds., *Profiles in International Social Work*. Washington, D.C.: NASW Press, 1992. London: Routledge, 1994. Included in this book are descriptions of social work in Chile; Great Britain; Hungary; India; Japan; Hong Kong, Singapore, South Korea, and Taiwan; South Africa; Sweden, Uganda, and the United States.

the few wealthy persons in the society, and various guilds (e.g., agricultural trade groups and civic organizations). This type of society is typically found among developing countries in Africa, Latin America, Asia, and elsewhere. In these societies, direct human services are most likely to be provided on a natural helping or volunteer basis, and social work practice tends to evolve as a macro social change profession. In these societies, social workers' efforts have been orientated toward *social development,* that is, social, economic, and political change to improve basic human conditions. Lusk and Horejsi, however, note a change now occurring in this approach, indicating that "social work in the developing world is setting aside its long standing preoccupation with political ideology and has shifted to a pragmatic effort to ameliorate poverty and social injustice."[2]

Another philosophy tends to emerge when industrialization begins to occur in a country. When this happens, individual and family mobility is required, urbanization increases, and people are viewed as commodities whose time and talent can be bought and sold. There is reliance on the market system to provide people with needed resources because the extended family may not be present or have the capacity to meet its members' social needs. Similarly, countries emerging from communist rule are typically in the process of creating or re-creating industrial economies and systems of delivering; human services that were abandoned under communism must be redeveloped. There must, therefore, be a backup to what can be done by a family or the market system, and a social welfare system is created. Thus a set of social programs and persons to deliver these programs evolves. It is in these postindustrial societies that professional levels of social work are most likely to develop.

Epsing-Anderson (1990) has developed a typology of three distinct social welfare systems that have emerged in postindustrial societies. Epsing-Anderson's typology is based on the analysis of the degree to which the social welfare system (1) treats people as having a right to services, and not just as commodities used in the production of goods and services; (2) redistributes money and other resources to achieve greater equality and reduce poverty; and (3) maintains a balance between the government and private sectors having responsibility for the well-being of people.[3] Examination of how countries differ on these three points (i.e., comparative social welfare) yields the following distinct variations in postindustrial welfare approaches—or social welfare states.

First, the *corporatist welfare state* is designed to maintain existing social class differences and the distribution of resources by the system. Services are distributed primarily by the private or corporate entities, and people are not viewed as having the right to services. This approach to social welfare is at the most conservative side of the continuum of approaches and attempts to maintain the status quo. Examples of countries where this approach is dominant include France, Italy, Spain, and Austria. In these countries, social workers' activities are primarily related to accommodating for material deficits (social provisions) and resolving marriage and family issues. Social work practice under this system is highly specialized, and most recognized social workers are required to hold a social work credential, usually with training at the vocational level.[4]

Second, the *liberal welfare state* is best represented by the United States, Canada, Great Britain, Australia, India, and Japan—although these countries differ in the degree to which each of the criteria for comparing welfare systems is embraced. These programs typically focus on redistributing income to the low-income population; are designed to reinforce the work ethic and view peoples' labor primarily as an economic commodity; maintain minimum standards of well-being through government programs, yet also subsidize the private for-profit and nonprofit welfare programs; tend to stigmatize people receiving services, thus maintaining social stratification; and only minimally treat people as having a right to services. In these countries social workers are expected to provide a range of services, from direct practice interventions to efforts to facilitate at least incremental change in social structures. Most professional social workers in these countries hold a professional social work credential at the undergraduate or graduate level.

Last, the *social democratic welfare state* provides universal services and contends that the peoples' work should not simply be treated as another commodity. Social programs in countries that have adopted this model (e.g., Norway, Sweden, the Netherlands) attempt to achieve maximum standards of human well-being through universal health insurance systems and are designed to socialize the costs of family living through governmental transfers such as children's allowances, sharing costs of caring for the aged and handicapped, and guaranteeing full employment to all who can work. In this type of welfare system, relatively few of the service providers hold a social work credential. Those who have credentials are prepared at the vocational or secondary levels, except when offering therapeutic services typically related to child behavior issues and parenting problems.[5]

In reality, no country exactly fits into any one of the welfare states in this typology and, indeed, social welfare systems are constantly changing. A country may move from one type to another, or closer to or more distant from any form of welfare state over time, yet understanding where this country stands at any one time is essential if there is to be a successful social technology transfer (e.g., adopting or adapting maternal leave programs or crisis intervention techniques).[6]

THE EMERGENCE OF SOCIAL WORK TRAINING AND EDUCATION

It is difficult to mark the beginning of a profession. In the United States, for example, the National Association of Social Workers designated 1998 as the centennial year for the profession, presumably because in 1898 the New York Charity Organization created a six-week training program known as the New York School of Philanthropy. If one holds social work up to all the criteria for professions proposed by Abraham Flexner and other experts on the sociology of professions (see Chapter 3), it is more likely that social work in the United States met the criteria to become a recognized profession somewhere around the late 1920s. Nevertheless, the initiation of education and training programs is usually well documented and thus is used to signal the advent of professions. It is informative, therefore, to note a few of the dates when significant training or education in social work was introduced in different countries throughout the world as a means of marking when social work began in each.*

1898	United States and Germany
1899	The Netherlands
1903	England
1920	Chile
1921	Sweden
1924	South Africa
1931	Ireland
1932	Spain
1936	India and Egypt
1963	Uganda
1989	Hungry
1992	Italy

Social work also varies in different countries in the educational levels recognized as preparation for practice. In some countries it is *training,* with no particular academic preparation (not even a high school diploma required). In others, high school or specific community college vocational training is the requisite preparation, while in many countries college-level professional education is the requirement to enter social work. In a few countries a professional master's degree is the terminal practice degree. Nowhere is a doctoral degree the expected preparation for social work practice.

A Global Approach to Social Work

The initial approach to developing a worldwide perspective on social work was termed *international social work* and was concerned with comparing social work as it exists in different cultures and countries. Increasingly, as social work has grown and matured worldwide, an effort has been made to address social work from a *global perspective,* that is, as one profession practicing in many different countries. A global approach requires the creation of international professional organizations to coordinate the formulation of a single concept of the profession, discover where

*The literature is somewhat inconsistent regarding the starting dates of educational programs and, therefore, the dates included in this list should be viewed as approximate.

common understanding exists, promote political positions regarding worldwide social problems, identify the common values of the profession and specify ethical guidelines for practice, clarify the roles and functions that are typical for all forms of social work practice, and develop professional education. What is the current status of global social work?

INTERNATIONAL PROFESSIONAL ORGANIZATIONS

Two international organizations provide the basic leadership for the globalization of social work. One, the International Federation of Social Workers (IFSW), is structured to work through various national professional membership organizations such as the National Association of Social Workers and the professional trade unions of social workers that exist in some countries. Begun in 1928 following the International Conference on Social Work held in Paris, today organizations from approximately 70 countries, representing 500,000 social workers, participate in the IFSW. The activities of IFSW include publication of a newsletter, maintaining a commission that advocates for the protection of human rights throughout the world, the development of a statement of ethical guidelines for social workers, and maintenance of updated policy positions on thirteen global social welfare issues.[7]

The second important international social work organization is the International Association of Schools of Social Work (IASSW), which was formed in 1948. This organization now includes more than 400 member social work education associations (e.g., Council on Social Work Education) and individual schools from seventy-seven countries. The IASSW is concerned with facilitating the inclusion of international content into social work education programs, providing consultation to the United Nations and the United Nations Children's Fund, and facilitating the transfer of academic credit among schools from different countries. With the IFSW, it publishes the journal *International Social Work*.[8]

DEFINING SOCIAL WORK GLOBALLY

Arriving at a generally accepted definition of social work in the United States proved difficult (see Chapter 2). Finding a definition that will encompass social work throughout the world is even more challenging. The International Federation of Social Workers (IFSW) established a Task Force for this purpose in 1996 and, a year later, the committee's deliberations resulted in agreement that, rather than being a collection of social professions, there was sufficient commonality to attempt to define social work as one profession, albeit at very different stages of development. The charge to the Task Force is to formulate a definition for consideration at the year 2000 meeting of the IFSW General Assembly,[9] although it may be much later before agreement on a definition is achieved. Until a definition of social work is adopted, a sanctioned "global" definition of social work will not exist.

VALUES AND ETHICS HELD BY SOCIAL WORKERS GLOBALLY

The underlying beliefs about the inherent value of people and the responsibility of societies to create conditions in which people can thrive are perhaps the glue that binds social workers together. These basic principles transcend the particular cultures and social welfare systems in various parts of the world and are the most universal expressions of the common beliefs that characterize social work globally.

The International Federation of Social Workers has given high priority to developing an international ethical code that includes twelve statements of the fundamental principles that underpin social work and provides a related set of guidelines for ethical practice. The following principles reflect social work's fundamental orientation to serving people.

1. Every human being has a unique value, which justifies moral considerations for that person.
2. Each individual has the right to self-fulfillment to the extent that it does not encroach upon the same right of others, and has an obligation to contribute to the well-being of society.
3. Each society, regardless of its form, should function to provide the maximum benefits for all of its members.
4. Social workers have a commitment to principles of social justice.
5. Social workers have the responsibility to devote objective and disciplined knowledge and skill to aid individuals, groups, communities, and societies in their development and resolution of personal–societal conflicts and their consequences.
6. Social workers are expected to provide the best possible assistance to anybody seeking their help and advice, without unfair discrimination on the basis of gender, age, disability, color, social class, race, religion, language, political beliefs, or sexual orientation.
7. Social workers respect the basic human rights of individuals and groups as expressed in the *United Nations Universal Declaration of Human Rights* and other international conventions derived from that Declaration.
8. Social workers pay regard to the principles of privacy, confidentiality, and responsible use of information in their professional work. Social workers respect justified confidentiality even when their country's legislation is in conflict with this demand.
9. Social workers are expected to work in full collaboration with their clients, working for the best interests of the clients but paying due regard to the interests of others involved. Clients are encouraged to participate as much as possible and should be informed of the risks and likely benefits of proposed courses of action.
10. Social workers generally expect clients to take responsibility, in collaboration with them, for determining courses of action affecting their lives. Compulsion, which might be necessary to solve one party's problems at the expense of the interests of others involved, should only take place after

careful explicit evaluation of the claims of the conflicting parties. Social workers should minimize the use of legal compulsion.

11. Social work is inconsistent with direct or indirect support of individuals, groups, political forces, or power structures suppressing their fellow human beings by employing terrorism, torture, or similar brutal means.

12. Social workers make ethically justified decisions, and stand by them, paying due regard to the *IFSW International Declaration of Ethical Principles*, and to the "International Ethical Standards for Social Workers" adopted by their national professional association.[10]

In addition to the basic values held by social workers, *the International Declaration of Ethical Principles of Social Work* provides guides to the ethical conduct of social work. Like the *NASW Code of Ethics* (see Chapter 7), this statement of ethical principles addresses the obligations of social workers to be fully prepared and to bring the most relevant knowledge and skill to the practice situation, to give priority to the interests of their clients, to be responsible to the agencies and organizations that employ them, to treat their colleagues with respect, and to contribute to the development of the social work profession.

GLOBAL VIEWS OF SOCIAL ISSUES

One direct result of the similar values held by social workers is that agreement has been reached regarding understanding and developing approaches to resolving social problems that are experienced throughout the world. Social workers can make comparative analyses of issues and adopt or adapt solutions that have been successful in other countries.

What are the social issues that are of primary concern to social workers on a worldwide basis? Clearly, social workers are in agreement that they want to make the world a better place for all people—and particularly for those who are most vulnerable to experiencing social problems. There is universal concern among social workers for improving the social, economic, and health conditions of the most vulnerable people throughout the world and in changing the political and social structures that have made these people likely to experience violations of basic human rights, hunger and other expressions of poverty (e.g., approximately one-fifth of the world's population lives in extreme poverty), disease, and/or various forms of abuse or oppression.

More specifically, social workers and organizations of social workers are concerned with such worldwide issues as achieving and preserving peace, preventing the use of landmines in wartime situations, distributing human and economic resources more equitably, protecting the rights and preventing the exploitation of children and youth, enhancing women's status and safety, minimizing substance abuse, facilitating appropriate international adoptions, and so on. Evidence of these concerns is found in the issues addressed in the IFSW policy statements that have been adopted to date.[11]

- Advancement of Women

- Child Welfare

- The Welfare of Elderly People

- Health

- HIV–AIDS

- Human Rights

- Migration

- Peace and Disarmament

- The Protection of Personal Information

- Refugees

- Conditions in Rural Communities

- Self-Help

- Youth*

The value of these position papers is not only to identify topics for which social workers are in general agreement throughout the world, but also to provide a more influential voice to international organizations such as the United Nations (UN). In that venue, social workers have been actively involved with a number of UN agencies including the United Nations Children's Fund (UNICEF), the UN Development Program, the Department of Policy Coordination and Sustainable Development, the UN High Commission for Refugees, and the World Health Organization.

Employment in International Social Work

Four forms of international practice are possible for a social worker. One form is to secure a position in an international organization that advances human services on a worldwide basis. The United Nations (UN) serves as the primary agency to coordinate the efforts of the various countries to overcome oppression, facilitate the delivery of health and welfare services that cross international boundaries, and promote social justice. Social work with UN agencies such as UNICEF, the Economic and Social Council, the World Health Organization, and the UN High Commission on Refugees are examples of such positions.

Second, the U.S. government, too, has positions concerned with international social welfare issues. The Department of Health and Human Services maintains an international affairs staff to give attention to worldwide human services issues, and its Office of Refugee Settlement is actively involved in promoting the safety, welfare, and rights of refugees. The International Development Cooperation Agency (USAID)

---

*All position papers are available from the IFSW Secretariat (P. O. Box 4649, Sofienberg, N-0506, Oslo, Norway) in English, French, and Spanish.

administers foreign aid programs in approximately 100 countries throughout the world, and the Peace Corps has provided developing countries with the human and technical resources to improve their physical infrastructure (e.g., water, sanitation, roads), health care, and human services.

Third, perhaps the most common form of international employment for social workers is to find a social work job in a government or voluntary agency in another country. These roles typically include service provision, consultation, and teaching or training activities. Particularly for countries that are in the process of developing services to individuals and families, the skills possessed by most U.S. social workers are highly valued. The reverse is true, too, for social workers from developing countries, who often have a strong social development background and bring a helpful expertise not typically found among U.S.-educated social workers.

Last, some international social work positions exist in multinational corporations that locate personnel in foreign countries. When families are relocated (or left behind), there are inevitable social adjustments to be made. As in other social work practice in business and industry, social workers provide direct services to help individuals and families to deal with their social problems, assist the company in sharpening its cultural sensitivity, and represent the company as a participant in the local community, making contributions to and interfacing with the human services delivery system.

How does one become prepared for international social work? Certainly, the demands on workers differ depending on the nature of a country's social welfare system and/or the type of position that the social worker holds. Specific preparation, then, cannot be identified that is essential for all positions. However, a few fundamental areas of preparation are somewhat universal.

First, become informed and stay current regarding international affairs, particularly issues of social and economic justice, human rights, and peace. Careful reading of both the social work literature on international issues and the general news sources is essential.

Second, develop competence in the use of one or more foreign languages. Although English is used for general communication in most parts of the world, it is respectful to others to attempt to speak their language (however faltering) and, particularly if providing direct services, much subtle meaning in communication is lost if one does not know the language.

Third, it is also essential to develop knowledge of the host county's culture. This is prerequisite to helping to avoid the tendency to believe that one's own culture is superior and, therefore, to force his or her way of doing things into the other culture. The concept of "the ugly American" reflects the reputation persons from the United States have developed by reflecting such cultural insensitivity. Just as in other forms of insensitivity (e.g., racism, sexism, ageism), the study of the other's culture and experience is a first step in increasing awareness and avoiding inadvertent acts of insensitivity.

Finally, the unique contribution that a professional social worker brings is his or her professional knowledge and skill. Experience in practicing social work after completing one's professional education is prerequisite for most international social work positions.

Although all the above competencies are necessary for successful international social work practice, one research project identified the basic social work principles of "individualizing the client," "maximizing client empowerment," "maximizing client participation," and "maximizing client self-determination"[12] as the factors most associated with successful Peace Corps and USAID projects. Ghavam's study of 74 projects throughout the world, found that "the greater the villagers' role and participation in start-up, assessment, and design phases of the projects resulted in more overall success of the development projects." This study also found that the project director's technical preparation for the position, experience in international work, and adequacy in the culture and language of the area were also associated with the overall success of the projects.[13] In short, good social work practice, plus orientation to the language and culture of the specific country, corresponds with successful international practice. The competent social worker already has a good start for international practice.

Concluding Comment

It can be argued that the Industrial Revolution created the need for the professional approach to helping represented by social work. As countries have become increasingly industrialized, traditional ways of meeting human needs have been supplemented by programs and personnel especially prepared to meet many human needs. It can be further argued that the Technological Revolution occurring today is moving social work from a profession oriented to its practice in a single country to one with an increasing global orientation.

As technology advances, the world shrinks. The presence of a worldwide economy makes countries increasingly interdependent. The ability of the media to immediately transmit information around the globe creates an unprecedented awareness of events as they occur in even remote areas of the world. And the availability of the World Wide Web and e-mail allows human services agencies and human services providers to exchange information through a virtually cost free and instantaneous process. Although some parts of the world have not yet fully experienced the Technological Revolution, in many ways international boundaries have become less significant.

Parallel to the diminishing isolation of individual countries, social work, too, is beginning to blur national distinctions and think of itself as a global profession. A challenge for the next generation of social workers will be to evolve a concept of social work that will bridge the differing philosophies of society's role in meeting human needs and yet maintain the social worker's unique function as the profession that addresses both individual and family needs and, simultaneously, is concerned with changing the society to reduce or eliminate factors that contribute to people's problems in social functioning.

KEY WORDS AND CONCEPTS

Social development

International social work

Global social work

International Federation of Social Workers

International Declaration of Ethical
Principles for Social Work

Corporatist welfare state

Liberal welfare state

Social democratic welfare state

International Association of Schools
of Social Work

Social technology transfer

SUGGESTED READINGS

Chatterjee, Pranab. *Repackaging the Welfare State.* Washington, D.C.: NASW Press, 1999.

Colton, Matthew, Casas, Ferran, Drakeford, Mark, Roberts, Susan, Scholte, Evert, and Williams, Margaret. *Stigma and Social Welfare: An International Comparative Study.* Brookfield, VT: Ashgate, 1997.

Healy, Lynne H. "International Social Welfare Organizations and Activities." In Richard I. Edwards, ed., *Encyclopedia of Social Work,* 19th Edition. Washington, D.C.: NASW Press, 1995, pp. 1499–1510.

Hokenstad, M. C., Khinduka, S. K., and Midgley, James, eds. *Profiles in International Social Work.* Washington, D.C.: NASW Press, 1992.

Lapidus, Gail W., and Swanson, Guy E., eds. *State and Welfare USA/USSR: Contemporary Policy and Practice.* Berkeley, CA: Institute of International Studies, 1988.

Lorenz, Walter. *Social Work in a Changing Europe.* London: Routledge, 1994.

Midgley, James. "International and Comparative Social Welfare." In Richard I. Edwards, ed., *Encyclopedia of Social Work,* 19th Edition. Washington, D.C.: NASW Press, 1995, pp. 1490–1498.

———. *Social Welfare in Global Context.* Thousand Oaks, CA: Sage, 1997.

Ramanathan, Chathapuram S., and Link, Rosemary J. *Principles and Resources for Social Work Practice in a Global Era.* Belmont, CA: Brooks/Cole–Wadsworth, 1999.

van Wormer, Katherine. *Social Welfare: A World View.* Chicago: Nelson-Hall, 1997.

ENDNOTES

1. Robin Wright, "World Population Reaches 6 Billion," *Los Angeles Times,* Part A, Saturday, July 17, 1999, p. A5.
2. Mark W. Lusk and Charles Horejsi, "Toward a Synthesis of International Social Development," *Indian Journal of Social Work* 60 (January 1999): p. 153.
3. Gøsta Epsing-Anderson, *The Three Worlds of Welfare Capitalism* (Princeton, NJ: Princeton University Press, 1990), pp. 21–29.
4. Matthew Colton, Ferran Casas, Mark Drakeford, Susan Roberts, Evert Scholte, and Margaret Williams, *Stigma and Social Welfare: An International Comparative Study* (Brookfield, VT: Ashgate, 1997), pp. 138–140.
5. Ibid.
6. Norma Berkowitz, Lowell Jenkins, and Eileen Kelly, "Reaching Beyond Your Borders: Social Technology Transfers." In Ka-Ching Yeung, chief editor, *Proceedings: Joint World Congress of the International Federation of Social Workers and International Association of Schools of Social Work, 1996,* p. 176 (publisher not identified, 1998).
7. International Federation of Social Workers, "General Information" [http://www.ifsw.org].

8. Lynne M. Healy, "International Social Welfare: Organizations and Activities," in Richard L. Edwards, ed., *Encyclopedia of Social Work,* 19th Edition (Washington, D.C.: NASW Press, 1995), pp. 1505–1506.

9. International Federation of Social Workers, "Activity Report: 1996–1998," [http://www.ifsw.org].

10. International Federation of Social Workers, "The Ethics of Social Work—Principles and Standards," [http://www.ifsw.org].

11. Ibid., "Activity Report."

12. Bradford W. Sheafor, Charles R. Horejsi, and Gloria A. Horejsi, *Techniques and Guidelines for Social Work Practice,* 5th ed. Boston: Allyn and Bacon, 2000, pp. 74–78.

13. Hamid Reza Ghavam, "Characteristics of External Activators in Third World Village Development." Unpublished Doctoral Dissertation, Colorado State University, Fort Collins, CO, pp. 148–149.

SUBJECT INDEX

Conditional loyalty, 118–19
Conduct, standards of, 139–40. *See also* Ethics
Confidentiality, 139
Conflict of values, 133
Conflict resolution skills, 156
Conflictual situations, dealing with, 177
Conservative philosophy, 82
Constitution, U.S., 5
Consultation
  in private practice, 124
  professional competence development and, 157
Consumer service model, 105
Consumers' League, 56
Corporate social responsibility model, 105
Corporatist welfare state, 213
Corrections, field of practice in, 97–98
COS, 56, 96
Council on Social Work Education (CSWE), 38, 59, 60, 62, 71, 72, 79–80, 82
Counseling
  family, 100
  skills in, 156
Court-based gang violence and homicide prevention programs, 192–93
Criminal justice, field of practice in, 97–98
Crisis intervention, 166
Crisis Intervention Network (Philadelphia), 192
CSWE, 38, 59, 60, 62, 71, 72, 79–80, 82
Culture(s), interpersonal helping and, 155
Curriculum development, 174
Curriculum Policy Statement of the Council on Social Work Education, 37

Data collection and assessment
  in interpersonal helping, 156
  skills in, 172
Decision-making
  in agencies, 170
  facilitating, 164
Defense expenditures, 12–13
Delivery system knowledge development, 162–64
Democratic ideals, American social values and, 134
Demographics. *See under specific racial and ethnic group*
Developmental Disabilities Assistance and Bill of Rights Act (Public Law 95-602), 98–99
Developmental disability, 98–99
Diagnostic and Statistical Manual for Mental Disorders (DSM-IV), 161
Diplomate in Clinical Social Work, 71

Direct service practitioners, 153
Disability(ies)
  field of practice in, 98–99
Dispute resolution, 169–70
Diversity, human, 27–28, 30
Division of labor, 117
Doctor of Philosophy (Ph.D.) degree, 38, 41, 42
Doctor of Social Work (DSW) degree, 38, 41, 42

Education
  family life, 100–101
  field of practice in, 99
  funding allocations to, 16, 17
  public, 180
  social work, 59, 71
    emergence of, 214–15
  social work evolution and, 57
Educational models of gang violence and homicide prevention, 191–92
Efficiency/effectiveness balance, 116–17
Emotional needs, 50
Employee service model, 105
Employment, 70–73
  in bureaucracies, 117
  in international social work, 219–21
Empowerment
  prevention and, 199–201
Enhancement programs, 18
Enjoyment, sense of, 135*n*
Enlightenment, French, 11
Entry to social work profession, 69–87
  with baccalaureate-level disciplines, 74–77
  as nonprofessional service providers, 74
  preparation and employment issues, 70–73
  professional practice, 77–85
    advanced, 39, 78, 84–85
    basic, 39, 62, 77–80, 82, 83
    independent, 39, 78, 84
    specialized, 39, 78, 80–83
  as volunteer, 73–74
Environment-person focus of social work, 33–34
Esteem needs, 8
Ethical issues, examples of, 146–48
Ethics. *See also* Values
  globally held, 217–18
  operation in practice, 142–46
Ethics code, 58, 61, 73, 131, 132, 140–42, 218
  Canadian, 141*n*
  interpersonal helping and, 155
  professional competence development and, 158